Birdwatching with American Women

BIRDWATCHING
with AMERICAN WOMEN *A Selection of Nature Writings*

EDITED BY DEBORAH STROM

W · W · NORTON & COMPANY

New York   London

First published as a Norton paperback 1989

Published simultaneously in Canada by Penguin Books Canada Ltd.,
2801 John Street, Markham, Ontario L3R 1B4
Printed in the United States of America.

The editor acknowledges the use of the following selections: Cornell
University Press for Anna Botsford Comstock's lesson reprinted from
Handbook of Nature Study, © 1939 by Comstock Publishing Company,
Inc. Christopher Publishing House for Althea Sherman's "The Old
Ornithology and the New," reprinted from *Birds of an Iowa Dooryard,* ©
1952. McGraw-Hill Company for Louise de Kiriline Lawrence's "The
Lovely," reprinted from *The Lovely and the Wild,* © 1968. Helen Gere
Cruickshank for her excerpt "Double-Crested Cormorants," reprinted
from *Bird Islands Down East,* © 1941, Macmillan Publishing Company.
W. W. Norton & Company, Inc. for Helen Blackburn Hoover's "The
Air Hunters," reprinted from *The Long-Shadowed Forest,* © 1963 by
Thomas Y. Crowell Company. Olin Sewall Pettingill for Eleanor Rice
Pettingill's "Kidney Island," reprinted from *Penguin Summer,* © 1960,
Clarkson N. Potter, Inc.

The text of this book is composed in Goudy Old Style,
with display type set in Kennerly. Composition by PennSet, Inc.
Manufacturing by The Murray Printing Company
Book design by Judith Henry

Library of Congress Cataloging in Publication Data
Main entry under title:
Birdwatching with American women.
1. Birds—Addresses, essays, lectures. 2. Bird watching—
Addresses, essays, lectures. I. Strom, Deborah.
QL673.B585   1986   589.2973   85-8822

ISBN 0-393-30598-8

W. W. Norton & Company, Inc.
500 Fifth Avenue, New York, N.Y. 10110

W. W. Norton & Company Ltd.
37 Great Russell Street, London WC1B 3NU

2 3 4 5 6 7 8 9 0

For Felton

CONTENTS

Editor's Note   ix

1 · OLIVE THORNE MILLER   3

2 · CELIA LEIGHTON THAXTER   16

3 · FLORENCE MERRIAM BAILEY   33

4 · NELTJE BLANCHAN DOUBLEDAY   52

5 · GENE STRATTON PORTER   67

6 · ANNA BOTSFORD COMSTOCK   84

7 · CORDELIA STANWOOD   92

8 · FANNIE HARDY ECKSTORM   99

9 · SARAH ORNE JEWETT   112

10 · ALTHEA SHERMAN   129

11 · MABEL OSGOOD WRIGHT   144

12 · MARY HUNTER AUSTIN   159

13 · MARGARET MORSE NICE   169

14 · LOUISE DE KIRILINE LAWRENCE   185

15 · FLORENCE PAGE JAQUES   206

16 · HELEN GERE CRUICKSHANK   226

17 · HELEN BLACKBURN HOOVER   242

18 · ELEANOR RICE PETTINGILL   261

Bibliography   285

Editor's Note

American women have been writing about birds with wit and style for more than a hundred years, but few readers or bird-watchers seem to know their work. In 1957 Roger Tory Peterson included only three samples of prose by women in a selection of eighty writers in *The Birdwatcher's Anthology*. None of the women he selected wrote before 1920, even though the first two decades of this century were fruitful ones for aspiring women nature writers. William Beebe in his 1945 anthology *The Book of Naturalists* included only one woman writer, Rachel Carson, who to Beebe's credit was not yet well known for her nature writing. The essays, sketches, and poems brought together here are meant to acquaint the reader with neglected and often unknown women bird writers. These selections represent a small fraction of the literature on birdwatching produced by women in the United States during the past hundred years. The quality of these writings would alone justify their being reprinted, but the all too frequent obscurity of women writers in American letters increases the justification for gathering this material together.

By far the richest body of bird literature by American women was produced in the first twenty years of the twentieth century. Women authors enjoyed a wide readership then and had little difficulty in finding publishers for their work. Gene

Stratton Porter, for example, took over the juvenile market with two novels thematically focused on the redemptive qualities of nature study for the American teenager. *Freckles* (see selection) and its sequel, *A Girl of the Limberlost*, sold more than eight million copies, making Porter the most popular writer of her day and probably the richest. But how many people today have heard of her or of her best friend Neltje Blanchan Doubleday, the publisher's wife and popular writer of books about birds? Doubleday's four volumes were attractively produced and illustrated with hand-colored photographs. Written with great brio, they were accurate to a reasonable degree and useful as guides for the backyard birdwatcher. There *was* some difficulty with her attitude about certain hawks (see selection), which she claimed were so harmful to small songbirds and game birds that they should be killed off by any means possible. Doubleday's books and the books by several other women in this anthology who shared her negative attitude toward raptors sold well enough for their misguided attitude to actually have some adverse influence on the hawk population. It was some time before bird enthusiasts were convinced that hawks were a necessary link in the ecological chain.

How many people today know about Mabel Osgood Wright, the president and founder of the Connecticut Audubon Society, associate editor of *Bird-Lore* (precursor of *Audubon* magazine), and author of more than a dozen novels? Her *Birdcraft*, a widely used field guide for young readers, was reissued nine times. She also wrote serious nature sketches for adult readers.

These are only three of the many women writers who, fired with enthusiasm for the study and preservation of North American birds, produced an amazing amount of natural history literature, most of it unread today and most of it worth the time to locate and enjoy.

Doubleday, Porter, and Wright were part of a larger move-ment initiated by a small group of ornithologists centered at the American Museum of Natural History in New York City and the Smithsonian Institution who banded together at the end of the nineteenth century in an intense and swiftly moving campaign to save the vanishing birdlife of North America. Before George Grinnell formed the first Audubon Society in 1886, bird study had been limited to the scientific side of the discipline, and the only broadly based organization for the bird student was the strictly professional American Ornithologists' Union. The fauna of the New World had to be classified and described before their beauties could be appreciated and their populations saved.

By the end of the nineteenth century the wilderness was dwindling and the birdlife of the continent, thought to be limitless, was in ruins. Extirpation threatened a host of species as a result of untrammeled hunting and the rapacious millinery trade. Feather hunters were known to slaughter entire nesting colonies of egrets, herons, pelicans, and terns to supply the demands of milliners in the United States and Europe. Frank Chapman, curator of birds at the American Museum of Nat-ural History, made the following list of birds he had identified on the hats of New York's fashionable ladies in 1886. His inventory was completed during only two afternoon walks on the streets of lower Manhattan:

robin, four	northern shrike, one
brown thrasher, one	pine grosbeak, one
bluebird, three	snow bunting, fifteen
blackburnian warbler, one	tree sparrow, two
blackpoll warbler, three	white-throated
Wilson's warbler, three	sparrow, one
scarlet tanager, three	bobolink, one

tree swallow, one
bohemian waxwing, one
cedar waxwing, twenty-
three
swallow-tailed flycatcher,
one
kingbird, one
kingfisher, one
pileated woodpecker, one
red-headed woodpecker,
two
flicker, twenty-one
saw-whet owl, one
mourning dove, one
prairie hen, one
ruffed grouse, two

meadowlark, two
Baltimore oriole, nine
purple grackle, five
blue jay, five
bob-white, sixteen
California Valley
quail, two
sanderling, five
greater yellowlegs, one
green heron, one
Virginia rail, one
laughing gull, one
common tern,
twenty-one
black tern, one
grebe, seven

Women bird enthusiasts fought a tough battle with pen and lectern to stop the unnecessary wearing of feathers and plumes, and to that end wrote diligently from a primarily feminine viewpoint for *Bird-Lore* and other magazines. Mabel Osgood Wright reported, for example, in an early issue of *Bird-Lore*:

. . . Every well-dressed, well-groomed woman who buys several changes of head-gear a year can exert a positive influence upon her milliner, if she is so minded, and by appearing elegantly charming in bonnets devoid of the forbidden feathers, do more to persuade the milliner to drop them from her stock than by the most logical war of words.

A glance at the holiday hats seen recently at many good shops, theaters, and in the streets of New York, was not without much that is encouraging.

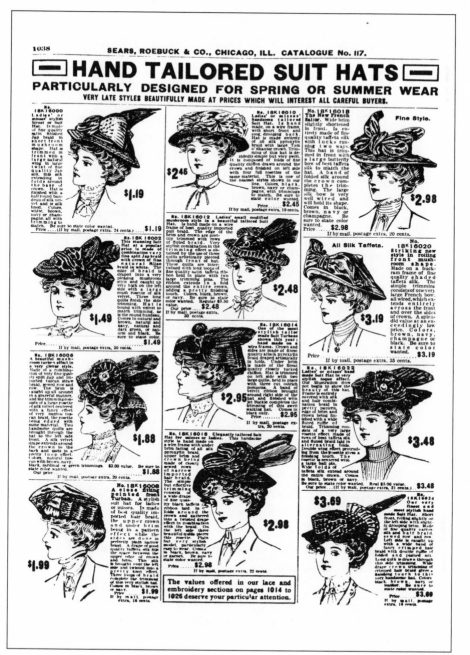

Velvet flowers of exquisite colors and workmanship, jeweled, gold, and steel ornaments, and pompons of lace and ribbons have largely taken the place of any but Ostrich feathers, with people of refined taste.

To be sure, bandeaux of separated feathers offer a Chinese puzzle as to their origin, Ptarmigan wings and questionable quills appear on walking hats, and the Egret still lingers as the apex of many a diamond hair ornament, but the *average is surely better*. Fewer Grebe muffs and capes are seen, and whole Terns seem, by common consent, to be relegated either to the wearer of the molted garments of her mistress or to the 'real lady,' who, in winter, with hat cocked over one eye, pink tie, scarlet waist, sagging automobile coat, rickety Louis heels, and rings instead of gloves, haunts the cheaper shops, lunching on either beer or soda water, and in summer rides a man's wheel, chews gum, and expectorates with seeming relish.

The headgear of a fashionable audience, gathered at the first night of a new play, was another encouraging sign. Those who arrived without bonnets wore in their hair a single flower, a filet of ribbons or some flexible metal, or lace choux. I only recognized half a dozen Egrets among them, and these were worn by women of the dubious age and complexion that may be excused from the shock of abandoning time-honored customs. During the five minutes' millinery show allowed, before the rise of the curtain causes the well-bred to unhat, absolutely no feathers were discoverable, save a few white breasts, Ostrich, and Maribou plumes; the effect of so much softly draped, delicately tinted gauze, mingled with gold, silver and flowers, giving greater brilliancy to the house than had a Bird of Paradise, a Humming-bird, or a Cockatoo been perched on every head.

We may ask ourselves if the change has any special significance. Is it a mere freak of fashion? Is it owed to the law or to the lady?

Let us credit it to the law *and* the lady, and hope that the two are standing with locked hands, as they exchange New Year's greetings and form a twentieth century alliance in the cause of Bird Protection, as they have so often done in other things that elevate the race.

In the end the anti–plume-hunting campaign was successful. Aided by the progressive conservation policies of Theodore Roosevelt and the herculean lobbying efforts carried out by distinguished scientists and members of the National Audubon Society (the name was National Association of Audubon Societies for the Protection of Wild Birds and Animals until 1940), birds were eventually protected and their slaughter for hats made illegal. Similar legislation was initiated on a state level by local Audubon societies. Stricter hunting laws were encouraged and implemented in many areas.

The nature study movement was born of this battle. Birds could only be protected from meaningless slaughter and harassment if children were taught at an early age to protect them. Thus women of the next generation would naturally refuse to wear feathers as decoration, and men would stop shooting songbirds for sport. The National Audubon Society launched a massive school program, headed by Mabel Osgood Wright, aimed at organizing a society chapter in every school in America. *Bird-Lore* published monthly educcational pamphlets for teachers; it sponsored poetry and birdhouse design contests for children and summer birdwatching courses for

Bird-Lore, *the magazine of the National Audubon Society, encouraged the nation's children to build bird boxes.*

LEFT *Mrs. F. T. Bicknell, president of the Los Angeles Audubon Society, as pictured in* Bird-Lore.

BELOW *Doylestown nature club on a canal outing in 1918.*

secondary school teachers at many colleges and universities. Wright wrote a teaching guide for bird study in novel form, *Grey Lady and the Birds*. A center for this movement grew up at Cornell University's College of Agriculture, where a series of pamphlets for teaching nature study was produced. Eventually a superb teaching guide, *A Handbook of Nature Study*, was written by Anna Botsford Comstock, another inexhaustible nature promoter (see selection). At Cornell the nature study movement was seen as an antidote to the agricultural depression then affecting the economy of New York State's country life, and the economics of nature conservation were especially encouraged to rekindle enthusiasm for farming.

As a result of the emphasis on education, early twentieth-century bird literature often has a strongly didactic flavor. In the pages of *Bird-Lore* women were exhorted to go out-of-doors to appreciate the beauties of nature firsthand. Bird photography was considered a particularly suitable hobby for women bird lovers, as indicated by Emma Turner's charming decription of the proper outfit for the bird photographer:

> I took up bird-watching and photography some sixteen years ago simply because I possessed a very thin skin, and some outdoor occupation was deemed necessary. Since then I have become hardened to every kind of exposure, and never take cold out-of-doors. This immunity is largely a matter of suitable clothes and, as I am writing for women, a word or two concerning dress is not out of place. . . . Personally, as most of my work has been done in marsh lands, I always avoid tweeds, because they soak up the moisture like a sponge. My working clothes . . . consist of a coat to my knees, well furnished with large outside pockets, wide enough to take at least two quarter-plate double

dark slides, and a watch-pocket for trifles; a short skirt which, if necessary, can be discarded, hence the length of coat; a thick woollen shirt to match, and a second and longer skirt. A light shirt is often seen through the peep-hole of one's tent, by a wary bird, and it is often too hot for a coat. The principal use of the second skirt is for calling on the powers-that-be, when permission is wanted to hunt in private grounds. Beside which, in time the short skirt shrinks in length to a mere kilt, and every economical woman knows that a coat will outlast two skirts. I am not writing for millionaires, but for working-women of limited means, whose special outfit will have to last several years. If well-cut to start with, and not made in the latest evanescent fashion, although it may have "taken on color from the atmosphere," such a suit as I am describing will always look well and workmanlike. . . .

Of course when really on the warpath, it is not easy for the bird-photographer to look respectable, and one must be prepared to sacrifice appearance. . . . Modern bird-photography has attained a pitch of luxurious ease undreamt of by the earlier workers. One used to lie for hours beneath a heap of rubbish till every muscle became numb. The light portable tent which any women can make for herself, the tilting table, lens-hood, and modern combination lenses—all these accessories have reduced the difficulties and discomforts to a minimum. But, at the same time, one loses the odd intimacy which frequently existed between the photographer and various stray birds. Many a time, when lying on the ground, lightly covered with litter, all kinds of birds have mistaken me for a heap of rubbish. . . . The hiding tent has done away with all this. One now sits in comparative ease, notebook in hand, with thermos flask and sandwiches, and sometimes a novel.

Turner, a British bird photographer of distinction and author of two books on birdwatching, went on to describe the ideal photographic kit for the aspiring American woman photographer. Such a kit was given to Gene Stratton Porter by her family one Christmas. She spent countless hours in the field taking pictures of birds, some of which she subsequently used to illustrate her book of birdwatching reminiscences, *Homing with the Birds*. Cordelia Stanwood was encouraged by Frank Chapman, *Bird-Lore*'s editor, to take photographs to serve as illustrations for her essays on the nesting birds of her home town, Ellsworth, Maine. She subsequently became an extremely skilled photographer (see pages 94–97). Photography then as now is a craft requiring patience, diligence, and above all, time. Most of these women had time on their hands and plenty of it to use in trying to capture moments in birdlife often inaccessible to the casual bird student. College girls went out on bird rambles, sometimes led by their professors. Fannie Hardy Eckstorm, an anthropologist and folklorist as well as bird student from Brewer, Maine (see selection), helped form an Audubon Club at Smith College and led her classmates on weekly bird walks. Vassar students were especially fortunate to have as their guide John Burroughs, the greatest nature writer of his day, who often took student groups on walks at his home across the Hudson River from Poughkeepsie. River from Poughkeepsie.

Today the didactic flavor of some of the bird prose may make it tiresome reading. Porter's books may seem cloyingly sentimental and Doubleday's absurdly gushing. Yet Wright's prose is still magical and Fannie Hardy Eckstorm's still pungently witty (see selections). It is difficult to understand why writers of such quality fell into obscurity, but male bird writers did as well. Few birdwatchers read John Burroughs today, though when he died in 1921 he was the most famous writer in America. Theodore Roosevelt fondly called him Oom John (Uncle John) and corresponded with him frequently. In his time, Burroughs was considered the greatest American nature writer since Thoreau.

It may be the leisurely pace of this kind of writing combined with its overtly positivistic flavor that puts us off. Today we are more accustomed to pessimistic prophecy rapidly dished out than to leisurely sentiments glorifying the beauties of nature.

Alongside these writers, primarily concerned with nature appreciation and study, are such writers as Sarah Orne Jewett, Mary Hunter Austin, and Celia Leighton Thaxter. Known for their fiction or in Thaxter's case poetry, they also wrote occasionally about birds. Both Thaxter and Jewett became somewhat caught up in the conservation movement. Thaxter wrote delightful poems about birds for children (see selections), and Jewett dedicated one of her finest short stories, "A White Heron" (see selection), to the conservation of birds. Mary Austin, primarily a novelist, was horrifed at the disregard for the California desert's natural beauties. In 1914 she wrote *The Land of Little Rain* to impress upon her readers the unique qualities of the desert ecology which she so admired and hoped to preserve (see selection). Thus the nature study movement reached beyond didactic writers such as Comstock and Doubleday to include the most distinguished women of American letters. No greater proof of the movement's impetus or size can be found.

The legacy of the early teachers and popularizers can be identified easily in the next generation of women birdwatchers and students. Margaret Morse Nice, one of the most distinguished ornithologists of this century, credits the earlier generation with firing her interest in birdwatching and nature study. Nice recalls requesting Mabel Osgood Wright's *Birdcraft* for her twelfth Christmas and the next year begging for any book by Olive Thorne Miller, author of several bird books for young readers (see selection). But whereas all of the women writing before World War I spoke in a strongly optimistic voice, the women writing during the Depression, the ominous rumblings of fascist Europe, and the nightmare of World War II turned to birds for different reasons. Some found in bird study a model for tranquility within a turbulent world. It was not escapism—rather, a fresh expression of the old transcendental theme: nature is the blueprint of God's will, a restorer of meaning in an inarticulate world.

A new seriousness, also, is evident in the depth of women's involvement in bird study. Few of the women prominent in bird study before the First World War thought of themselves as serious scientists. They were more likely to term themselves dedicated observers, the "watchers at the nest." But with the following generation, women who were in most respects amateurs in that they did not earn their living as scientists rose through self-education and dedication to become contributing ornithologists as well as practiced exponents of the bird essay. Margaret Morse Nice, the most distinguished of those women, undertook a major study of nesting behavior of the song sparrow, for which she invented a new method of field observation that is still considered the model for most ornithological field studies. What started as a mild interest in the activities of the birds around her became for Nice a self-redeeming obsession that led her to invent new ways of observing the birds being studied and new ways of interpreting the rich data the methods produced. In her autobiography she describes the moment in which observation of birds became for her the key to self-fulfillment and rescue from the stultifying routine of a life as housewife and mother:

> Under the great elms and cottonwoods on the river bank I watched the turbulent Canadian River and dreamed. The glory of nature possessed me. I saw that for many years I had lost my way. I had been led astray on false trails and had been trying to do things contrary to my nature. I resolved to return to my childhood vision of studying nature and trying to protect the wild things of the earth.
>
> I thought of my friends who never take walks in Oklahoma "for there was nothing to see." I was amazed and grieved at their blindness. I longed to open their eyes to the wonders around them, to persuade people to love and cherish nature. Perhaps I might be a sort of John Burroughs for Oklahoma.
>
> This August walk was a turning point in my life. It was a day of vision and prophecy. But what the future really held in store for me would have seemed to me utterly fantastic.

That future included a friendship with Konrad Lorenz, who thought her one of the greatest scientific minds of his time, and world fame as a ground-breaking field biologist.

Nice's popular account of the song sparrow study, *The Watcher at the Nest* (see selection), was not a commercial success. Today the book is recognized as a frank revelation of a research project so vast and so difficult that the mind boggles at the amount of time and patience required. It is a remarkable example of the sudden vagaries of taste that would allow Porter and Doubleday to be popular in their day but Nice to be unread in hers.

Nice inspired another woman of her generation, Louise

de Kiriline Lawrence. Lawrence started to watch birds in a desultory way at her wilderness home in northern Ontario to distract herself from worrying about her husband, then serving with the British Army in World War II. She only turned to serious bird study when urged by her friend Nice. The resulting monograph on woodpeckers is a classic. But her essays on birds are far more entertaining. Lawrence, more than Nice, is a born writer as well as nature student, and her essays are among the most intelligent by women bird students (see selection).

Although acknowledging debts to Wright, Porter, and their contemporaries, such women naturalists as Nice and Lawrence often conducted their lives with an intensity rarely found in the previous generation. This intensity resulted partly from their own intelligence and alienation from the normal roles allotted to women and partly from the times in which they lived. We are heirs to that intensity both in our reaction to nature and in the importance of nature study to many intellectuals.

The practice of writing entertaining and instructional bird essays did not die out altogether with World War I. A small group of women writers, including Florence Page Jaques, Helen Gere Cruickshank, and Helen Blackburn Hoover came of age in the years before the Second World War. They wrote in a typically American way. Humorous and relaxed, their prose is among the most genuinely American birdwatching literature.

All these women were married to professional naturalists—illustrators, photographers, field specialists—and all found themselves willy-nilly in the thick of a bird study, whether they liked it or not. A woman was more or less expected to devote herself to her husband's career, especially if that vocation involved a level of commitment and displacement unusual in other professions. Frank Chapman at the American

Museum of Natural History epitomized that attitude when he described his marriage:

> When a man wedded to his profession (ornithology) takes a mortal wife he commits a very dangerous type of bigamy. If the two spouses do not agree there arises a three-cornered conflict to determine which one of them will be widowed. . . . I was among the fortunate ones and when, on February 24, 1898, I married Fanny Bates Embury I acquired a helpmeet who ever since has made it the chief object of her life to advance the aims of mine.

Fanny Chapman was taken on a field expedition for her honeymoon. She proved herself a great sport, for during her first week of marriage she was taught how to skin birds for study specimens and became an indispensable member of her husband's research teams.

After one month of marriage Grace Murphy was left behind by her husband, Robert Cushman Murphy, a research ornithologist on the staff of the American Museum of Natural History. He stayed away on a field trip for a full year, and thereafter she refused to allow him to go alone on any long trips. Surprising to us today, her attitude is distinctly similar to Chapman's:

> As everything in this world is both give and take, somebody must return in part measure to the naturalist what he is giving out—without noticing it, of course— to everybody. The wife can be the bridge. The wife who stands by, frequently enduring loneliness and neglect, giving him anchorage, carrying her own respon-

sibilities and many of her man's, often meeting the children's problems almost singlehanded, moving from one home to another without help, and probably without her spouse more than half seeing either place, living on a meager income while her husband enjoys the fare of kings in foreign lands, somehow keeping up companionship when there is often almost nothing to keep it on—this wife should be the bridge.

It is time some word about her job was spoken rather loudly. Each young wife has learned that job alone. No one really notices her presence in the shadow of the lion, and our men are thoroughly and deservedly lionized. If I seem to blow our wifely horn, it is almost the first time that such loud blasts have sounded.

Murphy went on to become addicted to birdwatching, she says in her autobiography, but one wonders at the pluck it took to stay afloat as a personality in a marriage of such remarkable onesidedness.

The women in this group wrote books about their experiences alongside their husbands on countless research and pleasure trips to the wilderness. Their prose is strongly similar in style to Eleanor Roosevelt's ubiquitous daily column "My Day," which was widely read for decades. Hoover, Murphy, Jaques, and others seemed to model themselves on Roosevelt in additional ways, sporting a similar hair style and eschewing unnecessarily frivolous garb or makeup. This is not surprising since Roosevelt epitomized the woman who, firmly entrenched in the role of wife—and wife of a lion with unusual strength and needs—managed to carve out an identity and a life-style that was a giant step beyond wifely dependency. These women wrote in a natural, talky style totally without artifice. The modesty of their claims to a life of their own is reflected in the humor and honesty of their prose, and their books remain pleasant reading for us now. Their goal was to describe bird study fondly but without an intensity which might drive away the casual bird student. They wrote their books to earn enough money to augment their husbands' incomes because ornithology hardly paid a living wage. Some also wrote to supply an outlet for their husbands' illustrations. Francis Lee Jaques, for many years on staff at the American Museum of Natural History where he painted many of the diorama backgrounds, illustrated all of his wife's books. Some wrote to support their own identities. The difficulties faced on endless field trips such as those described by Helen Gere Cruickshank and Eleanor Rice Pettingill (see selections) and the dedication to their dependent roles lend dignity and worth to their birdwatching literature.

This kind of book, the "I-also-came-along" type, is probably permanently out of fashion. Women today observe nature for themselves, and no self-respecting woman writer would allow her inspiration to come strictly from her husband's profession. But Pettingill, Jaques, and Cruickshank broke ground in their own way. They were free from ordinary female vanities. They experienced appalling conditions in the field with uncomplaining camaraderie and set a wonderful example for the postwar generation of women to get out there and muck around in the wild. And certainly many American women now do.

The scope of this anthology has been defined somewhat arbitrarily, and a number of writers who might strictly be described as "modern" have not been included. My interest has been in tracing the evolution of nature writing by women and in reviving their writing for a new audience. The majority of the writers here were most active before World War II. Although a few, such as Helen Hoover and Louise de Kiriline

Lawrence, wrote as recently as ten or twenty years ago, their work frequently describes experiences that took place earlier.

Many librarians, catalogers, museum curators, and publishers made this anthology possible. To them I offer my warm thanks. Of all the authors included, only Helen Cruickshank and Louise de Kiriline Lawrence are alive today. I am indebted to them for their assistance and advice. Two modern nature writers, Mary Durant and Erma Fisk, helped with suggestions and encouragement. My thanks to them as well. Finally I am more than grateful to Barbara Kouts, Carol Houck Smith, Constance Stallings, Lynda Emery, and Lorna Mack for their practical and editorial assistance.

DEBORAH STROM
Hopewell, New Jersey
Ivy Rock Farm

WHICH WOULD YOU CHOOSE?
By T. GILBERT PEARSON.

Of all the nymphs that dwell in the world,
With dimpled cheek and tresses curled,
Who hark to the songs of the sea and land,
And gather each joy with an eager hand,
Which would you choose for life's short whirl—
The maid with the gun or the camera girl?

Down in the dell
That she loves so well,
Where the long moss waves
To the nonpareil,
Or anon on the hill
When the night is still,
And the mockingbird calls
To the whip-poor-will;
One dreams of the light
And the lens set right,
And the flash of wings
As the birds alight,
And the picture
The plate will fill.

In the autumn days when the purple haze
Softens and blends with the sunset rays,
Cheery and bright in the fading light
Comes the ringing note of the plump Bob-white.
There is one who's tanned on cheek and hand,
Who will listen and smile, and can understand,
If the pointers are working right.

Now which would you choose for life's short whirl,
The maid who can shoot or the camera girl?

Bird Lore, 1915.

Birdwatching with American Women

· 1 ·

OLIVE THORNE MILLER

(HARRIET MANN MILLER)

1831–1918

This anthology begins appropriately with the earliest and one of the most prolific of American woman birdwatchers, a writer who often used the pseudonym Olive Thorne Miller. Author of more than seven hundred and twenty-four books, eleven about birds, Miller was born in 1831 in upstate New York. Christened Harriet Mann, she was a shy and bookish child who wrote stories. Although she did not attend university, Miller, child of a prosperous family, was educated at a private girls' school in the Midwest. In 1854 she married Watts Todd Miller, a Chicago businessman. For a time she renounced the career in letters which she had envisaged for herself as a girl and raised four children. In 1871, however, as her family grew more independent, she again sought to be a writer. A woman of high intelligence and wit, she began modestly enough by writing short informative essays on practical activities for children. For over a decade she published hundreds of articles for both juvenile and adult audiences on such themes as the manufacture of household items like thread and china, on the life of the spider, and on oyster farming, to name just a few.

During this busy decade Miller also wrote five full-length children's books, among them *Little Folks in Feathers and Fur* in 1873 and *Little People of Asia* in 1882. These and her later books for children, including the vastly popular Kristy books, are not of any particular quality; had Miller stopped writing with them her name could be justifiably forgotten. But in about 1880 she discovered birdwatching when Chicago bird conservationist Sarah Hubbard visited Brooklyn, where Miller and her family had relocated in 1875. Hubbard insisted on going out to birdwatch in Prospect Park, and there Miller found a world of fascinating creatures which had utterly escaped her notice of fifty years. Remarkably, she was able to make up for lost time and within a few years was not only an expert birdwatcher but was writing intelligently about the birds she had so recently discovered. From 1885 until her death in 1918 she wrote her finest books, most of them about birdwatching at various summer vacation spots. *Nesting Time* appeared in 1888 and was followed quickly by *Little Brothers of the Air* in 1892. These two books were aimed at the juvenile audience and were early efforts at nature education, then gaining a nationwide foothold in public schools.

Miller's two finest books, both for adults, had their origins in her intense discovery of birds. *A Bird-Lover in the West* appeared in 1894, and her last book, *With the Birds in Maine*, in 1904. In the chapter from *A Bird-Lover in the West* reprinted here, Miller describes a summer journey she undertook unaccompanied at the age of 61 to a remote Colorado tourist camp where, freed from the responsibilities and strains of a busy urban life, she was able to restore her spirits through living closer to nature. The book is essentially in the mode of the nature travelog as practiced by Henry David Thoreau and exemplified in his *Cape Cod* or *The Maine Woods*.

Like Thoreau's *Cape Cod*, *A Bird-Lover in the West* is more than a transcendental polemic. It is a delightful travelog written in suave and elegant prose; from the vantage point of nearly a century later it still appears fresh. But the readability of Miller's prose, and particularly its scintillating wit, bely its ultimate seriousness of intent. *A Bird-Watcher in the West* was not intended as mere entertainment, nor can it be read seriously that way. In a prologue to the chapter included here, Miller stated her case quite plainly. Nature is to be sought out for the moral qualities its contemplation fosters. She went to Colorado to refresh her soul and hoped that by accompanying her the reader would do likewise.

Olive Thorne Miller, born three decades before the Civil War, was an extraordinary woman for her day. In her fifties she took up a new world of study. She forged a career independent of her husband and unaffected by her role as mother of four children. Her colleague and friend Florence Merriam Bailey recalled Miller as a woman of fierce spirit and independence. As one of America's earliest women bird writers, she would merit reprinting here. But as a writer of spirit and quality she can still be read with real pleasure.

In the Cottonwoods

A cottonwood grove is the nearest approach to our Eastern rural districts to be found in Colorado, and a cotton storm, looking exactly like a snowstorm, is a common sight in these groves. The white, fluffy material grows in long bunches, loosely attached to stems, and the fibre is very short. At the lightest breeze that stirs the branches, tiny bits of it take to flight, and one tree will shed cotton for weeks. It clings to one's garments; it gets into the houses, and sticks to the carpets, often showing a trail of white footprints where a person has come in; it clogs the wire-gauze screens till they keep out the air as well as the flies; it fills the noses and the eyes of men and beasts. But its most curious effect is on the plants and flowers, to which it adheres, being a little gummy. Some flowers look as if they were encased in ice, and others seem wrapped in the gauziest of veils, which, flimsy as it looks, cannot be completely cleared from the leaves.

It covers the ground like snow, and strangely enough it looks in June, but it does not, like snow, melt, even under the warm summer sunshine. It must be swept from garden and walks, and carted away. A heavy rain clears the air and subdues it for a time, but the sun soon dries the bunches still on the trees, and the cotton storm is again in full blast. This annoyance lasts through June and a part of July, fully six weeks, and then the stems themselves drop to the ground, still holding enough cotton to keep up the storm for days. After this, the first rainfall ends the trouble for that season.

In the midst of the cottonwoods, in beautiful Camp Harding, I spent the June that followed the journey described in the last chapter—

> "Dreaming sweet, idle dreams of having strayed
> To Arcady with all its golden lore."

The birds, of course, were my first concern. Ask of almost any resident not an ornithologist if there are birds in Colorado, and he will shake his head.

"Not many, I think," he will probably say. "Camp birds and magpies. Oh yes, and larks. I think that's about all."

This opinion, oft repeated, did not settle the matter in my mind, for I long ago discovered that none are so ignorant of the birds and flowers of a neighborhood as most of the people who live among them. I sought out my post, and I looked for myself.

There are birds in the State, plenty of them, but they are not on exhibition like the mountains and their wonders. No driver knows the way to their haunts, and no guide-book points them out. Even a bird student may travel a day's journey, and not encounter so many as one shall see in a small orchard in New England. He may rise with the dawn, and hear nothing like the glorious morning chorus that stirs one in the Atlantic States. He may search the trees and shrubberies for long June days, and not find so many nests as will cluster about one cottage at home.

Yet the birds are here, but they are shy, and they possess the true Colorado spirit—they are mountain-worshipers. As the time approaches when each bird leaves society and retires for a season to the bosom of its own family, many of the feathered residents of the State bethink them of their inaccessible cañons. The saucy jay abandons the settlements where he has been so familiar as to dispute with the dogs for their food, and sets up his homestead in a tall pine-tree on a slope which to look at is to grow dizzy; the magpie, boldest of birds, steals away to some secure retreat; the meadow-lark makes her nest in the monotonous mesa, where it is as well hidden as a bobolink's nest in a New England meadow.

The difficulties in the way of studying Colorado birds are several, aside from their excessive suspicion of every human being. In the first place, observations must be made before ten o'clock, for at that hour every day a lively breeze, which often amounts to a gale, springs up, and sets the cottonwood and aspen leaves in a flutter that hides the movement of any bird. Then, all through the most interesting month of June the cottonwood-trees are shedding their cotton, and to a person on the watch for slight stirrings among the leaves the falling cotton is a constant distraction. The butterflies, too, wandering about in their aimless way, are all the time deceiving the bird student, and drawing attention from the bird he is watching.

On the other hand, one of the maddening pests of bird study at the East is here almost unknown—the mosquito. Until the third week in June I saw but one. That one was in the habit of lying in wait for me when I went to a piece of low, swampy ground overgrown with bushes. Think of the opportunity this combination offers to the Eastern mosquito, and consider my emotions when I found but a solitary individual, and even that one disposed to coquette with me.

I had hidden myself, and was keeping motionless, in order to see the very shy owners of a nest I had found, when the lonely mosquito came as far as the rim of my shade hat, and hovered there, evidently meditating an attack—a mosquito hesitating! I could not stir a hand, or even shake my leafy twig; but it did not require such violent measures; a light puff of breath this side or that was enough to discourage the gentle creature, and in all the hours I sat there it never once came any nearer. The race increased, however, and became rather troublesome on the veranda after tea; but in the grove they were never annoying; I rarely saw half a dozen. When I remember the tortures endured in the dear old woods of the East, in spite of "lollicopop" and pennyroyal, and other horrors with which I have tried to repel them, I could almost decide to live and die in Colorado.

The morning bird chorus in the cottonwood grove where I spent my June was a great shock to me. If my tent had been pitched near the broad plains in which the meadow-lark delights, I might have wakened to the glorious song of this bird of the West. It is not a chorus, indeed, for one rarely hears more than a single performer, but it is a solo that fully makes up for want of numbers, and amply satisfies the lover of bird music, so strong, so sweet, so moving are his notes.

But on my first morning on the grove, what was my dismay—I may almost say despair—to find that the Western wood-pewee led the matins! Now, this bird has a peculiar voice. It is loud, pervasive, and in quality of tone not unlike our Eastern phoebe, lacking entirely the sweet plaintiveness of our wood-pewee. A pewee chorus is a droll and dismal affair. The poor things do their best, no doubt, and they cannot prevent the pessimistic effect it has upon us. It is rhythmic, but not in the least musical, and it has a weird power over the listener. This morning hymn does not say, as does the robin's, that life is cheerful, that another glorious day is dawning. It says, "rest is over; another day of toil is here; come to work." It is monotonous as a frog chorus, but there is a merry thrill in the notes of the amphibian which are entirely wanting in the song. If it were not for the light-hearted tremolo of the chewink thrown in now and then, and the loud, cheery ditty of the summer yellow-bird who begins soon after the pewee, one would be almost superstitious about so unnatural a greeting to the new day. The evening call of the bird is different. He will sit far up on a dead twig of an old pine-tree, and utter a series of four notes, something like "do, mi, mi, do," repeating them without pausing till it is too dark to see him, all the time getting lower, sadder, more deliberate, till one feels like running out and committing suicide or annihilating the bird of ill-omen.

I felt myself a stranger indeed when I reached this pleasant spot, and found that even the birds were unfamiliar. No robin or bluebird greeted me on my arrival; no cheerful song-sparrow tuned his little pipe for my benefit; no phoebe shouted the beloved name from the peak of the barn. Everything was strange. One accustomed to the birds of our Eastern States can hardly conceive of the country without robins in plenty; but in this unnatural corner of Uncle Sam's dominion I found but one pair.

The most common song from morning till night was that of the summer yellow-bird, or yellow warbler. It was not the delicate little strain we are accustomed to hear from this bird, but a loud, clear carol, equal in volume to the notes of our robin. These three birds, with the addition of a vireo or two, were our main dependence for daily music, though we were favored occasionally by others. Now the Arkansas goldfinch uttered his sweet notes from the thick foliage of the cotton-wood-trees; then the charming aria of the catbird came softly from the tangle of rose and other bushes; the black-headed grosbeak now and then saluted us from the top of a pine-tree; and rarely, too rarely, alas! A passing meadow-lark filled all the grove with his wonderful song.

And there was the wren! He interested me from the first; for a wren is a bird of individuality always, and his voice reminded me, in a feeble way, of the witching notes of the winter wren, the

> "Brown wren from out whose swelling throat
> Unstinted joys of music float."

This bird was the house wren, the humblest member of his musical family; but there was in his simple melody the wren quality, suggestive of the thrilling performances of his more gifted relatives; and I found it and him very pleasing.

The chosen place for his vocal display was a pile of brush beside a closed-up little cottage, and I suspected him of having designs upon that two-roomed mansion for nesting purposes. After hopping all about the loose sticks, delivering his bit of an aria a dozen times or more, in a most rapturous way, he would suddenly dive into certain secret passages among the dead branches, when he was instantly lost to sight. Then, in a few seconds, a close watcher might sometimes see him pass like a shadow, under the cottage, which stood up on corner posts, dart out the farther side, and fly at once to the eaves.

One day I was drawn from the house by a low and oft-repeated cry, like "Hear, hear, hear!" It was emphatic and imperative, as if some unfortunate little body had the business of the world on his shoulders, and could not get it done to his mind. I carefully approached the disturbed voice, and was surprised to find it belonged to the wren, who was so disconcerted at sight of me, that I concluded this particular sort of utterance must be for the benefit of his family alone. Later, that kind of talk, his lord-and-master style as I supposed, was the most common sound I heard from him, and not near the cottage and the brush heap, but across the brook. I thought that perhaps I had displeased him by too close surveillance, and he had set up housekeeping out of my reach. Across the brook I could not go, for between "our side" and the other raged a feud, which had culminated in torn-up bridges and barbed wire protections.

One day, however, I had a surprise. In studying another bird, I was led around to the back of the still shut-up cottage, and there I found, very unexpectedly, an exceedingly busy and silent wren. He did sing occasionally while I watched him from afar, but in so low a tone that it could not be heard a few steps away. Of course I understood this unnatural circumspection, and on observing him cautiously, I saw that he made frequent visits to the eaves of the cottage, the very spot I had hoped he would nest. Then I noted that he carried in food, and on coming out he alighted on a dead bush, and sang under his breath. Here, then, was the nest, and all his pretense of scolding across the brook was but a blind! Wary little rogue! Who would ever suspect a house wren of shyness?

I had evidently done him injustice when I regarded the scolding as his family manner, for here in his home he was quiet as a mouse, except when his joy bubbled over in trills.

To make sure of my conclusions I went close to the house, and then for the first time (to know it) I saw his mate. She came with food in her beak, and was greatly disturbed at sight of her uninvited guest. She stood on a shrub near me fluttering her wings, and there her anxious spouse joined her, and fluttered his in the same way, uttering at the same time a low, single note of protest.

On looking in through the window, I found that the cottage was a mere shell, all open under the eaves, so that the birds could go in and out anywhere. The nest was over the top of a window, and the owner thereof ran along the beam beside it, in great dudgeon at my impertinent staring. Had ever a pair of wrens quarters so ample—a whole cottage to themselves? Henceforth, it was part of my daily rounds to peep in at the window, though I am sorry to say it aroused the indignation of the birds, and always brought them to the beam nearest me, to give me a piece of their mind.

Bird babies grow apace, and baby wrens have not many inches to achieve. One day I came upon a scene of wild excitement: two wrenlings flying madly about in the cottage, now plump against the window, then tumbling breathless to the floor, and two anxious little parents, trying in vain to show their headstrong offspring the way they should go, to the openings under the eaves which led to the great out-of-doors. My face at the window seemed to be the "last straw." A much-distressed bird came boldly up to me behind the glass, saying by his manner—and who knows but in words?—"How can you be so cruel as to disturb us? Don't you see the trouble we are in?" He had no need of Anglo-Saxon (or even of American-English!). I understood him at once; and though exceedingly curious to see how they would do it, I had not the heart to insist. I left them to manage their willful little folk in their own way.

The next morning I was awakened by the jolliest wren music of the season. Over and over the bird poured out his few notes, louder, madder, more rapturously than I had supposed he could. He had guided his family safely out of their imprisoning four walls, I was sure. And so I found it when I went out. Not a wren to be seen about the house, but soft little "churs" coming from here and there among the shrubbery, and every few minutes a loud, happy song proclaimed that wren troubles were over for the summer. Far in among the tangle of bushes and vines, I came upon him, as gay as he had been of yore:—

"Pausing and peering, with sidling head,
As saucily questioning all I said;
While the ox-eye danced on its slender stem,
And all glad Nature rejoiced with them."

The chewink is a curious exchange for the robin. When I noticed the absence of the red-breast, whom—like the poor— we have always with us (at the East), I was pleased, in spite of my fondness for him, because as every one must allow, he is sometimes officious in his attentions, and not at all reticent in expressing his opinions. I did miss his voice in the morning chorus—the one who lived in the grove was not much of a singer—but I was glad to know the chewink, who was almost a stranger. His peculiar trilling song was heard from morning till night; he came familiarly about the camp, eating from the dog's dish, and foraging for crumbs at the kitchen door. Next to the wood-pewee, he was the most friendly of our feathered neighbors.

He might be seen at any time, hopping about on the ground, one moment picking up a morsel of food, and the next throwing up his head and bursting into song:—

> "But not for you his little singing,
> Soul of fire its flame is flinging,
> Sings he for himself alone,"

as was evident from the unconscious manner in which he uttered his notes between two mouthfuls, never mounting a twig or making a "performance" of his music. I have watched one an hour at a time, going about in his jerky fashion, tearing up the ground and searching therein, exactly after the manner of a scratching hen. This, by the way, was a droll operation, done with both feet together, a jump forward and a jerk back of the whole body, so rapidly one could hardly follow the motion, but throwing up a shower of dirt every time. He had neither the grace nor the dignity of our domestic biddy.

Matter of fact as this fussy little personage was on the ground, taking in his breakfast and giving out his song, he was a different bird when he got above it. Alighting on the wren's brush heap, for instance, he would bristle up, raising the feathers on head and neck, his red eyes glowing eagerly, his tail a little spread and standing up at a sharp angle, prepared for instant fight or flight, whichever seemed desirable.

I was amused to hear the husky cry with which this bird expresses most of his emotions—about as nearly a "mew," to my ears, as the catbird executes. Whether frolicking with a comrade among the bushes, reproving a too inquisitive bird student, or warning the neighborhood against some monster like a stray kitten, this one cry seemed to answer for all his needs, and, excepting the song, was the only sound I heard him utter.

Familiar as the chewink might be about our quarters, his own home was well hidden, on the rising ground leading up to the mesa—

> "An unkempt zone,
> Where vines and weeds and scrub oaks intertwine,"

which no one bigger than a bird could penetrate. Whenever I appeared in that neighborhood, I was watched and followed by anxious and disturbed chewinks; but I never found a nest, though, judging from the conduct of the residents, I was frequently "very warm" (as the children say).

About the time the purple aster began to unclose its fringed lids, and the mariposa lily to unfold its delicate cups on the lower mesa—nearly the middle of July—full-grown chewink babies, in brown coats and streaked vests, made their appearance in the grove, and after that the whole world might search the scrub oaks and not a bird would say him nay.

> "All is silent now
> Save bell-note from some wandering cow,
> Or rippling lark-song far away."

· 2 ·

CELIA LEIGHTON THAXTER

1835–1894

Celia Leighton Thaxter was born in Portsmouth, New Hampshire, in 1835 but spent most of her childhood on the Isles of Shoals, a group of rocky outcroppings nine miles off the coast of New Hampshire. Her father, Thomas Leighton, at first kept the lighthouse on White Island, a tiny island battered continuously by the relentless Atlantic. It was there that Thaxter grew up among the mysteries and difficulties of an island home. When she was twelve her father moved the family to Appledore Island, the largest of the Shoals. In partnership with Levi Thaxter, a young Harvard graduate with an aesthete's passion for the sea, he built a tourist hotel which opened in 1848. The hotel enjoyed a surprising popularity. Appledore's proximity to the mainland and its similarities to the Scottish Hebrides no doubt contributed to the hotel's charm. Distinguished New England intellectuals, among them Ralph Waldo Emerson, Nathaniel Hawthorne, Sarah Orne Jewett, and such painters as Childe Hassam and William Morris Hunt were frequent summer guests. The influence of these prominent creative minds was to dominate Celia Thaxter's later life.

At the age of sixteen Celia Leighton married Levi Thaxter, once her father's partner but at that time resident on Appledore Island as tutor to the Leighton children. For much of the ensuing two decades Celia Thaxter moved about New England, following her husband's sporadic and mostly unsuccessful attempts to establish a career. At one time Levi Thaxter taught school on Star Island, the center of habitation for the Shoals; another time at Newburyport, Massachusetts. In 1855, nearly killed in a shipwreck, Thaxter lost his taste for the sea and thereafter Celia Thaxter's life became a struggle between her keen desire to live on the islands of her youth and her duty to her husband and their three sons. Although she settled finally with husband and children in Newtonville, Massachusetts, near Boston, she returned each summer to Appledore, where she helped out at the prosperous hotel and continued her acquaintance with the prominent literateurs and artists among the guests.

Celia Thaxter was an engaging and lively hostess, her mainland home often filled with these same friends. Her first poem was published in the *Atlantic Monthly* without her knowledge in 1861 by James Russell Lowell. Minor literary successes followed with the frequent publication of poems in magazines such as *Scribner's* and *Harper's*. In 1872 her first collected volume of poems appeared, and in 1873 *Among the Isles of Shoals*, a gathering of essays describing the geography, natural history, and inhabitants of her island home. Based in form and style on Thoreau's famous travelog, *Cape Cod*, the book nonetheless demonstrates Thaxter's keen eye and spirited diction. (Her husband, a Browning scholar, served as advisor and critic for her work.) These qualities were evident also in her influential anti–plume-hunting essay entitled "Woman's Heartlessness," which appeared originally in 1887 in the first issue of George Bird Grinnell's short-lived *The Audubon Magazine* and was reprinted as a circular ten years later by the Pennsylvania Audubon Society.

In the 1870s Levi Thaxter's health began to fail, and he sought refuge in Florida with the two younger children. Celia Thaxter returned to Appledore with their oldest son, Karl, who had been mentally disturbed since early childhood. The Thaxters began to live more and more apart. Celia wintered on the mainland and summered on her beloved Appledore Island. Another volume, *Poems*, appeared in 1874. In 1880 the home in Newtonville was sold. The Thaxters wintered thereafter with their son John at his farm in coastal Maine.

In spring and summer Celia Thaxter continued to visit Appledore, where she had a small cottage for her personal use. She surrounded this house with a richly imaginative flower garden which she lovingly described in a volume of 1894 called *An Island Garden*. It was handsomely illustrated with watercolors by her longtime friend, Childe Hassam. She died in 1894.

Thaxter's work enjoyed a certain stylish popularity, thanks mainly to her close association with the influential critics in her circle. Today her poetry, strongly influenced by the transcendental philosophy of Emerson, Lowell and Whittier, appears densely packed and obscure. The rhetoric of the poetry for adults, her serious literary accomplishment, is strained and laborious. On the other hand, in a more informal mode her writing is readable and engaging. Charm is especially evident in her poems for children, which are primarily about birds. She became caught up to a degree in the nature education movement and determined to contribute to children's awareness of the birds around them. She especially despaired when the natives of the Isles of Shoals shot at the migrating birds that flocked in droves to the islands in fall and spring.

Her appreciation of native birds expanded through extensive correspondence with Bradford Torrey, a New England bird student and popular nature essayist. Through this correspondence Thaxter learned the identity and characteristics of the frequent migratory species that fetched up on her island home.

Thaxter's bird poems for children are droll and clever. Her witty personality, submerged in the rhetorically turgid formal poems, shines forth in this genre. Humor and grace are even more evident in the descriptive passages devoted to birds in *An Island Garden* and *Among the Isles of Shoals*. Thaxter was deeply moved by nature. Like other transcendentalists, especially Thoreau, nature was the source of her creative energies and her solace during an often difficult life. The delicacy of her touch is nowhere more evident than in the bird descriptions from her essays, which follow here. It is unlikely that Thaxter would be content with these selections. Her serious poetry was far more important to her than her ventures into nature writing. But it was when she was relaxed that her appreciation of nature becomes accessible to the modern reader.

Note: Celia Thaxter's cottage burned to the ground in 1914, but Cornell University, which operates Appledore Island as a research station, has restored her garden according to the descriptions provided by Thaxter and Childe Hassam in *An Island Garden*.

The Burgomaster Gull

The old-wives sit on the heaving brine,
　　White-breasted in the sun,
Preening and smoothing their feathers fine,
　　And scolding, every one.

The snowy kittiwakes overhead,
　With beautiful beaks of gold,
And wings of delicate gray outspread,
　Float, listening while they scold.

And a foolish guillemot, swimming by,
　Though heavy and clumsy and dull,
Joins in with a will when he hears their cry
　'Gainst the Burgomaster Gull.

For every sea-bird, far and near,
　With an atom of brains in its skull,
Knows plenty of reasons for hate and fear
　of the Burgomaster Gull.

The black ducks gather, with plumes so rich,
　And the coots in twinkling lines;
And the swift and slender water-witch,
　Whose neck like silver shines;

Big eider-ducks, with their caps pale green
　and their salmon-colored vests;
And gay mergansers sailing between,
　With their long and glittering crests.

But the loon aloof on the outer edge
　of the noisy meeting keeps,
And laughs to watch them behind the ledge
　Where the lazy breaker sweeps.

They scream and wheel, and dive and fret,
　And flutter in the foam;
And fish and mussels blue they get
　To feed their young at home:

Till hurrying in, the little auk,
 Brings tidings that benumbs,
And stops at once their clamorous talk—
 "The Burgomaster comes!"

And up he sails, a splendid sight!
 With "wings like banners" wide,
And eager eyes both big and bright,
 That peer on every side.

A lovely kittiwake flying past
 With a slippery pollock fine—
Quoth the Burgomaster, "Not so fast,
 My beauty! This is mine!"

His strong wing strikes with a dizzying shock;
 Poor kittiwake, shrieking, flees;
His booty he takes to the nearest rock,
 To eat it at his ease.

The scared birds scatter to left and right,
 But the bold buccaneer, in his glee,
Cares little enough for their woe and their fright—
 " 'Twill be *your* turn next!" cries he.

He sees not, hidden, behind the rock,
 In the sea-weed, a small boat's hull,
Nor dreams he the gunners have spared the flock
 For the Burgomaster Gull.

So proudly his dusky wings are spread,
 And he launches out on the breeze—
When lo! what thunder of wrath and dread!
 What deadly pangs are these!

The red blood drips and the feathers fly,
  Down drop the pinions wide;
The robber-chief, with a bitter cry,
  Falls headlong in the tide!

They bear him off with laugh and shout;
  The wary birds return—
From the clove-brown feathers that float about
  The glorious news they learn.

Then such a tumult fills the place
  As never was sung or said;
And all cry, wild with joy, "The base
  Bad Burgomaster's dead!"

And the old-wives sit with their caps so white,
  And their pretty beaks so red,
And swing on the billows, and scream with delight,
  For the Burgomaster's dead!

The Kingfisher

Could you have heard the kingfisher scream and scold at me
When I went this morning early down to the smiling sea!
He clamored so loud and harshly, I laughed at him for his
  pains,
And off he flew with a shattered note, like the sound of
  falling chains.

He perched on the rock above me, and kept up such a din,
And looked so fine with his collar snow-white beneath his
  chin,

And his cap of velvet, black and bright, and his jacket of
    lovely blue,
I looked, admired, and called to him, "Good morning!
    How do you do?"

But his kingship was *so* offended! He hadn't a pleasant word,
Only the crossest jargon ever screamed by a bird.
The gray sandpiper on one leg stood still in sheer surprise,
And gazed at me, and gazed at him, with shining bead-black
    eyes,

And pensively sent up so sweet and delicate a note,
Ringing so high and clear from out her dainty, mottled throat,
That echo round the silent shore caught up the clear refrain,
And sent the charming music back again, and yet again.

And the brown song-sparrow on the wall made haste with
    such a song,
To try and drown that jarring din! but it was all too strong.
And the swallows, like a steel-blue flash, swept past and
    cried aloud,
"Be civil, my dear kingfisher, you're far too grand and proud."

But it wasn't of any use at all, he was too much displeased,
And only by my absence could his anger be appeased.
So I wandered off, and as I went I saw him flutter down,
And take his place once more upon the seaweed wet and
    brown.

And there he watched for his breakfast, all undisturbed at
    last,
And many a little fish he caught as it was swimming past.
And I forget his harsh abuse, for, up in the tall elm-tree,
A purple finch sat high and sang a heavenly song for me.

An Island Garden
Boston: 1894

Another enemy to my flowers, and a truly formidable one, is my little friend the song-sparrow. Literally he gives the plot of ground no peace if I venture to put seeds into it. He obliges me to start almost all my seeds in boxes, to be transplanted into the beds when the plants are sufficiently tough to have lost their delicacy for his palate and are no longer adapted to his ideal of a salad. All the Sweet Peas, many hundreds of the delicate plants, are every one grown in this way. When they are a foot high with roots a foot long they are all transplanted separately. Even then the little robber attacks them, and, though he cannot uproot, he will "yank" and twist the stems till he has murdered them in the vain hope of pulling up the remnant of a pea which he judges to be somewhere beneath the surface. Then must sticks and supports be draped with yards of old fishing nets to protect the unfortunates, and over the Mignonette, and even the Poppy beds and others, I must lay a cover of closely woven wire to keep out the marauder. But I love him still, though sadly he torments me. I have adored his fresh music ever since I was a child, and I only laugh as he sits on the fence watching me with his bright black eyes; there is something quaintly comical and delightful about him, and he sings like a friendly angel. From him I can protect myself, but I cannot save my garden so easily from the hideous slug, for which I have no sentiment save only a fury of extermination.

❦

Day after day it is so pleasant working in the bright cool spring air, for as yet the New England spring is alert and brisk in temperature and shows very little softening in its moods. But by the seventh day of the month, as I stand pruning the Rosebushes, there is a flutter of glad wings, and lo! the first house martins! Beautiful creatures, with their white breasts and steel-blue wings, wheeling, chattering, and scolding at me, for they think I stand too near their little brown house on the corner of the piazza eaves, and they let me know their opinion by coming as near as they dare and snapping their beaks at me with a low gutteral sound of displeasure. But after a few days, when they have found they cannot scare me and that I do not interfere with them, they conclude that I am a harmless kind of creature and endure me with tranquility. Straightway they take possession of their summer quarters and begin to build their cosy nest within. Oh, then the weeks of joyful work, the love-making, the cooing, chattering, calling, in tones of the purest delight and content, the tilting against the wind on burnished wings, the wheeling, fluttering, co-quetting, and caressing, the while they bring feathers and straw and shreds and down for their nest-weaving—all this goes on till after the eggs are laid, when they settle down into comparative quiet. Then often the father bird sits and med-itates happily in the sun upon his tiny brown chimney-top, while the mother bird broods below. Or they go out and take a dip in the air together, or sit conversing in pretty cadences a little space, till mother bird must hie indoors to the eggs she dare not leave longer lest they grow chill. And this sweet little drama is repeated all about the island, on sunny roofs and corners and tall posts, wherever a bird house has been built for their convenience. All through April and May I watch them as I go to and fro about my business while they attend to theirs; we do not interfere with each other; they have made up their minds to endure, but I adore them! Flattered indeed am I if, while I am at work upon the flower beds below, father martin comes and sits close to me on the fence rail and chatters musically, unmindful of my quiet movements, quite fearless and at home.

᯼

Some morning in the first of May I sit in the sunshine and soft air, transplanting my young Pansies and Gillyflowers into the garden beds—father and mother martin on the fence watching me and talking to each other in a charming language, the import of which is clear enough, though my senses are not sufficiently delicate to comprehend the words. The song-sparrows pour out their simple, friendly lays from bush and wall and fence and gable peak all about me. Down in a hollow I hear the brimming note of the white-throated sparrow— brimming is the only word that expresses it—like "a beaker full of the warm South"—such joy, such overflowing measure of bliss! There is a challenge from a robin, perhaps, or a bobolink sends down his "brook o' laughter through the air," or high and far a curlew calls; there is a gentle lapping of waves from the full tide, for the sea is only a stone's-throw from my garden fence. I hear the voices of the children prattling not far away; there are no other sounds. Suddenly from the shore comes a clear cry thrice repeated, "Sweet, sweet, sweet!" And I call to my neighbor, my brother, working also in his garden plot, "The sandpiper! Do you hear him?" and the glad news goes from mouth to mouth, "The sandpiper has come!" Oh, the lovely note again and again repeated, "Sweet, sweet, sweet!" echoing softly in the stillness of the tide-brimmed coves, where the quiet water seems to hush itself to listen. Never so tender a cry is uttered by any bird I know; it is the most exquisitely beautiful, caressing tone, heard in the dewy silence of morning and evening. He has many and varied notes and calls, some colloquial, some business-like, some meditative, and his cry of fear breaks my heart to hear when any evil threatens his beloved nest; but this tender call, "Sweet, sweet," is the most enchanting sound, happy with a fullness of joy that never fails to bring a thrill to the heart that listens. It is like the voice of Love itself.

Then out of the high heaven above, at once one hears the happy chorus of the barn swallows; they come rejoicing, their swift wings cleave the blue, they fill the air with woven melody of grace and music. Till late August they remain. Like the martins', their note is pure joy; there is no coloring of sadness in any sound they make. The sandpiper's note is pensive with all its sweetness; there is a quality of thoughtfulness, as it were, in the voice of the song-sparrow; the robin has many sad cadences; in the fairy bugling of the oriole there is a triumphant richness, but not such pure delight; the blackbird's call is keen and sweet, but not so glad; and the bobolink, when he shakes those brilliant jewels of sound from his bright throat, is always the prince of jokers, full of fun, but not so happy as comical. The swallows' twittering seems an expression of unalloyed rapture—I should select it from the songs of all the birds I know as the voice of unshadowed gladness.

❧

I bring a mat from the house and kneel by the smooth bed of mellow brown earth, lay a narrow strip of board across it a few inches from one end, draw a furrow firmly and evenly in the ground along the edge of the board across it a few inches from one end, draw a furrow firmly and evenly in the ground along the edge of the board, repeating this until the whole

27

bed is grooved at equal distances across its entire length. Into these straight furrows the living seeds are dropped, the earth replaced over them (with a depth of about twice their diameter), and the board laid flat with gentle pressure over all the surface till it is perfectly smooth again. Then must the whole be lightly and carefully watered. With almost all the seeds sown in this bird-blest and persecuted little garden, I am obliged to lay newspapers or some protection over the planted beds, and over these again sheets of wire netting, to keep off the singing sparrows till the seeds are safely sprouted. Last year, one morning early in May, I put a border of Mignonette seeds round every flower bed. When I came to the garden again in the afternoon, it was alive with flirting wings and tails and saucy beaks and bright eyes, and stout little legs and claws scratching like mad; all white-throats and song-sparrows, and hardly a seed had these merry little marauders left in the ground. Around the edge of each bed a groove ran, nicely hollowed by their industrious feet, and empty as my hopes. I replaced the seed from my store, and this time took great pains to lay two laths side by side over the lines I had sowed, for safety. Next morning I found the birds again at it; they had burrowed under, kicked over, scratched away the light sticks, and again the seeds were all devoured. Patiently I planted once more, and this time dragged from a pile of lumber heavy square beams of different lengths, which I laid along the borders. The birds eyed the barricades, strove to burrow under, but were forced to give it up, and so at last I conquered. In the course of a week I turned over the protecting beams and found the little Mignonette plants white as potato shoots that have sprouted in a cellar, but safe, for which I was devoutly thankful! A day or two of sun and air made them green and strong, and all summer long I valued every fragrant spike of flowers they gave me, doubly, because of all the trouble

I had gone through to save them. I mention this little episode merely to illustrate the fact that the would-be gardener requires more patience than most mortals!

❧

At bird-peep, as the country folk have a charming way of calling the break of day, I am in my dear garden—planting and transplanting, hoeing, raking, weeding, watering, tying up and training those plants that need it, and always fighting for their precious lives against their legions of enemies. There is a time of great danger upon the island from the birds when they are migrating northward. They come suddenly down from the sky in myriads, on their way to the continent, and I have known them to strip the little plot of every green shoot in a single day, utterly bare. Nothing but fishing nets draped over the whole space will save the garden when these hungry hordes descend. But I do not lose patience with the birds, however sorely they try me. I love them too well. How should they know that the garden was not planted for them? Those belonging to the thrush tribe are the most mischievous; the others do not disturb the flower beds so much. The friendly robin, though a thrush, only comes for worms, to which he is more than welcome. Most of the other birds—bobolinks, kingbirds, orioles, purple finches, and many other beautiful creatures less familiar—stay with us for a short time only, on their passage north or south every year; but a single pair of kingbirds build every summer in the one tall elm-tree on the island, where also builds a cosy nuthatch and raises a numerous family, and one pair of most interesting kingfishers haunts the upper cove till late in the season. A Maryland yellow-throat began building here last summer. For several years one pair of cuckoos lingered through the summer, but at last ceased to come. A few blackbirds build, the white-throats stay late, but several varieties of swallows, the song-sparrows, and sandpipers remain and rear their broods. How we wish the robins would stay too, and the orioles and all the sweet company! But there are no trees to shelter them. Their coming and going, however, is a matter of the greatest interest to the little family on the island, and we are thrown into a state of the deepest excitement by the apparition of a scarlet tanager, or a rose-breasted grosbeak, or any of those unfamiliar beauties. Once a ferruginous thrush came and stayed a week with us in early June. Every day when he perched on a ridge-pole or chimney-top and sang, the whole family turned out in a body to listen, making a business of it, attending to nothing else while that thrilling melody was poured out on the silent air. That was a gift of the gods which we could, none of us, afford to neglect!

❧

14th. Sunday. A storm of wild wind and flooding rain, the storm the loons predicted! At breakfast my gardening brother said, "Well, my sweet peas are all gone!" "Oh," I cried in the greatest sympathy, "what has happened to them?" for he had planted six pounds or more and they had come up finely. "Sparrows," was his laconic reply. I flew to my boxes on the piazza: they were safe, only through a tiny crack in the net over one a bird had wriggled its little body, and pulled up and flung the plants to right and left all over the steps. But my brother's long rows, so green last night, were bare except for broken stems and withering leaves. Alas, it is so much trouble to cover such a large area with netting, he thought this time he would trust to luck, or Providence, or whatever one chooses to call it, but it is a fatal thing to do. Now he has to plant all over again, even though I shall share my boxes with him, and it will make his garden very late indeed. This time he will not fail to put nets over all! I sat on the piazza sheltered from the rain and watched the birds. Unmindful of the tempest, they skipped gayly round the garden, over and round the steps, examined all the tucked up boxes of Sweet Peas, wished they could get in, but finding it out of the question gave it up and resigned themselves to the inevitable. To and fro, here and there they went, peering into every nook and corner, behind every leaf and stick and board and stalk, busily pecking away and devouring something with the greatest industry. I drew nearer to discover what it could be, and to my great joy found it was the slugs which the rain had called forth from their hiding-places; the birds were working the most comprehensive slaughter among them. At that pleasing sight I forgave them on the spot all their trespasses against me.

Florence Merriam Bailey. Courtesy of Eithne Golden Sax.

FLORENCE MERRIAM BAILEY

1863–1948

Florence Merriam Bailey, a distinguished ornithologist and nature writer, was the first woman to be elected a fellow of the American Ornithologists' Union, a status not granted her until 1929 when she was sixty years old. For most of her life Bailey was part of the scientific community associated with the United States Biological Survey in Washington, D.C. This group numbered among its luminaries her older brother, C. Hart Merriam, first director of the United States Biological Survey and a scientific leader of great distinction.

Born in 1863, Florence grew up with her three siblings on the country estate of prosperous parents in Locust Grove, New York. The family had a strong love of natural history. Florence when a student at Smith College from 1882 to 1886 was already proficient enough in bird identification to take fellow students on bird rambles in the countryside around Northampton. She began to write about birds in her senior year. The several essays originally published in *Bird-Lore* appeared later, in 1899, in her volume, *Birds Through an Opera Glass*.

For a short while after college Bailey pursued a career as a social worker but contracted tuberculosis and was forced to seek a rest cure in the favorable climate of Utah and California. After spending the summer of 1893 in a Mormon village, an experience she later described in *My Summer in a Mormon Village*, she went on to Palo Alto, where in better health she attended classes at Stanford University. In the spring of 1894 she passed a few months on a ranch in a valley in San Diego County, riding horseback and observing birds. It is this halcyon adventure she described in her book *A-Birding on a Bronco* in 1896. Two years later she published *Birds of Village and Field*, a handy beginner's primer on birdwatching, attractively illustrated by Ernest Seton Thompson and Robert Ridgway.

Like so many women bird enthusiasts of her generation, Florence Bailey was deeply committed to nature education. When she returned east to take up residence with her brother, Hart, in Washington D.C., her activities centered around teaching Washingtonians about their native birds. In 1897 she helped to found the Audubon Society of the District of Columbia and in 1898 began to teach bird classes in both field and laboratory ornithology to public school teachers in the Washington area. Bailey continued these educational activities even after her marriage and subsequent devotion to field ornithology.

In 1899 Florence Merriam married Vernon Bailey, a young naturalist employed by her brother at the Biological Survey. For the remaining decades of her career, Bailey turned to more serious bird study as she accompanied her husband, who eventually became chief field biologist for the Survey, on numerous expeditions to Texas, California, Arizona, and New Mexico.

Vernon Bailey was notoriously parsimonious and austere in equipping his expeditions. From these arduous journeys, undertaken under difficult physical conditions on which Bailey evidently thrived, came her most serious books. It was not particularly unusual for a woman to accompany her husband on field expeditions. Both Frank Chapman's wife and Ernest Seton Thompson's wife, Grace, went along as their husbands' assistants. Florence Bailey, unlike these other women, fully participated in the scientific work. While her husband cataloged the mammals of the regions they explored, Florence amassed much needed information on their birdlife. In 1902 she published the *Handbook of Birds of the Western United States*, a book which went through several editions and was for many years the standard work in the field.

As a complementary volume to her husband's *Mammals of New Mexico*, Florence Bailey compiled a comprehensive report on the birds of that region. The *Birds of New Mexico*, published by the New Mexico Department of Game and Fish in 1928, was awarded the Brewster Medal for original scientific ornithological work by the American Ornithologists' Union. It was the first book by a woman to be so honored. In 1930 she was awarded an honorary degree by the University of New Mexico. She died in 1948, having outlived her partner in science and constant companion, Vernon Bailey, by six years.

There are many extraordinary aspects of Bailey's career: her steady production of serious ornithological writing, her egalitarian relationship with her scientist husband, her inexhaustible organizational and educational energies, her easy companionship with famous scientists who consistently found welcome at the Baileys' Washington home. But her travel writings about birdwatching probably remain her most distinctive contribution to the literature of natural history. I have chosen a chapter from *A-Birding on a Bronco* for its youthful exuberance and energy. Written when Bailey was thirty-three years old, the book described the months she spent in a California ranching valley while taking the cure for tuberculosis. The book is alive with the high spirits and optimism of a young woman freed from the trammels of urban society. With Bailey we inhale the crisp morning air of her mountain retreat. We rejoice with her in her freedom, and along the way we learn about the birds characteristic of the valley she explored on her calm little horse. *A-Birding on a Bronco* shimmers with the intelligence of a deeply gifted young woman who was later to fulfill her early promise with distinction.

Florence Merriam Bailey stands as an early example for contemporary women naturalists. With quiet determination and strong personal commitment, she lived a well-rounded and stimulating life which seems thoroughly modern.

Our Valley

"Climb the mountain back of the house and you can see the Pacific," the ranchman told me with a gleam in his eye; and later, when I had done that, from the top of a peak at the foot of the valley he pointed out the distant blue mountains of Mexico. Then he gave me his daughter's saddle horse to use as long as I was his guest, that I might explore the valley and study its birds to the best advantage. Before coming to California, I had known only the birds of New York and Massachusetts, and so was filled with eager enthusiasm at the thought of spending the migration and nesting season in a new bird world.

I had no gun, but was armed with opera-glass and note-book, and had Ridgway's Manual to turn to in all my perplexities. Every morning, right after breakfast, my horse was brought to the door and I set out to make the rounds of the valley. I rode till dinner time, getting acquainted with the migrants as they came from the south, and calling at the more distant nests on the way. After dinner I would take my camp-stool and stroll through the oaks at the head of the valley, for a quiet study of the nearer nests. Then once more my horse would be brought up for me to take a run before sunset; and at night I would identify my new birds and write up the notes of the day. What more could observer crave? The world was mine. I never spent a happier spring. The freedom and novelty of ranch life and the exhilaration of days spent in the saddle gave added zest to the delights of a new fauna. In my small valley circuit of a mile and a half, I made the acquaintance of about seventy-five birds, and without resort to the gun was able to name fifty-six of them.

My saddle horse, a white bronco who went by the musical name of Canello, had been broken by a Mexican whose cruelty had tamed the wild blood in his veins and left him with a fear of all swarthy things. Now he could be ridden bareback by the little girls, with only a rope noose around his nose, and was warranted to stand still before a flock of birds so long as there was grass to eat. He was to be relied on as a horse of ripe experience and mature judgment in matters of local danger. No power of bit or spur could induce him to set foot upon a piece of 'boggy land,' and to give me confidence one of the ranchman's sons said, "Wherever I've killed a rattlesnake from him he'll shy for years," and went on to cite localities where a sudden, violent lurch had nearly sent him over Canello's head! What greater recommendation could I wish?

If the old horse had had any wayward impulses left, his Mexican bit would have subdued them. It would be impossible to use such an iron in the mouth of an eastern horse. They say the Mexicans sometimes break horses' jaws with it. From the middle of the bit, a flat bar of iron, three quarters of an inch wide, extended back four inches, lying on the horse's tongue or sticking into the roof of his mouth, according to the use of the curb——there was no other rein. The bit alone weighed sixteen ounces. The bridle, which came from Ensenada in Lower California, then the seat of a great gold excitement, was made of braided raw-hide. It was all hand work; there was not a buckle about it. The leather quirt at the end of the reins was the only whip necessary. When I left the ranch the bridle was presented to me, and it now hangs beside my study door, a proud trophy of my western life, and one that is looked upon with mingled admiration and horror by eastern horsemen.

Canello and I soon became the best of friends. I found in him a valuable second—for, as I had anticipated, the birds were used to grazing horses, and were much less suspicious of an equestrian than a foot passenger—and he found in me a movable stake, constantly leading him to new grazing ground; for when there was a nest to watch I simply hung the bridle over the pommel and let him eat, so getting free hands for opera-glass and note-book. To be sure, there were slight causes of difference between us. He liked to watch birds in the high alfalfa under the sycamores, but when it came to standing still where the hot sun beat down through the brush and there was nothing to eat, his interest in ornithology flagged perceptibly. Then he sometimes carried the rôle of grazing horse too far, marching off to a fresh clump of grass out of sight of my nest at the most interesting moment; or when I was intently gazing through my glass at a rare bird, he would sometimes give a sudden kick at a horse-fly, bobbing the glass out of range just as I was making out the character of the wing-bars.

From the ranch-house, encircled by live-oaks, the valley

widened out, and was covered with orchards and vineyards, inclosed by the low brush-grown ridges of the Coast Mountains. It was a veritable paradise for the indolent field student. With so much insect-producing verdure, birds were everywhere at all times. There were no long hours to sit waiting on a camp-stool, and only here and there a treetop to 'sky' the wandering birds. The only difficulty was to choose your intimates.

Canello and I had our regular beat, down past the blooming quince and apricot orchard, along the brush-covered side of the valley where the migrants flocked, around the circle through a great vineyard in the middle of the valley, past a pond where the feathered settlers gathered to bathe, and so back home to the oaks again.

I liked to start out in the freshness of the morning, when the fog was breaking up into buff clouds over the mountains and drawing off in veils over the peaks. The brush we passed through was full of glistening spiders' webs, and in the open the grass was overlaid with disks of cobweb, flashing rainbow colors in the sun.

As we loped gayly along down the curving road, a startled quail would call out, "Who-are-you'-ah? who-are-you'-ah?" and another would cry "quit" in sharp warning tones; while a pair would scud across the road like little hens, ahead of the horse; or perhaps a covey would start up and whirr over the hillside. The sound of Canello's flying hoofs would often rouse a long-eared jack-rabbit, who with long leaps would go bounding over the flowers, to disappear in the brush.

The narrow road wound through the dense bushy undergrowth known as 'chaparral,' and as Canello galloped round the sharp curves I had to bend low under the sweeping branches, keeping alert for birds and animals, as well as Mexicans and Indians that we might meet.

A WOMAN TENDERFOOT

51

Costumes such as these were fashionable for the active woman
at the turn of the century.

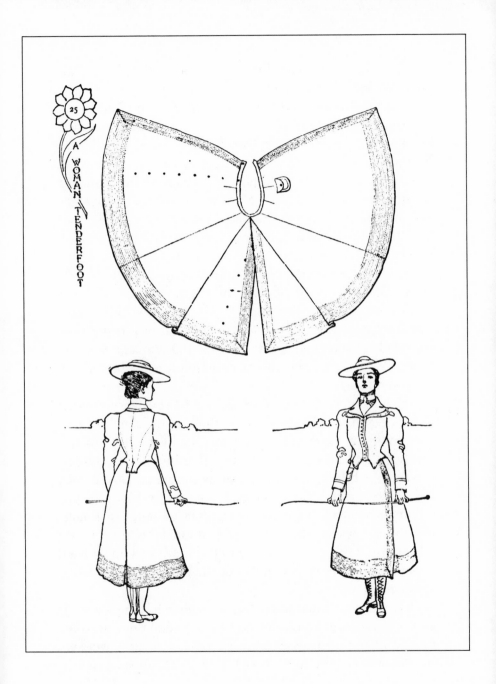

This corner of the valley was the mouth of Twin Oaks Canyon, and was a forest of brush, alive with birds, and visited only by the children whose small schoolhouse stood beside the giant twin oak from which the valley post-office was named. Flocks of migrating warblers were always to be found here; flycatchers shot out at passing insects; chewinks scratched among the dead leaves and flew up to sing on the branches; insistent vireos cried *tu-whip' tu-whip' tu-whip' tu-wee'-ah*, coming out in sight for a moment only to go hunting back into the impenetrable chaparral; lazuli buntings sang their musical round; blue jays—blue squawkers, as they are here called—went screaming harshly through the thicket; and the clear ringing voice of the wren-tit ran down the scale, now in the brush, now echoing from the boulder-strewn hills above. But the king of the chaparral was the great brown thrasher. His loud rollicking song and careless independent ways, so suggestive of his cousin, the mocking-bird, made him always a marked figure.

There was one dense corner of the thicket where a thrasher lived, and I used to urge Canello through the tangle almost every morning for the pleasure of sharing his good spirits. He was not hard to find, big brown bird that he was, standing on the top of a bush as he shouted out boisterously, *kick'-it-now, kick'-it-now, shut'-up shut'-up, dor'-a-thy dor'-a-thy*; or, calling a halt in his mad rhapsody, slowly drawled out, *whoa'-now, whoa'-now*. After listening to such a tirade as this, it was pleasant to come to an opening in the brush and find a band of gentle yellow-birds leaning over the blossoms of the white forget-me-nots.

There were a great many hummingbirds in the chaparral, and at a certain point on the road I was several times attacked by one of the pugnacious little warriors. I suppose we were treading too near his nest, though I was not keen-eyed enough to find it. From high in the air, he would come with a whirr, swooping down so close over our heads that Canello started uneasily and wanted to get out of the way. Down over our heads, and then high up in the air, he would swing back and forth in an arc. One day he must have shot at us half a dozen times, and another day, over a spot in the brush near us— probably where the nest was—he did the same thing a dozen times in quick succession.

In the midst of the brush corner were a number of pretty round oaks, in one of which the warblers gathered. My favorite tree was in blossom and alive with buzzing insects, which may have accounted for the presence of the warblers. While I sat in the saddle watching the dainty birds decked out in black and gold, Canello rested his nose in the cleft of the tree, quite unmindful of the busy warblers that flitted about the branches, darting up for insects or chasing down by his nose after falling millers.

One morning the ranchman's little girl rode over to school behind me on Canello, pillion fashion. As we pushed through the brush and into the opening by the schoolhouse, scattered over the grass sat a flock of handsome black-headed grosbeaks, the western representative of the eastern rose-breast, looking, in the sun, almost as red as robins. They had probably come from the south the night before. As we watched, they dispersed and sang sweetly in the oaks and brush.

In the giant twin oak under whose shadow the little school-house stood was an owl's nest. When I stopped under it, nothing was to be seen but the tips of the ears of the brooding bird. But when I tried to hoot after the manner of owls, the angry old crone rose up on her feet above the nest till I could see her round yellow eyes and the full length of her long ears. She snapped her bill fiercely, bristled up, puffing out her feathers and shaking them at us threateningly. Poor old bird! I was amused at her performances, but one of her little birds lay dead at the foot of the tree, and I trembled for the others, for the schoolchildren were near neighbors. Surely the old bird needed all her devices to protect her young. One day I saw on one side of the nest, below the big ears of the mother, the round head of a nestling.

It was pleasant to leave the road to ride out under the oaks along the way. There was always the delightful feeling that one might see a new bird or find some litttle friend just gone to housekeeping. One morning I discovered a bit of a wren under an oak with building material in her bill. She flew down to a box that lay under the tree and I dismounted to investigate. A tin can lay on its side in the box, and a few twigs and yellowish brown oak leaves were scattered about in a casual way, but the rusted lid of the can was half turned back, and well out of sight in the inside was a pretty round nest with one egg in it. I was delighted—such an appropriate place for a wren's nest—and sat down for her to come back. She was startled to find me there, and stopped on the edge of the board when just ready to jump down. She would have made a pretty picture as she stood hesitating, with her tail over her back, for the sun lit up her gray breast till it almost glistened and warmed her pretty brown head as she looked wistfully down at the box. After twisting and turning she went off to think the matter over, and, encouraged perhaps by my whistle, came back and hopped down into the little nest.

Two weeks later I was much grieved to find that the nest had been broken up. A horse had been staked under the tree, but he could not have done the mischief; for while the eggs were there, the nest itself was all jumbled up in the mouth of the can. I could not get it out of my mind for days. You become so much interested in the families you are watching that you feel as if their troubles were yours, and are haunted by the fear that they will think you have something to do with their accidents. They had taken me on probation at first, and at last had come to trust me—and then to imagine that I could deceive them and do the harm myself!

When Canello and I left the brushy side of the canyon and started across the valley, the pretty little horned larks, whose reddish backs matched the color of the road, would run on ahead of us, or let the horses come within a few feet of them, squatting down ready to start, but not taking wing till it seemed as if they would get stepped on. Sometimes one sat on a stone by the roadside, so busy singing its thin chattering song that it only flitted on to the next stone as we came up; for it never seemed to occur to the trustful birds that passers-by might harm them.

One of our most interesting birds nested in holes in the open uncultivated fields down the valley—the burrowing owl, known popularly, though falsely, as the bird who shares its nest with prairie dogs and rattlesnakes. Though they do not share their quarters with their neighbors, they have large families of their own. We once passed a burrow around which nine owls were sitting. The children of the ranchman called the birds the 'how-do-you-do owls,' from the way they bow their heads as people pass. The owls believe in facing the enemy, and the Mexicans say they will twist their heads off if you go round them times enough.

One of our neighbors milked his cows out in a field where the burrowing owls had a nest, and he told me that his collie had nightly battles with the birds. I rode down one evening to see the droll performance, and getting there ahead of the milkers found the bare knoll of the pasture peopled with ground squirrels and owls. The squirrels sat with heads sticking out of their holes, or else stood up outside on their hind legs, with the sun on their light breasts, looking, as Mr. Roosevelt says, like 'picket pins.' The little old yellowish owls who matched the color of the pasture sat on the fence posts, while the darker colored young ones sat close by their holes, matching the color of the earth they lived in. As I watched, one of the old birds flew down to feed its young. A comical little fellow ran up to meet his parent and then scudded back to the nest hole, keeping low to the ground as if afraid of being seen, or of disobeying his mother's commands. When the ranchman came with his cows, the small owls ducked down into their burrows out of sight.

Romulus, the collie, went up to the burrows and the old owls came swooping over his back screaming shrilly—the milkers told me that they often struck him so violently they nipped more than his hair! When the owls flew at him, Romulus would jump up into the air at them, and when they had settled back on the fence posts he would run up and start them off again. The performance had been repeated every night through the nesting season, and was getting to be rather an old story now, at least to Romulus. The ranchman had to urge him on for my benefit, and the owls acted as if they rather enjoyed the sport, though with them there was always the possibility that a reckless nestling might pop up its head from the ground at the wrong moment and come to grief. It would be interesting to know if the owls were really disturbed enough to move their nest another year.

When Canello and I faced home on our daily circuit of the valley we often found the vineyard well peopled. In April, when it was being cultivated, there was a busy scene. All the blackbirds of the neighborhood—both Brewer's and redwings—assembled to pick up grubs from the soft earth. A squad of them followed close at the plowman's heels, others flew up before his horse, while those that lagged behind in their hunt were constantly flying ahead to catch up, and those that had eaten all they could sat around on the neighboring grape-vines. The ranchman's son told me that when he was plowing the blackbirds were following him, two or three 'bee-birds,' as they call the Arkansas and Cassin's flycatchers, would take up positions on stakes overlooking the flock; and when one of the blackbirds got a worm, would fly down and chase after him till they got it away, regularly making their living from the blackbirds, as the eagles do from the fish hawks.

One day in riding by the vineyard, to my surprise and delight I saw one of the handsome yellow-headed blackbirds sitting with dignity on a grape-vine. Although his fellows often flock with redwings, this bird did not deign to follow the cultivator with the others, but flew off and away while I was watching, showing his striking white shoulder patches as he went. The distinguished birds were sometimes seen assembled farther down the valley; and I once had a rare pleasure in seeing a company of them perched high on the blooming mustard.

The son of the ranchman told me an interesting thing about the ordinary blackbirds. He said he had seen a flock of perhaps five hundred fly down toward a band of grazing sheep, and all but a few of the birds light on the backs of sheep. The animals did not seem to mind, and the birds flew from one to another and roosted and rode to their heart's content. They would drop to the ground, but if anything startled them, fly back to their sheep again. Sometimes he had seen a few of the blackbirds picking out wool for their nests by bracing themselves on the backs of the sheep, and pulling where the wool was loose. He had also seen the birds ride hogs, cattle, and horses; but he said the horses usually switched them off with their tails.

On our way home we passed a small pond made by the spring rains. Since it was the only body of water for miles

around, it was especially refreshing to us, and was the ren-
dezvous of all our feathered neighbors—how they must have
wished it would last all through the hot summer months! As
I rode through the long grass on the edge of the pond, dark
water snakes often wriggled away from under Canello's feet;
but he evidently knew they were harmless, for he paid no
attention to them, though he was mortally afraid of rattlers.
I did not like the feeling that any snake, however innocent,
was under my feet, so would pull him up out of the grass onto
a flat rock overlooking the pond.

In the fresh part of the morning, before the fog had entirely
melted away, the round pool at our feet mirrored the blue sky
and the small white clouds. If a breath of wind ruffled the
water into lines, in a moment more it was sparkling. Along
the margin of the water was a border of wild flowers, pink,
purple, and gold; on one side stood a group of sycamores, their
twisted trunks white in the morning sun and their branches
full of singing birds; while away to the south a line of dark
blue undulating hills was crowned by the peak from which we
had looked off on the mountains of Mexico. The air was
ringing with songs, the sycamores were noisy with the chatter
of blackbirds and bee-birds, and the bushes were full of sparrows.

There was an elder on the edge of the pond, and the
bathers flew to this and then flitted down to the water; and
when they flew up afterwards, lighted there to whip the water
out of their feathers and sun themselves before flying off. I
never tired watching the little bathers on the beach. One
morning a pipit came tipping and tilting along the sand, peeping in its wild, sad way. Another time a rosy-breasted linnet
stepped to the edge of the pond and dipped down daintily
where the water glistened in the sunshine, sending a delicate
circle rippling off from its own shadow. Then the handsome
white and golden-crowned sparrows came and bathed in ad-

joining pools. When one set of birds had flown off to dry their feathers, others took their places. A pair of blackbirds walked down the sand beach, but acted absurdly, as if they did not know what to do in water—it was a wonder any of the birds did in dry California! Two pieces of wood lay in the shallows, and the blackbirds flew to them and began to promenade. The female tilted her tail as if the sight of herself in the pond made her dizzy, but the male finally edged down gingerly and took a dip or two with his bill, after which both flew off.

On the mud flats on one side of the pond, bee-birds were busy flycatching, perching on sticks near the ground and making short sallies over the flat. Turtle doves flew swiftly past, and high over head hawks and buzzards circled and let themselves be borne by the wind.

Swallows came to the pond to get mud for their nests. A long line of them would light on the edge of the water, and then, as if afraid of wetting their feet, would hold themselves up by fluttering their long pointed wings. They would get a little mud, take a turn in the air, and come back for more, to make enough to pay them for their long journeys from their nests. Sometimes they would skim over the pond without touching the surface at all, or merely dip in lightly for a drink in passing; at others they would take a flying plunge with an audible splash. Now and then great flocks of them could be seen circling around high up against a background of clouds and blue sky.

One day I had a genuine excitement in seeing a snow-white egret perched on a bush by the water. I rode home full of the beautiful sight, but alas, my story was the signal for the ranchman's son to seize his gun and rush after the bird. Fortunately he did not find him, although he did shoot a green heron; but it was probably a short reprieve for the poor hunted creature.

Canello was so afraid of miring in the soft ground that it

was hard to get him across some places that seemed quite innocent. He would test the suspicious ground as carefully as a woman, one foot at a time; and if he judged it dangerous, would take the bits, turn around and march off in the opposite direction. I tried to force him over at first, but had an experience one day that made me quite ready to take all suggestions in such matters. This time he was deceived himself. We were on our homeward beat, off into the brush beyond the vineyard. I was watching for chewinks. We came to what looked like an old road grown up with soft green grass, and it was so fresh and tender I let Canello graze along at will; while keeping my eyes on the brush for chewinks. Suddenly Canello pricked up his ears and raised his head with a look of terror. Rattlesnakes or miring—it was surely one or the other! When I felt myself sinking, I knew which. I gave the horse a cut with the quirt to make him spring off the boggy ground, and looked off over his side to see how far down he was likely to go, but found myself going down backwards so fast I had to cling to the pommel. I lashed Canello to urge him out, and he struggled desperately, but it was no use. We were sinking in deeper and deeper, and I had to get off to relieve him of my weight. By this time his long legs had sunk in up to his body. On touching the ground I had a horrible moment thinking it might not hold me; but it bore well. Seizing the bridle with one hand and swinging the quirt with the other, I shouted encouragement to Canello, and, straining and struggling, he finally wrenched himself out and stepped on *terra firma*—I never appreciated the force of that expression before! The poor horse was trembling and exhausted when I led him up to high ground to remount, and neither of us had any desire to explore boggy lands after that.

On our morning round, Canello and I attended strictly to business—he to grazing, I to observing; but on our afternoon rides I, at least, felt that we might pay a little more heed to the beauties of the valley and the joys of horsebacking. Sometimes we would be overtaken by the night fog. One moment the mustard would be all aglow with sunshine; at the next, a sullen bank of gray fog would have risen over the mountain, obscuring the sun which had warmed us and lighted the mustard; and in a few moments it would be so cold and damp that I would urge Canello into a lope to warm our blood as we hurried home.

· 4 ·
NELTJE BLANCHAN
DOUBLEDAY
1865–1918

Neltje Blanchan Doubleday was born in Chicago in 1865. She attended the Misses Master's School in Dobbs Ferry and in 1886 married Frank N. Doubleday, who ten years later founded the publishing firm which today bears his name. They had three children, two boys and a girl. Although Neltje Doubleday was an enthusiastic birdwatcher, her debut in the publishing world came in 1889 with an anthropological book, the *Piegan Indians*. She subsequently wrote occasionally on Indian education and handicrafts, an interest she shared with other women naturalists of her day—Fannie Hardy Eckstorm was an expert on the Penobscot Indians, and Cordelia Stanwood learned Indian crafts such as basket weaving.

Doubleday's real passion, however, was for nature study. Her *Bird Neighbors* appeared in 1897 and was followed quickly by *Birds that Hunt and are Hunted*. She wrote two flower books as well—*Nature's Garden* in 1900 and the *American Flower*

Garden in 1909. She again turned to bird study in 1903 with *How to Attract the Birds* and finally, in 1917, with *Birds Worth Knowing,* which contained an excellent introductory essay on the value of wild birds to human beings. This last book was illustrated by Louis Agassiz Fuertes, the most respected bird artist of his time. Doubleday died suddenly in China in 1918 while she and her husband were traveling as members of an American Red Cross mission.

The Doubledays were a social couple, maintaining a residence in Oyster Bay as well as Manhattan. Neltje Doubleday counted among her friends the popular writer Gene Stratton Porter, whom she encouraged to write a book of birdwatching anecdotes. The result, *Homing with the Birds,* was published by Doubleday.

Neltje Doubleday's moral values reflected the attitudes of fashionable New York society at the end of the last century. Theodore Dreiser blamed her for the failure of *Sister Carrie* when it was published by the Doubleday firm. He was convinced that she was instrumental in having the book suppressed after a small number of copies were printed. Neltje Doubleday, like many of her contemporaries, was said to have found the subject matter of Dreiser's book repellent. And although firm proof of her involvement in the incident cannot be found, the moral tone of some of her writings adds credibility to the story.

Doubleday's books were lavishly produced in quarto size and extensively illustrated. They might have made delightful Christmas gifts for a nature-loving maiden aunt. But her outraged tone in describing the characteristics of hawks makes one wonder about the accuracy of her other work. Some inaccuracy is obvious in her observations of bird behavior in the 1903 book *How to Attract the Birds,* where the influence of the Reverend William J. Long can be felt. Long, a Con-

necticut clergyman, was a widely read nature essayist who
incurred the wrath of serious bird conservationists because of
his tall tales about the behavior of wild creatures. In her own
book, Doubleday describes odd activities she has observed,
not so much fabricating evidence as drawing clearly unsup-
portable conclusions. Reading Doubleday makes one think
that this earnest crusader and talented writer could have become an excellent writer of fiction as well.

Home Life

Sharp, ringing cries of alarm, then of terror, coming from a
pair of robins one morning in June, caused me to drop my
work suddenly, dash out of doors and follow the sound through
the garden, across the lane to a meadow where a vagrant cat,
with a now-or-never desperation, made a leap through the
grass even as I approached and, before my very eyes, snapped
up a baby robin in its cruel jaws. With as frantic a leap upon
the cat, I quickly pried its jaws apart and released the limp
and apparently dead bird. Three other young robins, which
had fallen out of the same nest in the cherry tree when a
heavy thunder shower weakened its mud-plastered walls the
night before, were squatting dejectedly on the ground, unable
to fly. So I gathered them up in my arms too, lest they fall a
certain prey to the cat, and deposited the little family in an
improvised flannel nest on a sunny upper balcony.

One might have supposed that the parents would find them
here, within fifty yards of their cherry tree home, and come
to feed them. Strangely enough, the old birds' cries of distress
were the last sign from either of them in the neighbourhood.
Did they flee the place in despair, thinking their babies foully

murdered by the cat and me? After waiting in vain for some response from them to the incessant, insistent *cheep, cheep,* from the balcony nursery, I could resist the cries of hunger no longer. Even the baby which had been literally snatched from the jaws of death had now recovered from his fright, not having received so much as a scratch, and was clamouring for food as loudly as the others, jerking himself upright with every *cheep,* as if stamping both feet with impatience at delay.

A Sixteen Hour Working Day

From that hour my preconceived ideas of bird life were radically changed. Once I had shared the popular notion of birds as rather idle creatures of pleasure, singing to pass the time away, free from every care while they flew aimlessly about in the sunshine, fed from the abundant hand of Nature. But bringing up those four feathered waifs taught me that birds doubtless work as hard for their living as any creatures on earth. At about four o'clock every morning sharp, hungry cries from the balcony wakened me. Perhaps it was because I was only a step-mother that I refused to go out on the lawn then in search of early worms. Another nap was more agreeably purchased by stuffing each little crop full of the yolk of hard boiled egg and baked potato mashed into a soft paste, the lumps washed down with a tiny trickle of fresh water from a stylographic pen-dropper. Such gaping yellow caverns as were stretched aloft to be filled while the little birds trembled with excitement, jostled one another and scrambled for first turn! Every hour regularly throughout the long day those imperious babies had to be satisfied. Ants' eggs from the bird store, a taste of mocking-bird food mixed with potato and an occasional cherry or strawberry agreed with the little gourmands perfectly. A small boy, who was subsidized to dig earthworms for them, called the bargain off after one day's efforts to supply their demand. Sixty worms had not been sufficient for creatures which eat at least their weight of food every twenty-four hours.

Doubtless they were spoiled babies from the first. At any rate they had me completely enslaved; all other interests were forgotten; not for anything would I have gone beyond their call. But real motherly joy in them came when their pin feathers fluffed out, their legs became stout enough to climb and hop over the wistaria vine on the balcony, stubby little tails fanned out pertly and full crops distended their speckled, thrush-like vests. When, after about two weeks spent on and around the balcony, the last of the quartette spread his strong wings and flew off to the strawberry patch to pick up his own living thenceforth, I realized as never before why the alert, military-looking, red-breasted robin of the spring becomes more and more faded and dejected as summer advances, and the joyous song of courting days diminishes until it ceases altogether after the father has helped his mate raise two broods. Yet with my utmost care I had probably not done half for those fledglings that their parents would have done.

What it Means to Rear a Brood

In a state of nature, what would a pair of robins do for their family? After the building of the nest—of itself no small labor—there follow fourteen long weary days and nights of confinement upon the eggs before they hatch. Thenceforth on the average of every fifteen minutes daily from dawn till dark both parents visit the nest, usually bringing in their bills food which they often travel far and work hard to find—earthworms, grasshoppers, locusts, beetles, the larvae of insects, choke cherries or other small fruits to be crammed with sharp but painless thrusts into the ever hungry mouths. The second an old bird alights on the home branch, up spring the little heads, every one agape, like jacks-in-the-box. In their loving zeal, the parents themselves often forget to eat. After every feeding, the nest must be inspected and cleaned, the excreta being either swallowed or carried away. Then the fledglings are picked over lest lice irritate their tender skins. Very many young birds die from this common pest of the nests, especially those whose cradles are lined with chicken feathers, which are nearly always infested.

Birds, like all wild creatures, live in a constant state of fear, but parenthood develops courage amazingly, just as it developes all the virtues. When climbing cats, snakes, small boys, hawks, crows, blue jays, red squirrels and other foes do not threaten the baby robins' safety, either heavy rains, high winds, or fierce sunshine may require the patient little mother to brood over her treasures. Before they are a week old their education begins. On the eleventh day, if all goes well, it is usually the mother who utters low endearing baby talk, coaxing the little fellows to hop out of the nest and about it. Coming near an ambitious youngster she stands but does not deliver a tempting morsel held just beyond his bill. Luring him with it farther and farther away, hopping and flying from branch to branch, she tantalizes the hungry baby, perhaps, but she educates him with no loss of time. When finally the young are able to trip lightly, swiftly over the grass after their parents, have learned to cock their heads to one side and listen with the intentness of veterans for the stirring of worms beneath the sod, to capture their own food and fly swiftly out of the presence of danger, their education is considered complete. The remainder they must acquire by experience, for even now their parents may be repairing the old nest or building a new one to receive a second brood.

Baby Birds' Diet

Walking along a hot, sandy road in Florda one morning, I met a young coloured woman with a little baby in her arms, pacing back and forth under a blazing sun. A glance sufficed to show that her baby was ill. It moaned piteously and its skin was burning hot, as well it might be even without fever.

"Come under this tree," said I, "and tell me why you are carrying that baby about in the heat."

" 'Cause he's sick and I'se waitin' fo' de doctor to happen along dis yeah road."

"What do you think is the matter with your baby?"

"I specks he done eat too much fried fish dis mornin'."

"Fried fish!" I exclaimed. "Why, the baby has no teeth!"

"No'm; he ain't got no teeth yet, but he's powerful fond of fried fish."

A Florida jay, which was noisily searching in the palmetto scrub behind us for a mouthful of food to carry home to her fledglings, was evidently more discriminating in her choice than the equally untaught human mother, for she rejected as unfit many insects which she, herself, would gladly have swallowed.

Many birds have one diet for their babies and another, quite different, for themselves, only the seed-eaters reverse our ideas and give their strongest meat to babes. However strict vegetarians certain of the finch tribe may be at maturity, they provide for the nursery a variety of insects. These are not often given alive and squirming, but after they have been knocked and bruised into a pulpy condition that is sure to cause no colic.

Even the birds which provide for their babies the same food that they themselves enjoy—which is by far the greater number—usually take the trouble to give it special preparation for the tender stomachs. Having no pepsin, lime-water or sterilizer at command, what could be a simpler way to prepare a perfectly digestible baby food, than to first swallow and digest it themselves, then pump it down the throats of offspring not yet old enough to be squeamish? In this way the young flickers, for example, are fed, but, as far as is known, no other wood-peckers. The flicker, or high-hole, collects a square meal of perhaps two or three thousand ants which partially digest while she is on her way home. Her approach is sure to summon the hungriest, or possibly the greediest youngster to the entrance of the tree cavity. Thrusting her bill far down his gaping throat, she uses force enough to impale him. One confidently expects the point to appear somewhere through the baby's back. With the same *staccato* motion used when drumming on a tree, she jerks her bill up and down so violently that the fledgling has all he can possibly do to hold on during the second or two it takes to pump part of the contents of her stomach into his. Yet the next baby pushes and scrambles for position when the first one slips back satisfied, just as if he anticipated a truly delightful experience! By this same method—regurgitation—are humming-birds, purple finches, and many other birds fed, doubtless many more than we suppose, for it is only a few years since the habits of so common a bird as the flicker were thoroughly studied. The vultures eject the contents of their stomachs at will. . . .

Fish-eating birds especially are wont to regurgitate their

food. While the cormorant is flying home with its babies' dinner safely stowed away, the fish's skin will be digested off completely, leaving the meat in prime condition for young stomachs. On the other hand, some fish eaters allow their babies to swallow skin, bones and all. The pelicans which ply the coast of Florida, searching for food, collect a quantity of fish in the great pouch which hangs from their lower bill like the silk bag which used to drop from beneath our grandmother's sewing tables. On returning to the nest, open flies the parent's bill displaying the fish. The eager, crowding babies are invited to thrust their heads into the pouch and help themselves. And how they prod and poke about among the morning's catch, to make the best selection possible! It is a wonder the skinny pouch is not torn asunder by such thrusts and stabs as the ill-mannered little gourmands give it. No sooner is the family larder emptied, and the parent's back is turned to refill it, than the dissatisfied youngsters begin to squabble over the contents of one another's pouches. Their greed seems even more insatiable than their appetites.

The hawks, owls, ospreys and some other birds should make the best of stepmothers, so bountifully do they provide for their nurseries. Mice, muskrats, eels, small fish, young rabbits, rats, woodcock and grouse, weighing over eighteen pounds in the aggregate, were the surplus food removed from the nest of a pair of horned owls, wherein two owlets only had to be supplied. Some birds of prey heap food about their offspring until they can scarcely see over the piles. Owls choose the brains only of most of their captives as food for their babies.

A remarkable provision is made for young pigeons during the first week of their lives. When the squabs thrust their bills into their parents' throats to be fed, there arises what is erroneously called "pigeon's milk" from the crops of both the father and the mother. This secretion, formed from the peeled

lining of the parents' crop—a result following incubation—
gradually becomes mixed with regurgitated food as the squabs
grow older, and it ceases only when their digestion is strong
enough to dispense with baby diet. Apparently this strange
secretion is peculiar to the pigeon tribe.

Lower and Upper Classes

The labour involved in rearing a family differs, of course, with
the species by reason of physical conditions, temperament,
and environment. Some birds of the lower orders have little
required of them by Nature, while others, more highly or-
ganized, are enslaved by family cares as if they were afflicted
with the New England conscience. But, generally speaking,
there are only two classes: the lower or precocial birds, including those which, fully clothed and wide awake when
hatched, are able to run or swim at once and pick up their
own living like our domestic fowls, ducks, Bob Whites, grouse,
plover and snipe; and the altricial birds—those which come
into the world blind, naked and helpless, or nearly so, like
the heron, kingfisher, woodpecker, robin, and all our song
birds. The precocial ruffed grouse develops from an egg that
is large in proportion to the size of the mother's body, the
heavy yolk nourishing the young bird during eighteen days of
incubation and even after, whereas the altricial vireo lays a
very small egg that hatches in one week. But even precocial
and altricial birds of the same size in maturity may have come
out of shells that differ as greatly as a silver dollar differs from
a quarter. And the length of the period of incubation is in
nearly, if not exact, ratio to the size of the egg. The largest
bird's egg we know, the ostrich's, requires forty days, some-

times a full six weeks, to hatch. As in all arbitrary divisions, it is not always possible to draw a sharp dividing line. Between precocial and altricial birds, innumerable gradations occur.

Among the lower bird forms, polygamy being common, there can be no home life, and it is fortunate these chicks are independent little creatures from the first. Indeed, it was John Fiske who contributed to science the fact that the advancement of all creatures—not of the human race alone—has been measured by the prolongation of the period of infancy. The longer the young are dependent on both parents, the stronger the tie becomes between mates, the more prolonged and beautiful the home life with all its strengthening physical and moral influences making for the uplift of the species, until, among civilized humans, home living becomes a life habit, far outlasting the presence of children beneath the roof. Let the so-called advanced woman, with her unscientific notions of a readjustment of the partition of labor between the sexes, remember that the males among the ostrich tribe, most nearly related to the reptiles, take entire charge of the young. Certain plover fathers, too, and phalaropes attend to nursery duties, even to sitting on the eggs, leaving their wives free to waste their strength on clubs, pink teas, or whatever may be the equivalent among "advanced" feathered females. On the other hand, the selfish, dandified drakes of some of our wild ducks desert their mates as soon as the first egg is laid.

Birds that Hunt and are Hunted

Sharp-shinned Hawk (*Accipiter velox*)
Called also: pigeon hawk; little blue darter
Length: Male 10 to 12 inches; female 12 to 14 inches

Male and Female: Upper parts slaty gray. Tail, which is about 3 inches longer than tips of wings and nearly square, is ashy gray, barred with blackish, and with whitish tip; throat white, streaked with blackish. Other under parts whitish, barred on sides and breast with rusty, buff and brown, lining of wings white, spotted with dusky; head small; tarsus slender and feathered half way; feet slender. Immature birds have dusky upper parts, margined with rufous; tail resembling adults. Under parts buff or whitish, streaked or spotted with rust or blackish.

Range: North America in general; nesting throughout the United States and wintering from Massachusetts to Guatemala.

Season: Permanent resident, except in northern parts of range.

A smaller edition of Cooper's hawk (to be distinguished from it chiefly by its square, instead of rounded, tail), like it, dashes through the air with a speed and audacity that spread consternation among the little song and game birds and poultry, once it appears, like a flash of "feathered lightening," in their midst. Cries of terror from many sympathizers when a sparrow, a goldfinch, a warbler, or some tiny victim is making desperate efforts to escape, first attract one's notice; but of what avail are the stones hurled after a hawk that swoops and dodges, twists and turns, in imitation of every movement of the panic stricken bird he presses after, closer and closer, until, at the end of a long chase when it is exhausted and almost worried to death, he strikes it with talons so sharp and long that they penetrate to the very vitals? Now alighting on the ground, he rends the warm flesh from its bones with a beak as savage as the talons. If the little bird had but known enough to remain in the thicket! A race for life in the open seems to the pursuing villain a fiendish satisfaction: let his little prey but dash toward the woods, where he knows as well as it does that it is safe, and one fell swoop cuts the journey short. There can be little said in praise of a marauder that boldly enters the poultry yard and devours dozens of chicks, attacks and worsts game birds quite as large as itself, and that eats very few mice and insects and an overwhelming proportion of birds of the greatest value and charm. The so called "hen-hawks" and "chicken hawks"—much slandered birds—do not begin to be so destructive as this little reprobate that, like its larger prototype and the equally villainous goshawk, too often escapes the charge of shot they so richly deserve.

Unhappily, the sharp-shinned hawk is one of the most abundant species we have. Doubtless because it is small and looks inoffensive enough, as it soars in narrow circles overhead, its worse than useless life is often spared.

Cac, cac, cac, very much like one of the flicker's calls, is this hawk's love song apparently, for it seldom, if ever, lifts its voice, except at the nesting season. Now it seeks the woods to make a fairly well constructed nest of twigs, lined with smaller ones, or strips of bark, with the help of its larger mate, from fifteen to forty feet from the ground. Strangely enough, the nest is not a common find, however abundant the bird, neither Nuttall nor Wilson having discovered one in all their tireless wanderings. Dense evergreens, the favorite nesting localities, conceal the nest, large as it is—much too large for so small a bird, one would think. A pair of these hawks may sometimes repair their last season's home but will never appropriate an old tenement belonging to others, as many hawks do. Late in May, or even so late as June, from three to six bluish or greenish white eggs, heavily blotched or washed with cinnamon red or chocolate brown, keep both parents busy incubating and, later, feeding a hungry family. Climb up to the nursery, and angry, fearless birds dash and strike at an intruder as if he were not larger than a goldfinch.

❦

American Goshawk (*Accipiter atricapillus*)

Called also: blue hen hawk; partridge hawk

Length: Male, 22 inches; female 24 inches

Male and Female: Upper parts bluish slate, darkish or blackish on head; white line over and behind eye; tall like back and banded with blackish bars, the last one the broadest, and the tip whitish. Entire under parts evenly marked with irregular wavy lines of gray and white, the barring usually most heavy on the flanks and underneath. Immature birds have dusky upper parts margined with chestnut, the tail brownish gray barred with black, the under parts white or buff streaked with black. Bill dark bluish. Feet yellow.

Range: Northern North America; nests from northern United States northward; winters so far south as Virginia.

Season: Permanent resident.

Another villain of deepest dye; what good can be said of it beyond that it wears handsome feathers, is a devoted mate and parent, a fearless hunter, and of some small, if disproportionate, value to the farmer in occasionally eating field mice and insects? Whitewashing is useless in the case of a bird known to be the most destructive creature on wings. No more daring marauder prowls above the poultry yards than the goshawk that drops like a thunderbolt from a clear sky at the farmer's very feet and carries off his chickens before his eyes. Grouse, Bob Whites, ducks, and rabbits—in fact, all sportsmen's pets and innumerable songbirds, are hunted down with a dash and spirit worthy of a better motive. Bloodthirsty, delighting in killing what it often cannot eat, marvelously keen sighted, a powerful, swift flyer, aggressive, and constantly on the alert, it is small wonder all lesser birds become panic-stricken when this murderer sails within striking distance.

Without a quiver of its wings it will sail and sail, apparently with the most innocent intent. Again, with strong wing beats, it will rush through the air and overtake a duck that flies at the rate of a hundred miles an hour, seize it by the throat, sever its windpipe and fly off with its burden. One very rarely sees the goshawk perching and waiting for prey to come to it. When it does so, it holds itself erect, elegant and spirited as ever. After tearing the legs off a rugged grouse, and plucking every feather, this villain has been known to prepare another and another until five were ready for an orgie, which consisted of only fragments of each, torn with its savage beak. Mr. H.D. Minot tells of watching a goshawk press into a company of pine grosbeaks and seize one in each foot. Happily the agony is short, for a hawk's talons penetrate the vitals.

Although a northern ranger, the goshawk nests early—in April or early May—and placing a quantity of twigs and grasses close to the trunk of a tree, anywhere from fifteen to seventy feet from the ground, both mates take turns in attending to the nursery duties after from two to four pale bluish green eggs that fade to dull white have been laid. Now the hawks are more audacious and vicious than ever, as their piercing cries indicate, and it is an irrepressible collector who dares rob them.

· 5 ·

GENE STRATTON
PORTER

1863–1924

Gene Stratton Porter was born in 1863 on a farm near Wabash, Indiana. She was educated in local schools and did not attend university. As a girl Porter took a passionate interest in nature. An apparently autobiographical statements appears in the *National Cyclopedia of American Biography* for 1914:

> Her mother was of Dutch extraction, and like all Dutch women had a passionate love of flowers, which the daughter inherited. The daughter, in fact, loved all living things, and very early roamed the woods, watched the birds, fed butterflies, made pets of the squirrels and rabbits, collected wild flowers, and as she grew older she gathered arrow points and goose quills for sale in Fort Wayne.

In 1886 she married Charles Darwin Porter, a druggist and farmer from Geneva, Indiana, a town close to Decatur. Their

Gene Stratton Porter. Courtesy of Indiana State Museum.

only child, Jeanette, was born in 1887 and later became her mother's collaborator and biographer.

In 1895 Porter's family bought her a camera outfit, and she began to photograph birds in a serious way. Her photographic work led to a writing career when publishers began to request texts to accompany her expert, delightful pictures. Oil had been found on the family property a few years earlier, and the income from leases had enabled her to build a fourteen-room cabin on the edge of the Limberlost Swamp near Geneva, where she and her family resided. The Limberlost Swamp became the setting and inspiration for her popular juvenile fiction.

Porter's first book, *The Song of the Cardinal* (1903), is a fictional account of birdlife and was illustrated with her own photographs. But with *Freckles* in 1904 and its sequel, *A Girl of the Limberlost* in 1909, she hit upon a combination of nature lore and romantic fiction which earned her instant fame, popularity, and wealth. It is estimated that at the time of her death Porter's books had sold between eight and nine million copies.

In 1913 when the Limberlost Swamp was drained for agriculture Porter moved to northern Indiana. She built an even larger rustic cabin staffed with numerous servants and equipped for large groups of guests. In 1919 she moved to California, built two houses, one in Bel Air and one on Catalina Island, and formed a production company to make commercial films based on her books. She died in an automobile accident in 1924.

Porter's stories have immediate appeal for the young reader, and her books still interest the young. A twelve-year-old girl recently found *A Girl of the Limberlost* "really good and not at all old-fashioned." The critics, however, never found merit in her work. In 1922 in an attempt to gain greater recognition she wrote an allegorical lyric poem, "Firebird," and a novel for adults, the *White Flag*. Neither was popular with readers or critics.

Porter was a product of middle class midwestern America. She believed passionately in the ability of the individual to rise above difficulties and disadvantages through moral worth and hard work. Strength of character, she believed, arose from strong identification with values embodied in nature. Thus her stories were always written with the moral improvement of children in mind.

The characters in her books are rarely without redeeming qualities and always change their personalities for the better because of an example set by the hero or heroine. The early chapter of *Freckles* reprinted here is an excellent example of the peculiarites as well as the charm of Porter's fiction writing. Freckles is a maimed orphan youth from the slums of Chicago who, seeking a new life, asks for and receives employment from the owner of a large and valuable timber tract in the Limberlost Swamp. Freckles is to guard the timber lines against poachers by walking them daily and checking for faults in the fences. He is given room and board by a plain but honest Scottish family also employed by the lumberman. Although Freckles is at first frightened by nature, the natural world soon becomes the great consolation of his life and an inspiration for diligence. Loveless and lonely, he finds in the birds and other creatures of the swamp the friends and family he never had.

Glamor is not altogether absent from Porter's story, for Freckles falls in love with his boss's daughter and, although poor and nameless, is allowed to marry her. In the end it is discovered that Freckles is actually the son of a wealthy Irish nobleman. So his goodness, inherent in the beginning of the story, is given the stamp of social respectability as well.

Porter is a superb storyteller. There is an unusual mixture of nature lore, social ambition, and plain old fantasy in her fiction which endears it to children and adults as well. Her insistence upon the beauty and moral worth of nature, and especially of birds, earns her a well-deserved place in the top ranks of the nature education movement in the early twentieth century.

Wherein Freckles Proves His Mettle and Finds Friends

Next morning found Freckles in clean, whole clothing, fed, and rested. Then McLean outfitted him and gave him careful instruction in the use of his weapon. The Boss showed him around the timber-line, and engaged him a place to board with the family of his head-teamster, Duncan, whom he had brought from Scotland with him, and who lived in a small clearing he was working out between the swamp and the corduroy. When the gang started for the south camp, Freckles was left to guard a fortune in the Limberlost. That he was under guard himself those first weeks he never knew.

Each hour was torture to the boy. The restricted life of a great city orphanage was the other extreme of the world compared with the Limberlost. He was afraid for his life every minute. The heat was intense. The heavy wading-boots rubbed his feet until they bled. He was sore and stiff from his long tramp and outdoor exposure. The seven miles of trail was agony at every step. He practised at night, under the direction of Duncan, until he grew sure in the use of his revolver. He cut a stout hickory cudgel, with a knot on the end as big as his fist, and it never left his hand. What he thought in those first days he himself could not recall clearly afterward.

His heart stood still every time he saw the beautiful marsh-grass begin a sinuous waving *against* the play of the wind, as McLean had told him it would. He bolted a half-mile with the first boom of the bittern, and his hat lifted with every yelp of the sheitpoke. Once he saw a lean, shadowy form following him, and fired his revolver. Then he was frightened worse than ever for fear it might have been Duncan's collie.

The first afternoon that he found his wires down, and he was compelled to plunge knee deep into the black swamp-muck to restring them, he became so ill from fear and nervousness that he scarcely could control his shaking hand to do the work. With every step, he felt that he would miss secure footing and be swallowed in that clinging sea of blackness. In dumb agony he plunged forward, clinging to the posts and trees until he had finished restringing and testing the wire. He had consumed much time. Night closed in. The Limberlost stirred gently, then shook herself, growled, and awoke around him.

There seemed to be a great owl hooting from every hollow tree, and a little one screeching from every knot-hole. The bellowing of monster bull-frogs was not sufficiently deafening to shut out the wailing of whip-poor-wills that seemed to come from every bush. Night-hawks swept past him with their shivering cry, and bats struck his face. A prowling wild cat missed its catch and screamed with rage. A straying fox bayed incessantly for its mate.

The hair on the back of Freckles' neck rose as bristles, and his knees wavered beneath him. He could not see whether the dreaded snakes were on the trail, or, in the pandemonium, hear the rattle for which McLean had cautioned him to listen. He stood motionless in an agony of fear. His breath whistled between his teeth. The perspiration ran down his face and body in little streams.

Something big, black, and heavy came crashing through the swamp close to him, and with a yell of utter panic Freckles ran—how far he did not know; but at last he gained control over himself and retraced his steps. His jaws set stiffly and the sweat dried on his body. When he reached the place from which he had started to run, he turned and with measured steps made his way down the line. After a time he realized that he was only walking, so he faced that sea of horrors again. When he came toward the corduroy, the cudgel fell to test the wire at each step.

Sounds that curdled his blood seemed to encompass him, and shapes of terror to draw closer and closer. Fear had so gained the mastery that he did not dare look behind him; and just when he felt that he would fall dead before he ever reached the clearing, came Duncan's rolling call, "Freckles! Freckles!" A shuddering sob burst in the boy's dry throat. But he only told Duncan that finding the wire down had caused the delay.

The next morning he started on time. Day after day, with his heart pounding, he ducked, dodged, ran when he could, and fought when he was brought to bay. If he ever had an idea of giving up, no one knew it; for he clung to his job without the shadow of wavering. All these things, in so far as he guessed them, Duncan, who had been set to watch the first weeks of Freckles' work, carried to the Boss at the south camp; but the innermost, exquisite torture of the thing the big Scotchman never guessed, and McLean, with his finer perceptions, came only a little closer.

After a few weeks, when Freckles learned that he was still living, that he had a home, and the very first money he ever had possessed was safe in his pockets, he began to grow proud. He yet sidestepped, dodged, and hurried to avoid being late again, but he was gradually developing the fearlessness that men ever acquire of dangers to which they are hourly accustomed.

His heart seemed to be leaping when his first rattler disputed the trail with him, but he mustered courage to attack it with his club. After its head had been crushed, he mastered an Irishman's inborn repugnance for snakes sufficiently to cut off its rattles to show Duncan. With this victory, his greatest fear of them was gone.

Then he began to realize that with the abundance of food in the swamp, flesh-hunters would not come on the trail and attack him, and he had his revolver for defence if they did. He soon learned to laugh at the big, floppy birds that made horrible noises. One day, watching behind a tree, he saw a crane solemnly performing a few measures of a belated nuptial song-and-dance with his mate. Realizing that it was intended in tenderness, no matter how it appeared, the lonely, starved heart of the boy sympathized with them.

Before the first month passed, he was fairly easy about his job, and by the next he rather liked it. Nature can be trusted to work her own miracle in the heart of any man whose daily task keeps him alone among her sights, sounds, and silences.

When day after day the only thing that relieved his utter loneliness was the companionship of the birds and beasts of the swamp, it was the most natural thing in the world that Freckles should turn to them for friendship. He began by instinctively protecting the weak and helpless. He was astonished at the quickness with which they became accustomed to him and the disregard they showed for his movements, when they learned that he was not a hunter and that the club he carried was used more frequently for their benefit than his own. He scarcely could believe what he saw.

From the effort to protect the birds and animals, it was only a short step to the possessive feeling, and with that sprang the impulse to caress and provide. Through fall, when brooding was finished and the upland birds sought the swamp in swarms to feast on its seeds and berries, Freckles was content with watching them and speculating about them. Outside of half a dozen of the very commonest, they were strangers to him. The likeness of their actions to humanity was an hourly surprise.

When black frosts began stripping the Limberlost, cutting the ferns, shearing the vines from the trees, mowing the succulent green things of the swale, and setting the leaves swirling down, he watched the departing troops of his friends with dismay. He began to realize that he was going to be left alone. He made especial efforts toward friendliness with the hope that he could induce some of them to stay. It was then that he conceived the idea of carrying food to the birds; for he saw that they were leaving for lack of it. But he could not stop them. Day after day, flocks gathered and departed. By the time the first snow whitened his trail around the Limberlost, there were left only the little black-and-white juncos, the sapsuckers, yellowhammers, a few patriarchs among the flaming cardinals, the blue jays, the crows, and the quail.

Then Freckles began his wizard work. He cleared a space of swale, and twice a day he spread a birds' banquet. By the middle of December the strong winds of winter had beaten most of the seed from the grass and bushes. The snow fell, covering the swamp, and food was very scarce and difficult to find. The birds scarcely waited until Freckles' back was turned to attack his provisions. In a few weeks they flew toward the clearing to meet him. During the bitter weather of January they came half-way to the cabin every morning, and fluttered around him as doves all the way to the feeding-ground. Before February they were so accustomed to him, and so hunger-driven, that they would perch on his head and shoulders, and the saucy jays would try to pry into his pockets.

Then Freckles added to wheat and crumbs, every scrap of refuse food he could find at the cabin. He carried to his pets the parings of apples, turnips, potatoes, stray cabbage-leaves, and carrots, and tied to the bushes meat-bones having scraps of fat and gristle. One morning, he found a gorgeous cardinal and a rabbit side by side sociably nibbling a cabbage-leaf, and that instantly gave to him the idea of cracking nuts, from the store he had gathered for Duncan's children, for the squirrels, in the effort to add them to his family. Soon he had them coming—red, grey, and black; and he became filled with a vast impatience that he did not know their names or habits.

So the winter passed. Every week McLean rode to the Limberlost; never on the same day or at the same hour. Always he found Freckles at his work, faithful and brave, no matter how severe the weather.

The boy's earnings constituted his first money; and when the Boss explained to him that he could leave them safe at a bank and carry away a scrap of money that represented the amount, he went straight on every pay-day and made his deposit, keeping out barely what was necessary for his board and clothing. What he wanted to do with his money he did not know, but it gave to him a sense of freedom and power to feel that it was there—it was his and he could have it when he chose. In imitation of McLean, he bought a small pocket account-book, in which he carefully set down every dollar he earned and every penny he spent. As his expenses were small and the Boss paid him generously, it was astonishing how his little hoard grew.

That winter held the first hours of real happiness in Freckles' life. He was free. He was doing a man's work faithfully, through every rigour of rain, snow, and blizzard. He was gathering a wonderful strength of body, paying his way, and saving money. Every man of the gang and of that locality knew that he was under the protection of McLean, who was a power, and it had the effect of smoothing Freckles' path in many directions.

Mrs. Duncan showed him that individual kindness for which his hungry heart was longing. She had a hot drink ready for him when he came from a freezing day on the trail. She knit him a heavy mitten for his left hand, and devised a way to sew and pad the right sleeve that protected the maimed arm in bitter weather. She patched his clothing—frequently torn by the wire—and saved kitchen-scraps for his birds, not because she either knew or cared anything about them, but because she herself was close enough to the swamp to be touched by its utter loneliness. When Duncan laughed at her for this, she retorted: "My God, mannie, if Freckles hadna the birds and the beasts he would be always alone. It was never meant for a human being to be sa solitary. He'd get touched in the head if he hadna them to think for and to talk to."

"How much answer do ye think he gets to his talkin', lass?" laughed Duncan.

"He gets the answer that keeps the eye bright, the heart happy, and the feet walking faithful the rough path he's set them in," answered Mrs. Duncan earnestly.

Duncan walked away appearing very thoughtful. The next morning he gave an ear from the corn he was shelling for his chickens to Freckles, and told him to carry it to his wild chickens in the Limberlost. Freckles laughed delightedly.

"Me chickens!" he said. "Why didn't I ever think of that before? Of course they are! They are just little, brightly coloured cocks and hens! But 'wild' is no good. What would you say to me 'wild chickens' being a good deal tamer than yours here in your yard?"

"Hoot, lad!" cried Duncan.

"Make yours light on your head and eat out of your hands and pockets," challenged Freckles.

"Go and tell your fairy tales to the wee people! They're

just brash on believin' things," said Duncan. "Ye canna invent any story too big to stop them from callin' for a bigger."

"I dare you to come see!" retorted Freckles.

"Take ye!" said Duncan. "If ye make juist ane bird licht on your heid or eat frae your hand, ye are free to help yoursel' to my corn-crib and wheat-bin the rest of the winter."

Freckles sprang in air and howled in holy joy.

"Oh, Duncan! You're too aisy," he cried. "When will you come?"

"I'll come next Sabbath," said Duncan. "And I'll believe the birds of the Limberlost are tame as barnyard-fowl when I see it, and no sooner!"

After that Freckles always spoke of the birds as his chickens, and the Duncans followed his example. The very next Sabbath, Duncan, with his wife and children, followed Freckles to the swamp. They saw a sight so wonderful it will keep them talking all the remainder of their lives, and make them unfailing friends of the birds.

Freckles' chickens were awaiting him at the edge of the clearing. They cut the frosty air around his head into curves and circles of crimson, blue and black. They chased each other from Freckles, and swept so closely themselves that they brushed him with their outspread wings.

At their feeding-ground Freckles set down his old pail of scraps and swept the snow from a small level space with a broom improvised of twigs. As soon as his back was turned, the birds clustered over the food, snatching scraps to carry to the nearest bushes. Several of the boldest, a big crow and a couple of jays, settled on the rim and feasted at leisure, while a cardinal, that hesitated to venture, fumed and scolded from a twig overhead.

Then Freckles scattered his store. At once the ground resembled the spread mantle of Montezuma, except that this mass of gaily coloured feathers was on the backs of living birds. While they feasted, Duncan gripped his wife's arm and stared in astonishment; for from the bushes and dry grass, with gentle cheeping and queer, throaty chatter, as if to encourage each other, came flocks of quail. Before anyone saw it arrive, a big grey rabbit sat in the midst of the feast, contentedly gnawing a cabbage-leaf.

"Weel, I be drawed on!" came Mrs. Duncan's tense whisper.

"Shu-shu," cautioned Duncan.

Lastly Freckles removed his cap. He began filling it with handfuls of wheat from his pockets. In a swarm the grain-eaters arose around him as a flock of tame pigeons. They perched on his arms and the cap, and in the stress of hunger, forgetting all caution, a brilliant cock cardinal and an equally gaudy jay fought for a perching-place on his head.

"Well, I'm beat," muttered Duncan, forgetting the silence imposed on his wife. "I'll hae to give in. 'Seein' is believin'.' A man wad hae to see that to believe it. We mauna let the Boss miss that sight, for it's a chance will no likely come twice in a life. Everything is snowed under and thae craturs near starved, but trustin' Freckles that complete they are tamer than our chickens. Look hard, bairns!" he whispered. "Ye winna see the like o' yon again, while God lets ye live. Notice their colour against the ice and snow, and the pretty skippin' ways of them! And spunky! Weel, I'm beat fair!"

Freckles emptied his cap, turned his pockets, and scattered his last grain. Then he waved his watching friends good-bye and started down the timber-line.

A week later, Duncan and Freckles arose from breakfast to face the bitterest morning of the winter. When Freckles, warmly capped and gloved, stepped to the corner of the kitchen for his scrap-pail, he found a big pan of steaming boiled wheat on the top of it. He wheeled to Mrs. Duncan with a shining face.

"Were you fixing this warm food for me chickens or yours?" he asked.

"It's for yours, Freckles," she said. "I was afeared this cold weather they wadna lay good without a warm bite now and then."

Duncan laughed as he stepped to the other room for his pipe; but Freckles faced Mrs. Duncan with a trace of every pang of starved mother-hunger he ever had suffered written large on his homely, splotched, narrow features.

"Oh, how I wish you were my mother!" he cried.

Mrs. Duncan attempted an echo of her husband's laugh.

"Lord love the lad!" she exclaimed. "Why, Freckles, are ye no bricht enough to learn without being taught by a woman that I am your mither. If a great man like yoursel' dinna ken that, learn it now and ne'er forget it. Ance a woman is the wife of any man, she becomes wife to all men for having had the wifely experience she kens! Ance a man-child has beaten his way to life under the heart of a woman, she is mither to all men, for the hearts of mithers are everywhere the same. Bless ye, laddie, I am your mither!"

She tucked the coarse scarf she had knit for him closer over his chest and pulled his cap lower over his ears, but Freckles, whipping it off and holding it under his arm, caught her rough, reddened hand and pressed it to his lips in a long kiss. Then he hurried away to hide the happy, embarrassing tears that were coming straight from his swelling heart.

Mrs. Duncan, sobbing unrestrainedly, swept into the adjoining room and threw herself into Duncan's arms.

"Oh, the puir lad!" she wailed. "Oh, the puir mither-hungry lad! He breaks my heart!"

Duncan's arms closed convulsively around his wife. With

a big, brown hand he lovingly stroked her rough, sorrel hair.

"Sarah, you're a guid woman!" he said. "You're a michty guid woman! Ye hae a way o' speakin' out at times that's like the inspired prophets of the Lord. If that had been put to me, now, I'd 'a' felt all I kent how to and been keen enough to say the richt thing. But dang it, I'd 'a' stuttered and stammered and got naething out that would ha' done onybody a mite o' good. But ye, Sarah! Did ye see his face, woman? Ye sent him off lookin' leke a white light of holiness had passed ower and settled on him. Ye sent the lad off too happy for mortal words, Sarah. And ye made me that proud o' ye! I wouldna trade ye an' my share o' the Limberlost with ony king ye could mention."

He relaxed his clasp, and setting a heavy hand on each shoulder, he looked straight into her eyes.

"Ye're prime, Sarah! Juist prime!" he said.

Sarah Duncan stood alone in the middle of her two-room log-cabin and lifted a bony, claw-like pair of hands, reddened by frequent immersions in hot water, cracked and chafed by exposure to cold, black-lined by constant battle with swamp-loam, and calloused with burns, and stared at them wonderingly.

"Pretty lookin' things ye are!" she whispered. "But ye hae juist been kissed. And by such a man! Fine as God ever made at His verra best. Duncan wouldna trade wi' a king! Na! Nor I wadna trade with a queen wi' a palace, an' velvet gowns, an' diamonds big as hazel-nuts, an' a hundred visitors a day into the bargain. Ye've been that honoured I'm blest if I can bear to souse ye in dish-water. Still, that kiss winna come off! Naething can take it from me, for it's mine till I dee. Lord, if I amna proud! Kisses on these old claws! Weel, I be drawed on!"

Gene Stratton Porter taught herself to photograph birds. Here, clockwise: a pied-billed grebe; warbler brood with cowbird chick; meadowlark nestlings; brooding king rail; black vulture chick. Courtesy of Indiana State Museum.

· 6 ·

ANNA BOTSFORD COMSTOCK

1854–1930

Anna Comstock, the first woman to achieve the rank of professor at Cornell University, was elected one of America's
twelve greatest living women by the League of Women Voters
in 1923. She received this honor for her contributions to the
nature study movement, which she helped to begin in New
York in 1895 and helped to flourish until her death in 1930.
Comstock's major work, the *Handbook of Nature Study*, a 1911
lesson manual for public school teachers, was translated into
eight languages and was reprinted twenty-four times. Although she was not exclusively a bird student or even primarily
a nature writer, Anna Comstock is included in this book
because of her conspicuous role in the nature study movement
in which birdwatching was prominently featured.

Anna Botsford Comstock was born in upstate New York
in 1854. As a freshman at Cornell, she enrolled in a zoology
course taught by her future husband, John Henry Comstock,

later to become one of America's foremost entomologists. They were married in 1878. Except for a brief stay in Washington, D.C., where John Comstock served in the United States Department of Agriculture, and short visits to Stanford University, the Comstocks lived and worked in Ithaca—John as professor of entomology at Cornell and Anna as his research assistant. In 1885 she completed her Bachelor of Science degree in natural history at Cornell. Discovering an aptitude for natural history illustration, she decided to undertake wood engraving to illustrate her husband's projected textbook of 1888, *An Introduction to Entomology,* and traveled to Cooper Union in New York for short courses in wood engraving to perfect her technique.

For the rest of her life, Comstock diligently prepared illustrations for her husband's and her own frequent publications. Her achievements in this genre cannot be described as more than proficient, but the concentration and patience required for these countless illustratons reveal an unusually high level of perseverance.

In 1895 Anna Comstock was named to the Committee for the Promotion of Agriculture, which was sponsored by a group of philanthropists concerned about the agricultural depression and consequent migration to the cities in New York State. Nature study was viewed as a means to reintroduce children to the world of the outdoors, including crop production and the rewards of animal husbandry. Anna Comstock initiated an experimental nature study program in the Westchester County schools. The project was subsequently expanded with funds from the New York State Legislature. Comstock served as the project's unofficial chief, becoming totally immersed in lecturing, teaching, writing, and organizing.

Comstock taught nature study regularly at Cornell's summer session and finally in 1920 earned the status of full professor for her efforts. She wrote several books intended for children and teachers, among them *Insect Life* of 1897 and *How to Know the Butterflies* of 1904, both illustrated with her own engravings. These activities culminated in 1911 in the massive *Handbook of Nature Study*. Seemingly indefatigable, Comstock also founded and then helped to edit *Nature Study Review,* a national journal for teachers of natural history, and served as poetry editor for *Country Life in America,* a magazine whose original purpose was to stimulate interest in rural life.

Anna Comstock's commitment to nature education was absolute. Like her contemporary Mabel Osgood Wright, she devoted a large portion of her life to a cause which paid her little. Under Comstock's guidance, school systems throughout the country incorporated her curriculum into their classrooms. Her *Handbook* served as the core of these programs. The *Handbook* opens with a lengthy primer on bird study; its opening lesson is reprinted here. In it Comstock reveals her exhaustive understanding of educational methods and a serviceable knowledge of ornithology. Although she occasionally reveals herself dependent upon slightly unreliable sources—references to the evil ways of hawks appear frequently—she nevertheless presents the material objectively and methodically. Her lesson plans are pleasantly written and display imagination and wit. Carried out according to her instruction, the lessons must have delighted schoolchildren.

The nature study movement petered out during the Depression and has never been revived. Do children today study birds in school, go for nature walks with their teachers, or grow vegetables in the schoolyard? The computer has replaced nature in the classroom. Anna Comstock would be horrified.

Animal Life

I. BIRD STUDY

The reason for studying any bird is to ascertain what it does; in order to accomplish what it is being simply a step that leads to a knowledge of what it does. But, to hear some of our bird devotees talk, one would think that to be able to identify a bird is all of bird study. On the contrary, the identification of birds is simply the alphabet to the real study, the alphabet by means of which we may spell out the life habits of the bird. To know these habits is the ambition of the true ornithologist, and should likewise be the ambition of the beginner, even though the beginner be a young child.

Several of the most common birds have been selected as subjects for lessons in this book; other common birds, like the phoebe and wrens, have been omitted purposely; after the children have studied the birds, as indicated in the lessons, they will enjoy working out lessons for themselves with other birds. Naturally, the sequence of these lessons does not follow scientific classification; in the first ten lessons, an attempt has been made to lead the child gradually into a knowledge of bird life. Beginning with the chicken there follow naturally the lessons with pigeons and the canary; then there follows the careful and detailed study of the robins and constant comparison of them with the blue birds. This is enough for the first year in the primary grades. The next year the work begins with the birds that remain in the North during the winter, the chickadee, nuthatch and downy woodpecker. After these have been studied carefully, the teacher may be an opportunist when spring comes and select any of the lessons when the bird subjects are at hand. The classification suggested for the woodpeckers and the swallows is for more advanced pupils, as are the lessons on the geese and turkeys. It is to be hoped that these lessons will lead the child directly to the use of the bird manuals, of which there are several excellent ones.

Beginning Bird Study in the Primary Grades

The hen is especially adapted as an object lesson for the young beginner of bird study. First of all, she is a bird, notwithstanding the adverse opinions of two of my small pupils who stoutly maintain that "a robin is a bird, but a hen is a hen." Moreover, the hen is a bird always available for nature-study; she looks askance at us from the crates of the world's marts; she comes to meet us in the country barnyard, stepping toward us sedately; looking at us earnestly, with one eye, then turning her head so as to check up her observations with the other; meantime she asks us a little question in a wheedling, soft tone, which we understand perfectly to mean "have you perchance brought me something to eat?" Not only is the hen an interesting bird in herself, but she is a bird with problems; and by studying her carefully we may be introduced into the very heart and center of bird life.

This lesson may be presented in two days: First, if the pupils live in the country where they have poultry at home, the whole series of lessons may best be accomplished through interested talks on the part of the teacher, which should be made at home and the results given in school in oral or written lessons. Second, if the pupils are not familiar with fowls, a hen and a chick, if possible, should be kept in a cage in the schoolroom for a few days, and a duck or gosling should be brought in one day for observation. The crates in which fowls are sent to market make very good cages. One of the teachers of the Elmira, N.Y. Schools introduced into the basement of the schoolhouse a hen, which there hatched her brood of chicks, much to the children's delight and edification. After the pupils have become thoroughly interested in the hen and are familiar with her ways, after they have fed her and watched her, and have for her a sense of ownership, the following lessons may be given in an informal manner, as if they were naturally suggested to the teacher's mind through watching the fowl.

Feathers as Clothing:
Teacher's Story

The bird's clothing affords a natural beginning for bird study because the wearing of feathers is a most striking character distinguishing birds from other creatures; also, feathers and flying are the first things the young child notices about birds.

The purpose of all of these lessons on the hen are: (a) To induce the child to make continued and sympathetic observations on the habits of the domestic birds. (b) To cause him involuntarily to compare the domestic with the wild birds. (c) To induce him to think for himself why the shape of the body, wings, head, beak, feet, legs and feathers are adapted in each species to protect the bird and assist it in getting its living.

The overlapping of the feathers on a hen's back and breast is a pretty illustration of nature's method of shingling, so that the rain, finding no place to enter, drips off, leaving the bird's underclothing quite dry. It is interesting to note how a hen behaves in the rain; she droops her tail and holds herself so that the water finds upon her no resting place, but simply a steep surface down which to flow to the ground.

Each feather consists of three parts, the shaft or quill, which is the central stiff stem of the feather, giving it strength. From this quill come off the barbs which, toward the outer end, join together in a smooth web, making the thin, fan-like portion of the feather; at the base is the fluff, which is soft and downy and near to the body of the fowl. The teacher should put on the blackboard this figure so that incidentally the pupils may learn the parts of a feather and their structure. If a microscope is available, show both the web and the fluff of a feather under a three-fourths objective.

The feathers on the back of a hen are longer and narrower in proportion than those on the breast and are especially fitted to protect the back from rain; the breast feathers are shorter and have more of the fluff, thus protecting the breast from the cold as well as the rain. It is plain to any child that the soft fluff is comparable to our woolen underclothing while the smooth, overlapping web forms a rain and wind-proof outer coat. Down is a feather with no quill; young chicks are covered with down. A pin-feather is simply a young feather rolled up in a sheath, which bursts later and is shed, leaving the feather free to assume its form. Take a large pin-feather and cut the sheath open and show the pupils the young feather lying within.

When a hen oils her feathers it is a process well worth observing. The oil gland is on her back just at the base of the tail feathers; she squeezes the gland with her beak to get the oil and then rubs the beak over the surface of her feathers and passes them through it; she spends more time oiling the feathers on her back and breast than those on the other parts, so that they will surely shed water. Country people say when the hen oils her feathers, it is a sure sign of rain. The hen sheds her feathers once a year and is a most untidy looking bird meanwhile, a fact that she seems to realize, and is as shy and cross as a young lady caught in company with curl papers; but she seems very pleased with herself when she finally gains her new feathers.

Lesson I
Feathers as Clothing

Leading thought—Feathers grow from the skin of a bird and protect the bird from rain, snow, wind and cold. Some of the feathers act as cloaks or mackintoshes and others as under-clothing.

Method—The hen should be at close range for this lesson where the children may observe how and where the different kinds of feathers grow. The pupils should also study separately the form of a feather from the back, from the breast, from the under side of the body, and a pin-feather.

Observations for pupils—1. How are the feathers arranged on the back of the hen? Are they like shingles on the roof? If so, what for?

2. How does a hen look when standing in the rain?

3. How are the feathers arranged on the breast?

4. Compare a feather from the back and one from the breast and note the difference.

5. Are both ends of these feathers alike? If not, what is the difference?

6. Is the fluffy part of the feather on the outside or next to the bird's skin? What is its use?

7. Why is the smooth part of the feather (the web) on the outside?

8. Some feathers are all fluff and are called "down." At what age was the fowl all covered with down?

9. What is a pin-feather? What makes you think so?

10. How do hens keep their feathers oily and glossy so they will shed water?

11. Where does the hen get the oil? Describe how she oils her feathers and which ones does she oil most? Does she oil her feathers before a rain?

CORDELIA STANWOOD

1865–1958

Cordelia Stanwood was born in Ellsworth, Maine, in 1865, the daughter of a prosperous merchant sea captain. After teaching school in various New England towns for seventeen years, she retreated in 1904 to her parental home, where she remained for the rest of her life. Stanwood had experienced a severe nervous collapse, the result of overwork and the difficulties of being an isolated spinster. She never taught school again and she never married, but she did gradually recover her strength and with it her interest in the out-of-doors. The rest of her life was devoted to bird study as she observed meticulously with camera and pen the birds that nested in the woods, orchards, swamps, and fields of her parents' homestead.

In 1916, when she wanted to publish some essays incorporating her observations of the nesting habits of warblers and thrushes, Stanwood wrote to Frank M. Chapman, editor of *Bird-Lore*, who made suggestions on improving her writing style but more importantly recommended that she take up

Cordelia Stanwood at the age of twenty-nine.
Courtesy of Cordelia Stanwood Wildlife Foundation.

photography. Chapman even helped her to acquire the proper outfit and provided detailed instructions on its use.

Although Stanwood published a few articles here and there, she was not a natural writer and found composition trying. Her essays are somewhat awkward and lack the ease of expression that characterizes fine nature writing. Her greatest effort,

Photographs by Cordelia Stanwood:
(right and below) Savannah Sparrow;
chickadee nestlings; (opposite)
immature yellow-bellied flycatchers;
immature golden-crowned kinglets.
Courtesy of Cordelia Stanwood
Wildlife Foundation.

Immature broad-winged hawks, photographed in a delightful series by Cordelia Stanwood. Cordelia Stanwood Wildlife Foundation.

a manual on New England birds, failed to find a publisher. But her talent for bird observation was fully realized in photography. For more than forty years she patiently photographed with astounding brilliance and clarity the birds she had so diligently studied. She died in 1958, penniless and unknown to all but a few ornithologists, among whom she was recognized as an exceptionally reliable reporter on the nesting behavior of woodland species, especially the fine points of nest building, brooding, and fledging of the wood warblers in Maine.

Today her home is a nature center dedicated to her solitary efforts at bird study. Her photographs are carefully preserved by the Cordelia Stanwood Wildlife Foundation. In the images reproduced here, Stanwood's sensitivity and skill are immediately apparent. In many ways her life was a personal tragedy. Increasingly isolated, eccentric, and poor, unable to find a publisher for her massive manuscript on New England birds, often ridiculed by the children of Ellsworth as a witch and hermit, Stanwood found solace only in the contemplation of birdlife. Enduring rain and sleet, mosquitoes and black flies, she regularly went forth into the woods to locate bird nests and photograph their contents. Some of the magic she perceived is still lovingly communicated to us in her photographs.

· 8 ·

FANNIE HARDY
ECKSTORM
1865–1946

Fannie Hardy Eckstorm is one of two distinguished writers from the state of Maine in this anthology. Born in 1865 in Brewer, a thriving mercantile port across the Penobscot River from Bangor, Eckstorm participated in the renaissance of regional enthusiasm which also stimulated Sara Orne Jewett to document the special qualities of Maine's culture, both aboriginal and European. But whereas Jewett's fiction was focused exclusively on the relationship of Maine's rural population to its extraordinary ecology, Eckstorm's work, primarily historical and scholarly, dealt with the Penobscot Indians and the lumber and fur industries that dominated her early life in the Penobscot Valley.

Eckstorm's father, Manly Hardy, was a typical product of the mercantile boom in Maine in the second half of the nineteenth century. His father had been a successful merchant with interests in fur, lumber, and shipping. The son concen-

Fannie Hardy Eckstorm.
Courtesy of Fannie Hardy Eckstorm Collection
Folger Library, University of Maine, Orono.

trated exclusively on the fur trade and during Eckstorm's life became the state's most successful fur trader, exporting directly to European markets. Fur trading brought the Hardys into close contact with the Penobscot Indians; the family was on intimate terms with the large Indian community centered in Brewer. Manly Hardy spoke their language and was expert in perilous travel through the wilderness from which the Penobscot Indians derived their living. He became a recognized expert on the mammals and birds of Maine. His collection of 3,300 mounted birds was almost complete for North America (lacking only twenty species) and was so valuable that it was purchased by the Rhode Island Audubon Society in 1912. Hardy's influence on Fannie, his oldest child, cannot be overestimated. She often accompanied him on wilderness expeditions and learned taxidermy to assist him in gathering specimens.

Fannie's extraordinary intellectual gifts were recognized by her parents, and she was enrolled in Smith College in 1885. While there she helped to found a college Audubon Society, leading groups of students in long bird walks in the country around Northampton. At Smith she discovered anthropology and determined to study the Penobscot culture when she returned home. In 1888, upon her graduation, Manly Hardy took his daughter on the first of several long, difficult canoe trips through the waterways of the northern wilderness. These expeditions served as the stimulus for much of Eckstorm's later scholarship.

For a short while Fannie Eckstorm served as superintendent in the Brewer schools but, like Henry David Thoreau earlier in Concord, she found the town elders rigid and ignorant in their attitudes toward education, and she resigned to begin what was to become a distinguished literary and scholarly career.

In 1891, while working for a year in Boston as an editorial assistant, Fannie Hardy met her future husband, Jacob Andreason Eckstorm, a Norwegian-American Episcopal cleric. They were married in 1893. Her husband died in 1898 in Providence, and Fannie was left with two small children. She returned to Brewer to live in a house down the block from her parental home.

Eckstorm's earliest books, after her resettlement in Brewer, were concerned with birds—*The Bird Book* (undated), a text for children intended to stimulate their appreciation of nature, and *Woodpeckers* of 1901, more scientific but still for the amateur bird enthusiast. During the same decade she contributed occasional articles to *Bird-Lore* and the *Auk*.

This period for Eckstorm proved a trial on several fronts. Her small daughter died in 1901, only three years after her husband, and her father's health was failing. At the same time she could see the ravages of the fur and lumber industries on the wilderness that had nurtured her. To offset the rapid disappearance of the Maine frontier, Eckstorm determined to preserve what she knew of the early days of industry in the Penobscot Valley. In *Penobscot Man* (1904) she retold the oral history of the lumbermen with whom she had grown up.

In collaboration with Mary Winslow Smith of Elmira College she published in 1927 *The Minstrelsy of Maine*, a scholarly history of folk songs from the backwoods. In 1929 *British Ballads from Maine* appeared, to critical acclaim. While Eckstorm's interest in birds and folklore remained strong, her flexible intellect again turned to another area, Indian philology and mythology. Several journal articles were followed in 1941 by her monumental *Indian Place Names of the Penobscot Valley and the Maine Coast*. Her final work, *Old John Neptune and Other Maine Indian Shamans*, was published in 1945, a year before her death.

Eckstorm was a woman of manifold talents and interests. Her anthropological scholarship has endured along with her reputation as a regional writer of considerable depth. Her writing on birds, some of which is reprinted here, is flawless. The essay about the "Whiskey John" demonstrates her prodigious ability as well as her trenchant Yankee humor. The essay seeks to teach the reader about a particular species of bird in a painless and amusing way. At the same time Eckstorm's point of view is strictly factual. The gray jay is neither sentimentalized nor humanized.

Concerning the Bad Reputation of Whiskey John

In these days every bird has his apologist, but I should rather not be the advocate to defend Whiskey John. He is the worst thief, the greatest scoundrel, the most consummate hypocrite abroad in feathers, with his Quaker clothes, his hoary head, his look of patriarchal saintliness. He is a thief, a thief, a thief!

A friendly bird-lover who would loyally whitewash the character of the arch-fiend provided he was a *feathered* biped, argues that to admit of birds having a glimmering of moral sense would make them accountable for their actions in cherry-time, and that therefore the negative must be sustained. The vicious circle in the proof appears at once when we bring forward Whiskey Jack as a bird indubitably lacking moral sense, and inquire what would happen if all other birds were equally defective in their ethical notions. The sum of all the charges against Whiskey Jack is that he knows nothing and cares nothing about morals. Whether he does or does not know the difference between *meum* and *tuum*, he has a decided preference for what is not his own. He steals from pure love of pilfering, and shows not the slightest compunctions of conscience. He steals not alone to satisfy his own wants, but those of his brothers and sisters and wife's relations, and his third, fourth and fifth cousins, and after that he keeps right on stealing for posterity. He takes not only articles for which he has a use and an appetite, but others which he never saw before, doesn't know the uses of, doesn't like the taste of, and can never learn to enjoy or use. I am willing to share generously my cherries and strawberries with the birds; I am ready to divide my last meal of bread and meat with them, but I draw the line at allowing any bird to eat my *soap*. Soap is soap in the Maine woods, forty miles from a store, and even if it were something else it is debatable whether half a cake (of soap) is better for birds than no bread. But, as old Jed Prouty said of the dog that wanted the moon, Whiskey Jack is "cov'tous."

If he were a better-known bird his ill-repute would be in everybody's mouth; his isolation saves him. But all fur-hunters and all who travel the great spruce woods, from Atlantic to Pacific, know and revile Whiskey John. He goes by many names, of which this, being only a corruption of the Indian *Wis-ka-tjon* (but wouldn't one like to know what this means in Indian!) is as complimentary as any. In Maine he is most commonly called the Moose-bird or Meat-bird; in the Adirondacks he is the Camp-robber; in books he is the Canada Jay. If you would know how he looks do not go to the scientific books that tell you every feather on him, but take down your *Lorna Doone* and turn to those pages where that wily old scoundrel, Counsellor Doone, running away with Lorna's diamond necklace, almost persuades John Ridd that he is a good man cruelly misnamed. Whiskey Jack is the bird counterpart of Counsellor Doone. He looks like him, acts like him and has the same undesirable expertness in acquiring property not his own. Newcomers to the woods dread bears, wolves and snakes. What they fear will never harm them; it is the weak things of the wilderness that are exceedingly strong. There is a certain large-winged, tiny-bodied little fly, so feeble and appealing that in pity for his frailty you tenderly brush him aside—and then learn that he is the bloody butcher who is flaying your neck and ears; there is this clear-eyed, mild-mannered, trustful bird, for whose good behavior you would go bonds—until he eats your soap. These two and the mosquito are the real enemies of man in the wilderness.

Suppose that you are paddling along one of the still, thicket-bordered, moose-haunted streams of northern Maine, the "Sis," on Caucomgomoc, for example. There is a whistling, and confabulating ashore and down scales a medium-sized gray bird, whitish beneath and with a white forehead which gives him a curiously venerable and bald-headed look. He stretches out his black legs and alights with an uncertain hover on your canoe-bow. "*Ca-ca-ca?* Who are you anyway?" he inquires, looking boldly at you. You are new to this sort of thing and the woods are big and lonely; it seems like getting into a city to go where nobody cares about you, and this confidence man takes you in at once. He flits ashore and tells the others that it is So-and-so, of New York. Then back he comes; he never stays long anywhere. "*Ca-ca-ca?* Got any meat today?" says he, seating himself again upon the bow. Perhaps the guide has given you a hint, and this time you bat at him with the paddle and bid him begone for a thief. That hurts his feelings; he puffs out his waistcoat feathers in ruffled innocence till you forget that it would take half a dozen such thistle-down birds as he to weigh a pound, and he says: "Look at me, do you imagine that a fellow as old and gray-headed and respectable as I am would steal?" You do look at him—a little, stout, white-headed old gentleman with a clear hazel eye, like a superannuated clergyman who had gone into business too late in life to learn the ways of a wicked world, and you apologize profoundly—that is, if you are a novice in the woods; if you have already paid for your introduction to Mr. Whiskey John, you remark, "Pecksniff, get out!" and resort to the argument of the paddle.

He flits away forgiving you; Whiskey Jack is never above such mean revenges. When he comes back, as he is pretty sure to do, it is with the nonchalant impudence of a private detective. "If you don't mind," says he, "I think I'll just take a look at this outfit; I'm a sort of game-warden and have a right to overhaul your baggage." The next minute you hear the guide's paddle bang the middle bar of the canoe. "That there blame Meat-bird's a-stealin' our saddle of deer," he explains briefly.

This time Whiskey John is irritated and he flies off talking jay-talk, a most profane language, threatening to follow you to your camping ground and bring with him every last relative that he has.

He does it, too. When you have put your stuff ashore and begin to pitch your tent you know that you have a part of a saddle of deer, a big trout cleaned and split, a Partridge in the leg of one wading boot and a Wood-duck in the other, thrust there hunter-fashion to safe-guard them from accidental loss. You turn your back for a few moments, hear nothing unusual, suspect no mischief; but when you turn again you find the trout is a drabbled rag, rolled in dirt, the roast of venison which was to be the best part of your feast, is riddled above the kidneys (which are the favorite morsel of most meat-eating birds), and both the Duck and the Partridge have been dragged from their concealment and chiseled down the breast till there is nothing left. This is lesson number one. It teaches that the Meat-bird will destroy an incredible amount of meat in a very brief time.

You are now prepared to proceed to lesson number two, which is that if his appetite is limitless yet nothing comes amiss to it. The tent is up; the guide is off to get water from the spring; the fire crackles and the potatoes, boiling in their kettle, are knocking at the cover of it; the bread is baking in the open baker and the nice little collops of venison are lying in a tin plate before the fire all ready for the pan; you lie back on your blanket and dream dreams. Nothing happens till the guide returns, and then you hear a muttered growl about leaving a "sport" to keep a camp. There is the guide, looking at an empty plate, and there on a bush sits a Meat-bird with a very bloody breast. The connection is unmistakable.

Never mind; there is more meat where that came from, and a bird that, in addition to all his other work, has just stolen the dinner for two men cannot be hungry. But he doesn't appear to have lost his interest in your affairs. Instead, he tip-toes around on a limb, with wings and tail half spread, whistling and talking, and no sooner is a fresh supply of meat in the pan than he sweeps down in the smoke and heat and balances a moment on the long handle of the frying-pan, calculating the risks of stealing from the pan. Reluctantly he gives up the project and disappears around the corner of the tent. Presently other things begin to disappear. There is a little hollow in the ground, so that the sides of the tent are not pegged down closely. Entering here, he goes to work within three feet of your elbow, being hidden by a box, and, with the tireless industry which is his only virtue, he applies himself to whatever is nearest. You have some cherished candles, your only light for reading; he drags them off by the wicks. There was a dipper of grease for making pitch; that vanishes. You had pinned a rare bug to a chip; he eats it. You had saved some Duck's wings for the children at home; they are overhauled. The guide left his piece of pork unrolled, and it probably goes off in company with your tobacco, which never turns up after this visitation of Whiskey Jack. When you start to wash up for dinner, there is the rascal eating your soap for dessert! Those who have summered and wintered him say that the only article he has never been seen to steal is kerosene. "Him eat moccasins, fur cap, matches, anything," says an Indian to one observer. As for the amount that they will devour and carry off, there is no likelihood of any one ever having a patience to equal their—their "cov'tousness," as Jed puts it. There is in this typical account of their actions nothing exaggerated except the probability of its happening in one day.

The Canada Jay is not found everywhere even in Maine. One might camp for years in our woods and never see a Jay, for they are the most local bird that we have in the woods. Roughly speaking, the line of his frontier very nearly coincides with the route of the Canadian Pacific railway where it crosses this state. For example, he is found on the Grand Lakes of St. Croix, but not on Dobsy and Nicatowis, four ranges of townships to the south. In that region, which seems perfectly adapted to him, I have camped eight weeks; and my father, in the course of twenty-five years, has spent as many months; yet, with one exception, we have neither seen nor heard a Canada Jay in all that wilderness. On collating the experiences of four good observers, I find that they can mention but two instances of a Canadian Jay being seen within fifteen miles of Bangor, and one of these was fully thirty ears ago and the other not less than sixty years since; yet hardly more than fifty miles away they are a common resident. Why do they never straggle a short day's journey? Why is it that an om-nivorous bird, intelligent, restless, enterprising, fearless, ap-parently capable of adaptations and certainly attracted by the neighborhood of man, belonging to an order of birds which is eminently civilizable, is so closely restricted in its distri-bution? There is no climatic barrier; there is no noteworthy difference in the vegetal faunas of places within and with-out his limits; there is no dietary restriction as in the case of some local birds. Here is a very interesting ornithological puzzle.

The nest and eggs of the Canada Jay I have never seen. A standing offer of two dollars apiece for the eggs, though repeated several years, failed to bring in a single specimen. Woodsmen seem very ignorant of their breeding habits, and the only positive statement that I remember was the remark-able information volunteered by a lumberman that the "Beef-bird" nested and had young every month in the year. It is well known, however, that they nest in March when the snow is still very deep in the woods. The first of June I have seen the young, fully feathered and larger than parents, and with the edges of their bills still yellow. They were a very dark blackish slate, wholly unlike the adult. This plumage seems not to have been generally noticed, though it is worn some time.

On considering the evident reluctance of woodsmen to hunt up the nests of this bird, I have suspected that there may be some superstition connected with the bird similar to that which Mr. L. M. Turner records of the Labrador sub-species. The Indians there believe that "if a person sees the eggs in the nest, and especially if he counts them, some great mis-fortune will befall him." This is curiously substantiated in Mr. E. W. Nelson's account of the Alaska sub-species, where he notes that the natives refused large bribes rather than take the risk of angering the bird by stealing its nest. The super-stition applies only to the eggs, and is, I suspect, coincident with the distribution of the bird, though I never thought to inquire of our hunters and Indians on the subject. Indeed, unless it were chanced upon, its authenticity as a superstition would be doubtful, as the legend-hunter in Maine has only to state what he wants and he gets all he pays for. The seekers of the marvelous are sure to be satisfied.

How the native hunters always hated Whiskey Jack! They never had a good word for him, and a bullet was their usual greeting. The camper came home to find his hut invaded; the deer-stalker had his carcasses of venison riddled by their sharp bills and unfit for market; the trapper's sable were half-ruined in the traps, and, more provoking yet, his traps were robbed of their bait within five minutes after they had been set. It was hard work to plod all day through the lonesome, snowy wilderness, carrying a heavy bag of bait, and to feel that he was doing nothing but feed these gray wolves in feathers, who robbed him of his chance to get a fisher, lynx or sable almost before he was out of sight. And there is a side to this enmity between the hunter and the Meat-bird that is gruesome. It is years since, but some of us still recollect the tale, of an old outlaw and murderer—more than once a murderer if reports were true—who after haunting the woods for a year, a terror to those who crossed his path, fell finally in his turn, the victim of a man as evil as himself. He was shot by his partner and left alone to starve to death in his camp. And after three weeks of utter abandonment and despair, as he saw his end approaching, with no possibility of escaping it, he crept to the cold fireplace and got a black coal with which he scrawled a message on a shred of birch bark. And they found him later, dead and alone, with a tin basin protecting his face, so that, as the writing said, "the Meat-birds might not pick his face after he was dead."

A dread like that, shadowing the last hours of such a man, directing his last words and last act: what a revelation it is of the character of the bird and of the inveterate enmity with which the hunter regards him!

· 9 ·

SARAH ORNE JEWETT

1849–1909

The work of Sarah Orne Jewett is not often associated with birdwatching or even the broader category of natural history. Jewett is one of the recognized masters of the short story in American letters, and it is fortunate that the central theme of "A White Heron," bird conservation, justifies the story's inclusion in this anthology.

Sarah Orne Jewett was born in 1849 in South Berwick, Maine, on the southern boundary of the state. Although as an adult she passed several months each year in the Boston home of Annie Adams Fields, wife and then widow of publisher James T. Fields, Jewett spiritually never departed from the small town of her birth. She died in her parental home in 1909 at the age of sixty. Jewett's father, Theodore, was a country doctor. Sarah, a sickly child from birth, often accompanied him on his medical rounds; it was thought that the fresh air would do the child good. But the salubrious effects of the excursions were not limited to Sarah's health. For Jewett through these visits became deeply acquainted with the inhabitants of the small farms and settlements in rural Maine. This acquaintance formed the subject matter for all of her mature fiction. Jewett's attention to detail and the authenticity of her voice contributed to the strong reputation she enjoys as an American regionalist. She was primarily a master of the fictive sketch.

Jewett began publishing short stories before she was twenty. Her first collection of stories, *Deephaven*, appeared in 1877; others were published frequently thereafter. *A White Heron and Other Stories* of 1886 is the product of her mature art. Although Jewett rarely left New England, she was no literary provincial. Like Celia Thaxter, her close neighbor and occasional correspondent, she was well acquainted with the Boston aristocracy of letters. John Greenleaf Whittier, James Russell Lowell, and Henry James were among her friends. She was a serious student of European fiction and took particular pains with her writing style. This dedication is evident in her acknowledged masterpiece of 1896, *The Country of the Pointed Firs*, in which her subtle control of language is completely successful.

"A White Heron" is a particularly fine example of Jewett's mastery of the demanding short story genre. But unlike most of her other work, which generally treats the culture of rural Maine from the viewpoint of its relationship to the backwoods as a frontier, the theme of "A White Heron" is the conservation of birds. The story foreshadows the later widespread consciousness that the American frontier was rapidly being destroyed by the incursions of civilization and that birds were among the first populations to suffer.

Jewett sets the story, something of a moral parable, in the Maine backwoods where a small sickly child from the city lives with her grandmother in order to regain her health in the fresh air and pure atmosphere of the wilderness. The child is a nature student and knows about the birds and their nesting habits in her grandmother's woods. Into this ambience of tranquility and innocence an amateur ornithologist from the city arrives. Armed with a gun, he is determined to collect a specimen of a rare Maine visitor at that time, the little white heron (snowy egret). Although the child knows where to find the bird and its nest deep in the marshes near her home, she decides not to inform the ornithologist.

The story can be read as a plea for the conservation of the egret, a species under crippling pressure since egret feathers were in vogue as millinery decoration. It is also a severe condemnation of specimen gathering, a hobby fashionable among bird enthusiasts and scientists well into the twentieth century and one that was responsible for weakening the populations of several already endangered bird species. On a deeper level the story is a polemic against the incursions of civilization as embodied by the sophisticated urban naturalist who enters the idyllic world of unspoiled nature represented by the child.

As a conservation polemic "A White Heron" is remarkable for its early date. In 1886 the bird conservation movement was in its infancy and the gunning of birds all but uncontrolled. A small coterie of Boston ornithologists was just beginning to arouse public interest in the plight of species like the magnificent egret. Jewett's story is her personal attempt to stimulate awareness of the dangers, later overcome when bird conservation legislation was passed in the first decades of the twentieth century.

A White Heron

I.

The woods were already filled with shadows one June evening, just before eight o'clock, though a bright sunset still glimmered faintly among the trunks of the trees. A little girl was driving home her cow, a plodding, dilatory, provoking creature in her behavior, but a valued companion for all that. They were going away from whatever light there was, and striking deep into the woods, but their feet were familiar with the path, and it was no matter whether their eyes could see it or not.

There was hardly a night the summer through when the old cow could be found waiting at the pasture bars; on the contrary, it was her greatest pleasure to hide herself away among the huckleberry bushes, and though she wore a loud bell she had made the discovery that if one stood perfectly still it would not ring. So Sylvia had to hunt for her until she found her, and call Co'! Co'! with never an answering Moo, until her childish patience was quite spent. If the creature had not given good milk and plenty of it, the case would have seemed very different to her owners. Besides, Sylvia had all the time there was, and very little use to make of it. Sometimes in pleasant weather it was a consolation to look upon the cow's pranks as an intelligent attempt to play hide and seek, and as the child had no playmates she lent herself to this amusement with a good deal of zest. Though this chase had been so long that the wary animal herself had given an unusual signal of her whereabouts, Sylvia had only laughed when she came upon Mistress Moolly at the swampside, and urged her affectionately homeward with a twig of birch leaves. The old cow was not inclined to wander farther, she even turned in the right direction for once as they left the pasture, and stepped along the road at a good pace. She was quite ready to be milked now, and seldom stopped to browse. Sylvia wondered what her grandmother would say because they were so late. It was a great while since she had left home at half-past five o'clock, but everybody knew the difficulty of making this errand a short one. Mrs. Tilley had chased the hornéd torment too many summer evenings herself to blame any one else for lingering, and was only thankful as she waited that she had Sylvia, nowadays, to give such valuable assistance. The good woman suspected that Sylvia loitered occasionally on her own account; there never was such a child for straying about out-of-doors since the world was made! Everybody said that it was a good change for a little maid who had tried to grow for eight years in a crowded manufacturing town, but, as for Sylvia herself, it seemed as if she never had been alive at all before she came to live at the farm. She thought often with wistful compassion of a wretched geranium that belonged to a town neighbor.

" 'Afraid of folks,' " old Mrs. Tilley said to herself, with a smile, after she had made the unlikely choice of Sylvia from her daughter's houseful of children, and was returning to the farm. " 'Afraid of folks,' they said! I guess she won't be troubled no great with 'em up to the old place!" When they reached the door of the lonely house and stopped to unlock it, and the cat came to purr loudly, and rub against them, a deserted pussy, indeed, but fat with young robins, Sylvia whispered that this was a beautiful place to live in, and she never should wish to go home.

The companions followed the shady woodroad, the cow taking slow steps and the child very fast ones. The cow stopped long at the brook to drink, as if the pasture were not half a swamp, and Sylvia stood still and waited, letting her bare feet cool themselves in the shoal water, while the great twilight moths struck softly against her. She waded on through the brook as the cow moved away, and listened to the thrushes with a heart that beat fast with pleasure. There was a stirring in the great boughs overhead. They were full of little birds and beasts that seemed to be wide awake, and going about their world, or else saying good-night to each other in sleepy twitters. Sylvia herself felt sleepy as she walked along. However, it was not much farther to the house, and the air was soft and sweet. She was not often in the woods so late as this, and it made her feel as if she were a part of the gray shadows and the moving leaves. She was just thinking how long it seemed since she first came to the farm a year ago, and wondering if everything went on in the noisy town just the same as when she was there; the thought of the great red-faced boy who used to chase and frighten her made her hurry along the path to escape from the shadow of the trees.

Suddenly this little woods-girl is horror-stricken to hear a clear whistle not very far away. Not a bird's-whistle, which would have a sort of friendliness, but a boy's whistle, determined, and somewhat aggressive. Sylvia left the cow to whatever sad fate might await her, and stepped discreetly aside into the bushes, but she was just too late. The enemy had discovered her, and called out in a very cheerful and persuasive tone, "Halloa, little girl, how far is it to the road?" and trembling Sylvia answered almost inaudibly, "A good ways."

She did not dare to look boldly at the tall young man, who carried a gun over his shoulder, but she came out of her bush and again followed the cow, while he walked alongside.

"I have been hunting for some birds," the stranger said kindly, "and I have lost my way, and need a friend very much. Don't be afraid," he added gallantly. "Speak up and tell me what your name is, and whether you think I can spend the night at your house, and go out gunning early in the morning."

Sylvia was more alarmed than before. Would not her grandmother consider her much to blame? But who could have foreseen such an accident as this? It did not seem to be her fault, and she hung her head as if the stem of it were broken, but managed to answer "Sylvy," with much effort when her companion again asked her name.

Mrs. Tilley was standing in the doorway when the trio came into view. The cow gave a loud moo by way of explanation.

"Yes, you'd better speak up for yourself, you old trial! Where'd she tucked herself away this time, Sylvy?" But Sylvia kept an awed silence; she knew by instinct that her grandmother did not comprehend the gravity of the situation. She must be mistaking the stranger for one of the farmer-lads of the region.

The young man stood his gun beside the door, and dropped a lumpy game-bag beside it; then he bade Mrs. Tilley goodevening, and repeated his wayfarer's story, and asked if he could have a night's lodging.

"Put me anywhere you like," he said. "I must be off early in the morning, before day; but I am very hungry, indeed. You can give me some milk at any rate, that's plain."

"Dear sakes, yes," responded the hostess, whose long slumbering hospitality seemed to be easily awakened. "You might fare better if you went out to the main road a mile or so, but you're welcome to what we've got. I'll milk right off, and you make yourself at home. You can sleep on husks or feathers," she proffered graciously. "I raised them all myself. There's good pasturing for geese just below here towards the ma'sh. Now step round and set a plate for the gentleman, Sylvy!" And Sylvia promptly stepped. She was glad to have something to do, and she was hungry herself.

It was a surprise to find so clean and comfortable a little

dwelling in this New England wilderness. The young man had known the horrors of its most primitive housekeeping, and the dreary squalor of that level of society which does not rebel at the companionship of hens. This was the best thrift of an old-fashioned farmstead, though on such a small scale that it seemed like a hermitage. He listened eagerly to the old woman's quaint talk, he watched Sylvia's pale face and shining gray eyes with ever growing enthusiasm, and insisted that this was the best supper he had eaten for a month, and afterward the new-made friends sat down in the door-way together while the moon came up.

Soon it would be berry-time, and Sylvia was a great help at picking. The cow was a good milker, though a plaguy thing to keep track of, the hostess gossiped frankly, adding presently that she had buried four children, so Sylvia's mother, and a son (who might be dead) in California were all the children she had left. "Dan, my boy, was a great hand to go gunning," she explained sadly. "I never wanted for pa'tridges or gray squer'ls while he was to home. He's been a great wand'rer, I expect, and he's no hand to write letters. There, I don't blame him, I'd ha' seen the world myself if it had been so I could."

"Sylvy takes after him," the grandmother continued affectionately, after a minute's pause. "There ain't over a foot o' ground she don't know her way over, and the wild creaturs counts her one o' themselves. Squer'ls she'll tame to come an' feed right out o' her hands, and all sorts o' birds. Last winter she got the jay-birds to bangeing here, and I believe she'd a scanted herself of her own meals to have plenty to throw out amongst 'em, if I had n't kep' watch. Anything but crows, I tell her, I'm willin' to help support—though Dan he had a tamed one o' them that did seem to have reason same as folks. It was round here a good spell after he went away. Dan an' his father they didn't hitch—but he never held up his head ag'in after Dan had dared him an' gone off."

The guest did not notice this hint of family sorrows in his eager interest in something else.

"So Sylvy knows all about birds, does she?" he exclaimed, as he looked round at the little girl who sat, very demure but increasingly sleepy, in the moonlight. "I am making a collection of birds myself. I have been at it ever since I was a boy." (Mrs. Tilley smiled.)

"There are two or three very rare ones I have been hunting for these five years. I mean to get them on my own ground if they can be found."

"Do you cage 'em up?" asked Mrs. Tilley doubtfully, in response to this enthusiastic announcement.

"Oh no, they're stuffed and preserved, dozens and dozens of them," said the ornithologist, "and I have shot or snared every one myself. I caught a glimpse of a white heron a few miles from here on Saturday, and I have followed it in this direction. They have never been found in this district at all. The little white heron, it is," and he turned again to look at Sylvia with the hope of discovering that the rare bird was one of her acquaintances.

But Sylvia was watching a hop-toad in the narrow footpath.

"You would know the heron if you saw it," the stranger continued eagerly. "A queer tall white bird with soft feathers and long thin legs. And it would have a nest perhaps in the top of a high tree, made of sticks, something like a hawk's nest."

Sylvia's heart gave a wild beat; she knew that strange white bird, and had once stolen softly near where it stood in some bright green swamp grass, away over at the other side of the woods. There was an open place where the sunshine always seemed strangely yellow and hot, where tall, nodding rushes grew, and her grandmother had warned her that she might sink in the soft black mud underneath and never be heard of more. Not far beyond were the salt marshes just this side the sea itself, which Sylvia wondered and dreamed much about, but never had seen, whose great voice could sometimes be heard above the noise of the woods on stormy nights.

"I can't think of anything I should like so much as to find that heron's nest," the handsome stranger was saying. "I would give ten dollars to anybody who could show it to me," he added desperately, "and I mean to spend my whole vacation hunting for it if need be. Perhaps it was only migrating, or had been chased out of its own region by some bird of prey."

Mrs. Tilley gave amazed attention to all this, but Sylvia still watched the toad, not divining, as she might have done at some calmer time, that the creature wished to get to its hole under the doorstep, and was much hindered by the un-usual spectators at that hour of the evening. No amount of thought, that night, could decide how many wished-for trea-sures the ten dollars, so lightly spoken of, would buy.

The next day the young sportsman hovered about the woods, and Sylvia kept him company, having lost her first fear of the friendly lad, who proved to be most kind and sympathetic. He told her many things about the birds and what they knew and where they lived and what they did with themselves. And he gave her a jack-knife, which she thought as great a treasure as if she were a desert-islander. All day long he did not once make her troubled or afraid except when he brought down some unsuspecting singing creature from its bough. Sylvia would have liked him vastly better without his gun; she could not understand why he killed the very birds he seemed to like so much. But as the day waned, Sylvia still watched the young man with loving admiration. She had never seen anybody so charming and delightful; the woman's heart, asleep in the child, was vaguely thrilled by a dream of love. Some premonition of that great power stirred and swayed these young creatures who traversed the solemn woodlands with soft-footed silent care. They stopped to listen to a bird's song; they pressed forward again eagerly, parting the branches—speaking to each other rarely and in whispers; the young man going first and Sylvia following, fascinated, a few steps behind, with her gray eyes dark with excitement.

She grieved because the longed-for white heron was elusive, but she did not lead the guest, she only followed, and there was no such thing as speaking first. The sound of her own unquestioned voice would have terrified her—it was hard enough to answer yes or no when there was need of that. At last evening began to fall, and they drove the cow home together, and Sylvia smiled with pleasure when they came to the place where she heard the whistle and was afraid only the night before.

II.

Half a mile from home, at the farther edge of the woods, where the land was highest, a great pine-tree stood, the last of its generation. Whether it was left for a boundary mark, or for what reason, no one could say; the woodchoppers who had felled its mates were dead and gone long ago, and a whole forest of sturdy trees, pines and oaks and maples, had grown again. But the stately head of this old pine towered above them all and made a landmark for sea and shore miles and miles away. Sylvia knew it well. She had always believed that whoever climbed to the top of it could see the ocean; and the little girl had often laid her hand on the great rough trunk and looked up wistfully at those dark boughs that the wind always stirred, no matter how hot and still the air might be below. Now she thought of the tree with a new excitement, for why, if one climbed it at break of day could not one see all the world, and easily discover from whence the white heron flew, and mark the place, and find the hidden nest?

What a spirit of adventure, what wild ambition! What fancied triumph and delight and glory for the later morning when she could make known the secret! It was almost too real and too great for the childish heart to bear.

All night the door of the little house stood open and the whippoorwills came and sang upon the very step. The young sportsman and his old hostess were sound asleep, but Sylvia's great design kept her broad awake and watching. She forgot to think of sleep. The short summer night seemed as long as the winter darkness, and at last when the whippoorwills ceased, and she was afraid the morning would after all come too soon, she stole out of the house and followed the pasture path through the woods, hastening toward the open ground beyond, listening with a sense of comfort and companionship to the drowsy twitter of a half-awakened bird, whose perch she had jarred in passing. Alas, if the great wave of human interest which flooded for the first time this dull little life should sweep away the satisfactions of an existence heart to heart with nature and the dumb life of the forest!

There was the huge tree asleep yet in the paling moonlight, and small and silly Sylvia began with utmost bravery to mount to the top of it, with tingling, eager blood coursing the channels of her whole frame, with her bare feet and fingers, that pinched and held like bird's claws to the monstrous ladder reaching up, up, almost to the sky itself. First she must mount the white oak tree that grew alongside, where she was almost lost among the dark branches and the green leaves heavy and wet with dew; a bird fluttered off its nest, and a red squirrel ran to and fro and scolded pettishly at the harmless house-breaker. Sylvia felt her way easily. She had often climbed there, and knew that higher still one of the oak's upper branches chafed against the pine trunk, just where its lower boughs were set close together. There, when she made the dangerous pass from one tree to the other, the great enterprise would really begin.

She crept out along the swaying oak limb at last, and took the daring step across into the old pine-tree. The way was harder than she thought; she must reach far and hold fast, the sharp dry twigs caught and held her and scratched her like angry talons, the pitch made her thin little fingers clumsy and stiff as she went round and round the tree's great stem, higher and higher upward. The sparrows and robins in the woods below were beginning to wake and twitter to the dawn, yet it seemed much lighter there aloft in the pine-tree, and the child knew she must hurry if her project were to be of any use.

The tree seemed to lengthen itself out as she went up, and to reach farther and farther upward. It was like a great main-mast to the voyaging earth; it must truly have been amazed that morning through all its ponderous frame as it felt this determined spark of human spirit wending its way from higher branch to branch. Who knows how steadily the least twigs held themselves to advantage this light, weak creature on her way! The old pine must have loved his new dependent. More than all the hawks, and bats, and moths, and even the sweet voiced thrushes, was the brave, beating heart of the solitary gray-eyed child. And the tree stood still and frowned away the winds that June morning while the dawn grew bright in the east.

Sylvia's face was like a pale star, if one had seen it from the ground, when the last thorny bough was past, and she stood trembling and tired but wholly triumphant, high in the tree-top. Yes, there was the sea with the dawning sun making a golden dazzle over it, and toward that glorious east flew two hawks with slow-moving pinions. How low they looked in the air from that height when one had only seen them before far up, and dark against the blue sky. Their gray feathers were as soft as moths; they seemed only a little way from the tree, and Sylvia felt as if she too could go flying away among the clouds. Westward, the woodlands and farms reached miles and miles into the distance; here and there were church steeples, and white villages, truly it was a vast and awesome world!

The birds sang louder and louder. At last the sun came up bewilderingly bright. Sylvia could see the white sails of ships out at sea, and the clouds that were purple and rose-colored and yellow at first began to fade away. Where was the white heron's nest in the sea of green branches, and was this wonderful sight and pageant of the world the only reward for having climbed to such a giddy height? Now look down again, Sylvia, where the green marsh is set among the shining birches and dark hemlocks; there where you saw the white heron once you will see him again; look, look! a white spot of him like a single floating feather comes up from the dead hemlock and grows larger, and rises, and comes close at last, and goes by the landmark pine with steady sweep of wing and outstretched slender neck and crested head. And wait! wait! do not move a foot or a finger, little girl, do not send an arrow of light and consciousness from your two eager eyes, for the heron has perched on a pine bough not far beyond yours, and cries back to his mate on the nest and plumes his feathers for the new day!

The child gives a long sigh a minute later when a company

·

of shouting cat-birds comes also to the tree, and vexed by their fluttering and lawlessness the solemn heron goes away. She knows his secret now, the wild, light, slender bird that floats and wavers, and goes back like an arrow presently to his home in the green world beneath. Then Sylvia, well satisfied, makes her perilous way down again, not daring to look far below the branch she stands on, ready to cry sometimes because her fingers ache and her lamed feet slip. Wondering over and over again what the stranger would say to her, and what he would think when she told him how to find his way straight to the heron's nest.

"Sylvy, Sylvy!" called the busy old grandmother again and again, but nobody answered, and the small husk bed was empty and Sylvia had disappeared.

The guest waked from a dream, and remembering his day's pleasure hurried to dress himself that might it sooner begin. He was sure from the way the shy little girl looked once or twice yesterday that she had at least seen the white heron, and now she must really be made to tell. Here she comes now, paler than ever, and her worn old frock is torn and tattered, and smeared with pine pitch. The grandmother and the sportsman stand in the door together and question her, and the splendid moment has come to speak of the dead hemlock-tree by the green marsh.

But Sylvia does not speak after all, though the old grandmother fretfully rebukes her, and the young man's kind, appealing eyes are looking straight in her own. He can make them rich with money; he has promised it, and they are poor now. He is so well worth making happy, and he waits to hear the story she can tell.

No, she must keep silence! What is it that suddenly forbids her and makes her dumb? Has she been nine years growing and now, when the great world for the first time puts out a hand to her, must she thrust it aside for a bird's sake? The murmur of the pine's green branches is in her ears, she remembers how the white heron came flying through the golden air and how they watched the sea and the morning together, and Sylvia cannot speak; she cannot tell the heron's secret and give its life away.

Dear loyalty, that suffered a sharp pang as the guest went away disappointed later in the day, that could have served and followed him and loved him as a dog loves! Many a night Sylvia heard the echo of his whistle haunting the pasture path as she came home with the loitering cow. She forgot even her sorrow at the sharp report of his gun and the sight of thrushes and sparrows dropping silent to the ground, their songs hushed and their pretty feathers stained and wet with blood. Were the birds better friends than their hunter might have been—who can tell? Whatever treasures were lost to her, woodlands and summer-time, remember! Bring your gifts and graces and tell your secrets to this lonely country child!

Althea Sherman. Iowa State Historical Department, Des Moines.

· 10 ·
ALTHEA SHERMAN
1853–1943

Althea Sherman is by far the most eccentric personality in this book. Ostensibly, her life was conventionally defined and quietly lived. Yet the strong contours of her personality can be discerned both in the projects she undertook as a serious amateur ornithologist and in the numerous articles and essays she wrote for the *Auk*, the *Wilson Bulletin*, *Bird-Lore*, and other periodicals. Like most genuine eccentrics, Sherman emerges as an opinionated, colorful, and often exasperating character. Although we may delight in the evident oddities of her personality, her family and neighbors must surely have found her at times exasperating if not downright enraging.

Sherman, born in 1853, was one of two daughters of a prosperous farming and entrepreneurial family in National, Iowa, a tiny hamlet six miles from the Mississippi River in the northeastern corner of the state. Althea first pursued a general education at Oberlin College, where she received the Bachelor of Arts degree in 1875. She taught for four years in public schools and then studied art for a short while at the

Chicago Art Institute and the Art Students League in New York City. From 1882 to 1887 she was an instructor of drawing at Carleton College in Minnesota; from 1892 to 1895 she served as supervisor of drawing in the city schools of Tacoma, Washington. Among her many accomplishments, Sherman's drawings—especially her pastel portraits of birds—stand out as more than proficient amateur representations. They are remarkably accomplished. No other woman included here drew birds so seriously or so expertly.

In 1895 Sherman returned to National, Iowa, to look after her aging parents. There she remained on the family homestead with her sister, Amelia, the only local doctor. The sisters were the leading lights of their rural village, known to all and fully involved in community affairs. Redoubtable spinsters of wide learning and sophistication, the two sisters were utterly dependent upon each other, according to local tradition. "It can be said with certainty that after their parents were gone the only person that influenced either of them was the other of them," reports Althea's biographer. Although their personalities were both sharply defined—Althea was free with money, Amelia parsimonious, for example—a photograph at middle age shows the sisters to have gradually blended together into one persona. They are shown seated on their porch, white hair arranged in conservative chignons, postures erect and studious, dressed in black with lace at throat and wrist, each clasping a copy of her favorite professional journal.

Althea Sherman evidently had always been interested in birds, but after returning to rural Iowa began to observe them seriously. Like Louise de Kiriline Lawrence and her contemporary Cordelia Stanwood, Sherman was uninterested in exotic birds from foreign places. And although she and her sister made one grand tour of Europe and the Middle East, Althea devoted herself completely to studies of the ordinary work-a-day birds of her backyard, which consisted of a farmyard, small orchard, and adjacent fresh-water swamp. Sherman's earliest articles dating from the first decade of this century are exclusively concerned with demonstrating the richness of native ecology.

It was to her home environment that she turned for her ornithological research. The lengths to which she went to facilitate her studies is a clear measure of her obsession with birds. Sherman's most ambitious project was the building of a swift observation tower, a clapboard structure thirty feet high and nine feet square with viewing holes cut in the sides. The purpose of this curious edifice was the study of chimney swift nesting behavior. Sherman could take up position at one of the viewing openings and observe the entire cycle from start to finish. The tower became a local attraction. Year after year Sherman played host to scores of visitors who were attracted to her bird experiments. Visitors recall fondly the generous dinners which were served up on these occasions.

Sherman frequently wrote up her meticulously observed results of nesting and feeding behavior for ornithological journals. She was an active participant in the American Ornithologists' Union's annual meetings, where she became friends with Margaret Morse Nice, whose work far outdistances Sherman's but whose interest in birds was no more ardent. Sherman often wrote less scientific articles for the more popular journals to encourage birdwatchers to enjoy their native songbirds.

Her ornithological observations are almost always sound, but her lack of scientific training is manifest in her inability to draw any general conclusions from the data she gathered. Thus her own claims to serious scientific inquiry were somewhat exaggerated.

Nothing can better demonstrate Sherman's eccentricity of mind than the article reprinted here. The author lashes out at nature fakers and gushers in a manner far from lighthearted. She was obsessed with the need for seriousness in her research and in the writings and research of others. In a letter to Margaret Morse Nice she wrote, "I am glad to welcome another woman to our ranks. Too many are dabblers."

Althea Sherman died in 1943, two years after her sister.

The Old Ornithology and the New

It seems necessary at the outset to define the two schools of ornithology to be discussed in this paper. The old school deals with ornithology: "That branch of natural science which investigates and treats of the form, structure, and habits of birds." Its members respect the derivation of the word, meaning to discourse about a bird, and call themselves "ornithologists." They abide by the definition quoted which states that ornithology is a science and that it investigates or studies birds; in other words, they do scientific work following the rules for scientific research.

Various writers have been busy defining science in our scientific magazines, even in some newspapers. None of them get far beyond the dictionary's definition: that science is concerned with knowledge, with truth; meaning true knowledge, not mistaken notions that all too often pass for knowledge and truth. In this connection may be quoted the words of Dr. Theodore W. Richards, our first native American to receive the Nobel prize in science. He wrote, "First and foremost I should emphasize the overwhelming importance of perfect sincerity and truth." To this he added, "And then patience, patience! Only by unremitting, persistent labour can a lasting outcome be reached." Clearly then truth and hard work are

Charcoal drawing of robin nestlings by Althea Sherman.
Courtesy of Iowa State Historical Department, Des Moines.

the exactions of science. Conformity to this requirement is the role for ornithologists of the old school. Their work is research, the spirit of their gatherings can be told in the words of Paul by the substitution of a single word: "For all the Athenians and the strangers which were there spent their time in nothing else, but either to tell, or to hear some new thing." ("About birds," are two words to be added). The old school may be divided into two classes, the professionals and the amateurs. Of the latter class William Brewster is a notable example.

The followers of the new school of ornithology far outnumber the members of the old school. They shy from using the word "ornithologists" (perhaps it is too hard for them to pronounce), and call themselves "bird lovers"; and again they shy away from "ornithology," naming their twaddle "bird talks." They do no research work themselves, and have so slight regard for the truth about birds, that they neglect, sometimes positively refuse, to read the truths published by others. They will not take the bird magazines nor buy worthy books. One sentence fully describes them. They dabble a little in bird lore in order to gabble about birds.

The members of the new school also may be divided into two classes, the professionals and the amateurs. The professional class comprises those who are striving for fame or gain, or both; those who are panting for publicity, who imagine that they are on the road to world-wide fame by giving their "bird talks" before Women's Clubs or at gatherings of Community Clubs. As examples illustrative of this class will be taken two cases chosen from my own observations. The first place will be given to the man, who, when passing a singing bird on a telephone wire, expressed his very high appreciation of the Song Sparrow's music. When questioned, he admitted that he referred to the song of the bird on the telephone wire, and was told that it was a Dickcissel. His counterpart is found in a woman. Her story has been told once, but it so fitly illustrates this class of fame seekers that its repetition, possibly, may be pardoned. We met, and, as can readily be believed, I soon spoke of the exceedingly evil habits of the House Wren. She said, "I never heard of the House Wren." Following a brief description of the bird she exclaimed: "Oh, I know now what you mean! *You* call it a House Wren; *I* always call it a Jenny Wren." She is only one of the many instructors about birds who refuse to take bird magazines, who refuse also to learn the most elementary facts about birds. There are thousands of babblers, like her, and how they do love to babble about birds! They are the teachers of the amateur class in the new school.

Passing now to the class who for gain lay defiling hands on the birds, quotations will be given from their writings, published in the highest class of popular magazines. The first example given was published in 1909, when magazines were paying twenty-five cents per line for poetry. One gem entitled "The Shipwrecked Sailor," reads:

"Yet he smiled
Abandoning hope and drowning unaware,
Til a great sea-bird, tern, or ptarmigan
Caught by the whiteness of his lonely face
Swooped low exultantly; huge swish of wings
Measuring his body, as he struck him once.
Thud of ribbed beak, like the call to arms
Stirred the wounded soldier. . . ."

Since 1909, when these lines won two dollars for the author, there have been the terrible shipwrecks of the Titanic and of the Vestris from which some of the victims escaped with their lives. None of them told of suffering blood-curdling attacks from ribbed-beaked birds, either tern or ptarmigan, hence we must conclude that this was a rare case of the man-eating ptarmigan going to sea.

On account of the high cost of living, poetry prices mounted to a dollar per line in 1929. The quality of the outpourings seems to be about the same. Here is a sample from a poem entitled "Home":

"There shall be towels as fresh as the clover
Stored on the cedar-wood shelves down the hall,
A kitchen as white as the eggs of the plover,
And candlestick lights for the library wall."

Between the lines one may read a romance: The author, con-templating matrimony, plans a home; he is a modern youth and travels; he goes to Great Britain; he samples everything; he eats; he calls for plovers' eggs and is served with the eggs of a Bantam hen. Moreover, he is served rightly.

In sharp contrast with these nature fakes there come to mind, whenever the October leaves are falling, the lines of one who must have sat at the feet of Nature, perhaps in her very lap. They were found in a scientific magazine without a taint of money about them. Quite likely the author was a college professor who did not work for money. Except a little tautology, what fault is there in them?

"The autumn leaves are falling,
Falling, falling, everywhere.
Some are falling through the atmosphere,
And some are falling through the air."

Again wonder thrills us upon reading some of the prose effusions about nature that have been accepted and published by the highest class of popular magazines. Some of these look like a big yellow cotton patch on a blue silk dress. Now and then they contain some remarkable statements relating to ornithology which may be quoted. When snow was lying deep on the ground in Vermont a writer said she saw a Rosebreasted Grosbeak on March 12. The same magazine published the story of a November blizzard in Michigan. In it we are told that in the thickness of the storm water fowl were rushing south and among them "Swallows twittered and swept low across the water." A well-known British writer tells a story that, as a story, is an erotic, neurotic, idiotic mess, but when he lays his defaming hands on the birds it is time for us to protest. His heroine is "twenty and loverless." She knew all the birds, she watched for the spring arrivals of cuckoo, swallow, sedge warbler, and kestrel; as they came she scattered millet for them. Her bounty halted these solely insectivorous, or flesh-eating birds, and as they ate her millet they hopped through the lilacs and sang to her. Late one afternoon she wandered forth and met a stranger. Cupid smote both of them with his famous darts. As night deepened they sat beneath the boughs of a tree, "they heard a tiny commotion in the tree overhead; it was like the breaking of most fragile glass. He pointed through the branches to a nest. She knew what he meant; a new-born traveller was fighting his way out of the shell into the wind-swept world." What marvelous acuity of hearing had these love-lorn creatures! But their British creator evidently had failed to read Professor C. O. Whitman and to note his statement that birds' eggs do not hatch in the night, and rarely after three o'clock in the afternoon, even though the shells may be pipped; that the hatching bird has its time for sleep and like its parents it sleeps in the night.

The Reverend Dean Inge has said, "Perhaps the great struggle of the future will be between science and sentimentalism, and it is by no means certain that the right side will win." It may be that the great struggle is now taking place in regard to the birds and that the ignorant sentimentalists will seal the fate of the few birds now left to us. They comprise the vast mass of people who belong to the new school of ornithology. They are the amateurs who in their own language *"just love the birds."* They refuse to study, even to read the truth that days, months, and years of hard delving by the disciples of the old school have brought to light. To them the words, even the names, of the great leaders in ornithological science have no more meaning than they would have if quoted to a Bushman or a Hottentot. Moreover, they refuse to believe these same words, when told of them orally. By them all birds are to be loved and protected, even though they are the birds that are destroying other birds at an alarming rate.

A prolific source of information (perhaps the only source) for these amateurs of the new school seems to be the newspapers. If some of the men who supply the columns of these papers with their stories of bird life, containing "facts" unknown to scientists, have any true knowledge of birds they fail to demonstrate it. One marvels over the announcements of the results of some of their original research investigations. Among them may be mentioned the statement that Catbirds and Brown Thrashers use mud in the construction of their nests. One of these men declares that in northeastern Iowa there has been a "ruthless slaughter of blackbirds," and he adds: "A peculiarity of this species is that the male bird comes north in the spring two weeks in advance of the female, after mating in the southland. How they find each other is one of the mysteries of bird instinct." True, indeed, the "mystery" is sufficient to hold one spellbound! But this research student of the new school of ornithology failed to tell us the name of the blackbird of his remarkable discovery, whether it is the amorous, polygamous Cowbird or that sweet singer, the Bronzed

Grackle. You may be sure he emphasized the insectivorous habits of his song bird, yet he gave no hint that the "ruthless slaughter," whether of Cowbird or Bronzed Grackle, might be the means of saving hundreds of other and better insectivorous birds. There are other things besides food habits to be considered in the evaluation of birds. Some such consideration ought to have saved our birds from the introduction of their pestiferous foes, the English Sparrow and the Starling. Many years ago the Encyclopaedia Britannica under the heading "Birds" made the statement that the Starling "constantly dispossesses the Green Woodpecker." Its habits remain the same after its transplanting to America. It usurps the homes of our native woodpeckers, yet seldom is a voice raised against it. That 4,000 Starlings in Washington, D.C., and 600 in Ohio were banded, *then released*, is an offense against our woodpeckers that scarcely can be understood or forgiven.

Returning again to the choice excerpts from popular magazines, for several months one of them offered numerous things new to science. The bold young man who writes these things begins by telling us about the Brown Creeper "who is a true warbler according to ornithologists," he confidently asserts. This statement was published in April, 1923. In February, 1926, another of our leading magazines shows an excellent picture of a Brown Creeper, bearing beneath it this legend, "Little Willie Woodpecker," and the text that accompanies the picture implies that under the *alias* of Willie Woodpecker the Brown Creeper is a beneficial bird. Thus it may be seen that in the short space of thirty-four months the changeling creeper metamorphosed from a warbler into a woodpecker.

Turning once more to the magazine of the bold young man, we may read of his trip taken through southern Ohio in July. He says of it: "The most conspicuous bird seen in the Ohio region was a male butcher bird or great northern shrike, along a roadside, industriously feeding a voracious young bird of the same species." Where were all the southern Ohio ornithologists of the old school, that the noteworthy breeding of Northern Shrikes in their very midst should be left to the discovery of this young tourist? The same young man is no less interesting when he wanders into the realms of history and mammalogy. He invades my own home neighborhood, when attempting to give the origin of the name of Prairie du Chien, Wisconsin. People, having knowledge of Upper Mississippi Valley history, recall that the early French explorers found an Indian called "The Dog" living on the prairie at the mouth of the Wisconsin River and they called the locality Prairie du Chien, a name it has borne ever since. All those, having the least bit of knowledge of the prairie dog, know that the eastern boundary of its range is several hundred miles west of the Mississippi River. But our bold young man has this to say about it: "Many similar and rather absurd instances might easily be cited; notably the 'prairie dog,' which of course, isn't a 'dog' at all, but a member of the *rat* family. For that particular misnomer we probably have to thank the French settlers who so named 'Prairie du Chien' because the locality was full of 'prairie dogs' whose outward resemblance to a dog happened to be that they had four legs, and a *tail*, which latter they wagged vigorously."

Time is lacking for tarrying longer with the many delightful things published by the new school of ornithology. Those quoted are treasures garnered while reading a very limited range of popular magazines. Doubtlessly wider reading would disclose thousands like them. No space for their like has ever been found in the bird magazines. Yet every week the *Literary Digest* can fill a page and the *Journal of the American Medical Association* does fill three columns with the gems that sparkle in their own special fields of knowledge.

There is no implication in the preceding pages that ornithologists of the old school never make mistakes. They would be more than supermen, if that were true. But their mistakes are not delightful and joy-giving, on the other hand they are painfully saddening. Since ornithology is a science; since the purpose of science is knowledge, truth, perfect truth, the aims of most ornithologists are to contribute to truthful, exact knowledge as far as in them lies. The purposes of science are not attained by copying old, time-worn errors, nor in neglecting to read the many truths that research workers are constantly bringing to light. The case of Professor Tweezers amply illustrates this point. He decided to publish a life history of the birds of his state, to repeat once more the many things already told in various state histories, which have appeared in ponderous forms of one to four volumes. Since it is utterly impossible for one man to have thorough, first-hand knowledge of the habits of all the birds of one state he was obliged to draw very largely from previous publications. But to make his book salable and to give it an appearance of original research he invited aid from his neighbors, from the Sam Smiths of Hazelbush Hollow, and the Mary Joneses of Metropolisville, whose observations as quoted are no better than scores of similar ones already published. All this is according to custom and quite justifiable. It is when Tweezers publishes ancient errors, adds some of his own, and refuses to read numerous life histories, that others have published, that he becomes reprehensible. Well might he be arrested for "cruelty to animals" when he hustles callow Purple Martins out of their nest, when the duration of the nest period is half completed, when the quills of their wing-feathers have not yet burst. His untruths about this species might more readily be pardoned if Dr. Brownesque and several others had not given him the correct data.

Professor Tweezers is not alone in his bookmaking projects, there are several other members of his family. Some of these Tweezers would refuse to change the figures you have placed on a bank check, but they do not hesitate to mutilate the correct figures you have given in a bird history. There is a certain Tweezers who showed his masculine strength by slashing off a half day from the incubation period given for one bird. It is strange that he did not show his superiority in a bolder, braver, more heroic way by slashing off a whole day. So far as respect for truth is concerned, five or ten days might have been cut off with equal reason. If science seeks knowledge and truth, there ought to be protest against those Tweezers who seize upon the outcome of days, weeks, or months of hard work done by others, only to mutilate it or to turn and twist it to suit their own ignorance or prejudice.

To emphasize the injustice they do both to truth and to bird students I take one example selected from my own experience. I had made as careful a study of nesting Sparrow Hawks as I could and it was published in the *Auk*. It seemed to please one of the Tweezers, the reason soon became apparent: he needed it to use in his book. He used it, giving my name and paraphrasing the whole nest history. To that no one could object, if he had not inserted a downright, inexcusable falsehood. He said that I wrote that these hawks fed their nestlings "insects." And there that lie will stand as long as the writings of this particular Tweezers shall endure. To some people this may appear a small matter. It is not. Besides being a gratuitous untruth, it suggests a habit that is beyond credibility. Besides never seeing it done, two seasons of close study of nesting Sparrow Hawks lead me to believe that no mother hawk of this species would be willing to approach the nest carrying insect food.

The case just cited calls to mind another class of people

that may be mentioned: They are the "half-castes" or hybrids between the old school and the new school of ornithology. With a smattering knowledge of a few birds they are busy trying to whitewash the reputations of certain birds proved to be bad. While they deify a bird they are at great pains to damn the characters of the people who have made known its evil habits. They forget that time is long; that after them will come bird students and ornithologists who will recognize the truth and forcibly denounce the errors and untruths in which these mongrel "half-castes" delight to revel.

11

MABEL OSGOOD WRIGHT

1859–1934

Mabel Osgood Wright, one of the most dedicated bird con-servationists, was a close friend of Frank M. Chapman, who served as curator of birds at the American Museum of National History and for thirty years edited *Bird-Lore*, which later became the official magazine of the National Audubon Society. Wright served as Chapman's associate editor of *Bird-Lore* for eleven years and was its first education editor. She also founded and then headed the Connecticut Audubon Society and from 1905 to 1928 was a director of the National Audubon Society. Author of several books with birds as their central theme, Wright dedicated most of her active life to bird study, appreciation, and conservation. She is one of the forgotten heroes of the American conservation movement. All her books, fiction as well as nonfiction, are out of print. Yet her *Birdcraft*, one of the earliest and most popular guides for amateur bird-watchers, went into eleven editions, and her novels, more than ten in number, sold consistently well.

Mabel Osgood Wright was born in New York City in 1859. Her father, a scholarly Episcopal priest, was a member of Manhattan's literary elite dominated after the Civil War by the poet William Cullen Bryant. Although Mabel Wright did not attend college, her private education was sophisticated and broad. In 1884 she married an Englishman, James Osborne Wright, who was an antiquarian bookseller. The couple settled in Fairfield, Connecticut. The gardens, orchards, and fields of their home often served as backgrounds for her writing.

How or why Wright learned so much about birds or why she felt compelled to fight for their protection is not known. Although when semiretired she wrote an autobiographical book called *My New York*, her private life was her own. *My New York*, which is a series of dreamlike childhood reminiscences, included few personal revelations. It is not even clear whether Wright had children, although it seems unlikely that she did.

What is clear is Wright's long-term commitment to bird conservation, both as an organizational activist and as a writer. Her lively columns for *Bird-Lore* are invariably well focused and humorous. Her greatest talent was her ability to produce under pressure consistently good polemical prose for the magazines to which she frequently contributed. Her novels, chatty and conventional in theme, are of no particular literary distinction. But in her birdwatching literature Wright found a suitable vehicle for a fundamentally mundane literary style. Her sparkling humor was also particularly well suited for children's literature. Wright's 1897 *Citizen Bird*, an early attempt at nature education for children, was among the first books to be illustrated by Louis Agassiz Fuertes, now considered the greatest American bird artist since John James Audubon.

Wright's knowledge of birdlife was profound. Although she casts her avian characters in human roles in *Citizen Bird*, a chapter of which follows, her anthropomorphism is purposive and didactic. In her bird essays for adults, her scientifically pragmatic point of view is rarely sentimental or blurred. She was a highly gifted writer, and this talent is evident in *The Friendship of Nature*, from which an essay is also reprinted here. In this essay her language attains a lyric intensity that is the hallmark of good nature writing.

Wright was on intimate terms with the great men of the bird conservation and education movement. She was the only woman to have shared fully in the activities of such luminaries as Chapman, Elliott Coues (with whom she wrote *Citizen Bird*), and National Audubon Society leader T. Gilbert Pearson. Her service to the cause of bird conservation was unselfish and complete. Upon her retirement from *Bird-Lore* Chapman doubted that he could continue his stewardship of the journal without her. Wright's unfailingly gracious and humorous personality was an indispensable ingredient of the magazine's success during its critical early years. She retired from active participation in the Audubon Society in 1910 to develop a small bird sanctuary in Fairfield which she named Birdcraft. Birdcraft Museum and Sanctuary is a nature center now maintained by the Connecticut Audubon Society. She died in 1934.

Overture by the Birds

"We would have you to wit, that on eggs though we sit,
  And are spiked on the spit, and are baked in a pan;
Birds are older by far than your ancestors are,
  And made love and made war, ere the making of man."
                                        (*Andrew Lang*)

A party of Swallows perched on the telegraph wires beside the highway where it passed Orchard Farm. They were resting after a breakfast of insects, which they had caught on the wing, after the custom of their family. As it was only the first of May they had plenty of time before nest-building, and so were having a little neighborly chat.

If you had glanced at these birds carelessly, you might have thought they were all of one kind: but they were not. The smallest was the Bank Swallow, a sober-hued little fellow, with a short, sharp-pointed cloak, fastened in front by a neckband between his light throat and breast.

Next to him perched the Barn Swallow, a bit larger, with a tail like an open pair of glistening scissors and his face and throat a beautiful ruddy buff. There were so many glints of color on his steel-blue back and wings, as he spread them in the sun, that it seemed as if in some of his flights he must have collided with a great soap-bubble, which left its shifting hues upon him as it burst.

This Barn Swallow was very much worried about something, and talked so fast to his friend the Tree Swallow, that his words sounded like twitters and giggles; but you would know they were words, if you could only understand them.

The Tree Swallow wore a greenish-black cloak and a spotless white vest. He was trying to be polite and listen to the Barn Swallow as well as to the Purple Martin (the biggest Swallow of all), who was a little further along on the wire; but as they both spoke at once, he found it a difficult matter.

"We shall all be turned out, I know," complained the Barn Swallow, "and after we have as good as owned Orchard Farm these three years, it is too bad. Those meddlesome House People have put two new pieces of glass in the hayloft window, and how shall I ever get in to build my nest?"

"They may leave the window open," said the Bank Swallow soothingly, for he had a cheerful disposition; "I have noticed that hayloft windows are usually left open in warm weather."

"Yes, they may leave it open, and then shut it some day after I have gone in," snapped Barney, darting off the perch to catch a fly, and grasping the wire so violently on his return, that the other birds fluttered and almost lost their footing.

"What is all this trouble about?" asked the Martin in his soft rich voice. "I live ten miles further up country, and only pass here twice a year, so that I do not know the latest news. Why must you leave the farm? It seems to be a charming place for Bird People. I see a little box under the barn eaves that would make me a fine house."

"It *is* a delightful place for us," replied the Barn Swallow; "but now the House People who own the farm are coming back to live here themselves, and everything is turned topsy-turvy. They should have asked us if we were willing for them to come. Bird People are of a *much* older race than House People anyway; it says so in their books, for I heard Rap, the lame boy down by the mill, reading about it one day when he was sitting by the river."

All the other birds laughed merrily at this, and the Martin said, "Don't be greedy, Brother Barney; those people are quite welcome to their barns and houses, if they will only let us build in their trees. Bird People own the whole sky and some of our race dive in the sea and swim in the rivers where no House People can follow us."

"You may say what you please," chattered poor unhappy Barney, "everything is awry. The Wrens always built behind the window-blinds, and now these blinds are flung wide open. The Song Sparrow nested in the long grass under the lilac bushes, but now it is all cut short; and they have trimmed away the nice mossy branches in the orchard where hundreds of the brothers built. Besides this, the Bluebird made his nest in a hole in the top of the old gate post, and what have these people done but put up a new post with *no hole in it!*"

148

"Dear! dear! Think of it, *think* of it!" sang the Bluebird softly, taking his place on the wire with the others.

"What if these people should bring children with them," continued Barney, who had not finished airing his grievances—"little BOYS and CATS! Children who might climb up to our nests and steal our eggs, boys with *guns* perhaps, and striped cats which no one can see, with feet that make no sound, and *such* claws and teeth—it makes me shiver to think of it." And all the birds shook so that the wire quivered and the Bank Swallow fell off, or would have fallen, if he had not spread his wings and saved himself.

The Martin had nothing to say to this, but the little Bank Swallow, though somewhat shaken up, whispered, "There *may* be children who do not rob nests, and other boys like Rap, who would never shoot us. Cats are always sad things for birds, but these House People may not keep any!" And then he moved down a wire or two, frightened at having given his opinion.

At that moment a Chimney Swift joined the group. This Swift, who nests in chimneys, is the sooty-colored bird that flies and feeds on the wing like a Swallow, and when he is in the air looks like a big spruce cone with wings. He was followed by a Catbird, who had been in a honeysuckle, by one of the farmhouse windows, and peeped inside out of curiosity. Both were excited and evidently bubbling over with news, which half the birds of the orchard were following them to hear.

"I know all about it," cried the Swift, settling himself for a long talk.

"I've *seen* the House People!" screamed the Catbird.

"They wish well to the Bird People, and we shall be happier than before!" squeaked the Swift, breathless and eager. "Listen!"—and the birds all huddled together. "This morning when I flew down the chimney, wondering if I should dare build my nest there again, I heard a noise on the outside, so I dropped as far as I could and listened.

"A voice said, 'Mammy Bun, we will leave this chimney for the birds; do not make a fire here until after they have nested!' I was so surprised that I nearly fell into the grate."

"And I," interrupted the Catbird, "was looking in the window and saw the man who spoke, and Mammy Bun too. She is a very big person, wide like a woodchuck, and has a dark face like the House People down in the warm country where I spend the winter."

"There are children at the farm. *I've* seen them too," cried the Phoebe, who usually lived under the eaves of the cow-shed; "three of them—one big girl, one little girl, and a BOY!"

"I told you so!" lisped the Barn Swallow; and a chorus of *ohs* and *ahs* arose that sounded like a strange message buzzing along the wires.

"The BOY has a pocket full of pebbles and a *shooter*," gasped the Phoebe, pausing as if nothing more shocking could be said.

"Yes, but the big girl coaxed the shooter away from him," said the Chimney Swift, who was quite provoked because his story had been interrupted: "she said, 'Cousin Nat, father won't let you shoot birds here or do anything to frighten them away, for he loves them and has spent half his life watching them and learning their ways, and they have grown so fearless hereabouts that they are like friends.'

"But Nat said, 'Do let me shoot some, Cousin Olive. I don't see why Uncle Roy likes them. What good are birds anyway? They only sit in the street and say "chuck, chuck, chuck" all day long.'

" 'You say that because you have always lived in the city and the only birds you have watched are the English Sparrows, who are really as disagreeable as birds can possibly be,' said the big girl; 'but here you will see all the beautiful wild birds.'

"Then the little girl said, 'Why, brother, you always loved our Canary!'

" 'Yes, but he is different; he is nice and yellow, and he knows something and sings too like everything; he isn't like these common tree birds.' "

"Common tree birds indeed!" shrieked the Catbird.

"That is what the boy called us," said the Chimney Swift, who then went on with his story about what he had heard the children say.

" 'Why you silly dear!' cried the big girl, laughing a sweet little laugh like the Bobolink's song, 'that only proves how little you know about wild birds. Plenty of them are more brightly colored than your Canary, and some of those that wear the plainest feathers sing more beautifully than all the Canaries and cage birds in the world. This summer, when you have made friends with these wild birds, and they have let you see their homes and learn their secrets, you will make up your mind that there are no *common birds*; for every one of them has something very uncommon about it.'

"Then our brother B. Oriole began to sing in the sugar maple over the shed. The sun was shining on his gay coat; the little girl pointed to him and whispered, 'Hush, Nat! you see Olive is right; please empty the stones out of your pocket.' "

The Chimney Swift had hardly finished his story when there was another excitement.

"News, more news!" called the Bank Swallow joyfully. He had been taking a skim over the meadows and orchard. "These House People do *not* keep cats!"

"They may not have any now, but that doesn't prove they never will," said a Robin crossly. He had just flown against a window, not understanding about the glass, and had a head-ache in consequence.

"They *never will keep cats*," insisted the little Swallow boldly.

"How do *you* know?" asked the birds in one breath.

"Because they keep *dogs!*" said Bankey, twittering with glee; "two nice dogs. One big and buff and bushy, with a much finer tail than the proudest fox you ever saw; and the other small and white with some dark spots, and as quick as a squirrel. This one has a short tail that sticks up like a Wren's and a nose like a weasel; one ear stands up and the other hangs down; and he has a *terrible* wink in one eye. Even a poor little Bank Swallow knows that where one of *these* dogs lives the Bird People need not fear either cats or rats!"

"I love dogs," said the black-and-white Downy Wood-pecker, running up a telegraph pole in search of grubs; "dogs have bones to eat and I like to pick bones, especially in winter."

"Me too," chimed in the Nuthatch, who walks chiefly head down and wears a fashionable white vest and black neck-tie with a gray coat; "and sometimes they leave bits of fat about. Yes, dogs are very friendly things indeed."

Then a joyful murmur ran all along the wires, and Farmer Griggs, who was driving past, said to himself, "Powerful lot of 'lectricity on to-day; should think them Swallers would get shock't and kil't." But it was only the birds whispering to-gether; agreeing to return to their old haunts at Orchard Farm and give the House Children a chance to learn that there are no such things as "common birds."

A New England May-Day

"That it was May, thus dremede me."
Romaunt of the Rose

Do you know the tale of the months, the ancient Bohemian legend—how by a fire which never goes out, sit twelve
silent men each with a staff in his hand? The cloaks of three
are white as snow, and three are green like the spring willow,
and three are gold as the ripened grain, and three are blood-
red like wine. The fire that never fails is the sun; the silent
men are the months of the year. Each in his turn stirs the fire
with his staff; for each has his office, and if one month should
sleep and a turn be made amiss, then the snow would fall,
bringing blight in spring, or drought would sere the harvest.
This year [1893] April has overslept, and March has rudely
jostled May, who in confusion takes up April's task, leaving
its own for June.

Here in New England, we have no calendar of Nature,
no rigid law of season, or of growth. The climate, a caprice,
a wholly eerie thing, sets tradition at defiance and forces our
poets to contradict each other. The flower which one declares
the harbinger of spring may be a lazy vanguard in another
year; the fringed gentian, set by Bryant in frayed and barren
fields, frosty and solitary, usually follows the cardinal flower,
in late September.

Come into the garden. The wind blows sharply from the
north, where the snow still lies, and the clouds hang low, yet
it is May-day, and a catbird is singing in the arbour. It is a
much-trodden path in a long-discovered country, but each
one discovers anew when he first sees it for himself. The golden
touch, the guinea-stamp of Nature, is the dandelion in the

grass border; flattened close to the sward, the wind passes over it, but bends and twists the masses of paler daffodils. The honeysuckles show pinched yellow leaves; the shrubs are bare, only the forsythia is budded.

With what green intensity the pines are thrown into relief by the surrounding barrenness! In the top of one, a pair of crows are building, stealing forward and back with the distrust that is born of their small natures. Below, in a sheltered rock, patches of hardy violets are blooming: the little white violets that our grandmothers cherished, the odorous dark purple of the English garden-alleys, and the pansy-like variety from the Russian Steppes, which, as they bloom, laugh at our frosty weather. In spots where the sun has rested, the cowslip shows its budded panicles, and a friendly hedge shelters a mat of yellow primroses, the flower of Tory dames. The same hedge harbours each season innumerable birds. Hark! that broken prelude is from the veery, or Wilson's thrush, as he darts into his shelter. Where the stone wall gathers every ray of heat, are rows of hyacinths, with ponderous trusses of bloom, rivalling in variety and richness of colouring any bulbous growth, and hordes of bees are thumping about them. If you wish to study colour, then stay awhile by these pansies, that jostle and overrun the borders like a good-natured crowd of boys. It is strange that we rarely see the most beautiful varieties in the markets or the flower shows. The trade florists grow them more for size and less for jewel-like markings. Here are solid colours, hues, veinings, tracings, and varied casts of expression, harlequin, sober, coquettish, as if continual hybridization had placed human intelligence in them.

Not a leaf as yet on the hardy roses, and the sweet peas are only piercing the soil. The trellis skirting the garden is a lattice-work of wintry branches, but in the wren-boxes cleaning and building is advancing. Birds are not like flowers; the climate with them matters little; the food supply is the great question, and many a bird, sent south to winter by the ornithologists, will remain contentedly here, if grubs and berries are in plenty. The wren is, perhaps, the most capable bird of the garden, at once a cheerful, melodious singer, a thrifty provider, and a Board of Health in the care of its dwelling. Nothing that is dirty is allowed to remain about its snug quarters, and by a simple and comprehensive plan its local drainage is made perfect.

Go from the garden down through the lane to the meadow. What a burst of bird music greets you, solo, quartet, and chorus, led by the vivacious accentor, the golden-crowned thrush, with his crescendo of "Teacher—teacher—teacher!" This is the time and season to study the birds, while their plumage is fresh and typical, and they never sing so freely as in the first notes of their love song. The most puzzling part of the task is their modifications of plumage; for not only in many species are males and females totally different, but the male also changes his coat after the breeding season, and the nestlings wear a hybrid dress, half father, half mother. Does the gunner know that the bobolink, the jaunty Robert of Lincoln, whose glossy black coat, patched with white and buff, is so conspicuous in the lowlands when in May and June he rings out his delicious incoherent song, but who becomes silent in August and changed to a sober brown, is the reed-bird that he slaughters?

New songsters are arriving daily, some as birds of passage only, and others to remain. The bushes along the lane are alive with twittering guests. Now it is the wood-pewee, with his plaintive cry, or his brother the phoebe-bird, twisting and turning, who has built his nest under the porch for many a season, and out in the pasture the chipping sparrow is gleaning fibres and hairs for her nest. The spring of clear water in the dell is a great attraction to them; and as they bathe and drink, we can, with a field-glass, easily distinguish their markings. The robins have been building for a week, and high upon a hickory trunk a golden-winged woodpecker and a squirrel are contending loudly for a hole, which both claim for a nest. The sparrow tribe is appearing in force. That flock of brown and ash-coloured birds with white-striped crowns and white-patched throats are peabody birds, or white-throated sparrows; and if you look overhead, you will see that the charming little soprano is the song-sparrow. He is Nature's bugler who sounds a reveille from the March alders, and calls, "Lights out," to the smouldering autumn fires. Yesterday a flock of red-brown fox-sparrows, the largest of the family, were drinking at the spring, but to-day they have passed northward.

Look at the bank where the sun, peeping through, has touched the moss; there is saxifrage, and there are violet and white hepaticas, pushing through last year's leaves; lower down the wool-wrapped fronds of some large ferns are unfolding. The arbutus in the distant woods is on the wane, a fragrant memory. At the shady side of the spring are dog-tooth violets; and on the sunny side the watercourse is traced by clusters of marsh-marigolds, making a veritable golden trail. On a flat rock, almost hidden by layers of leaf mould, the polypody spreads its ferny carpet, and the little dicentra—or Dutchmen's breeches, as the children call it—huddles in clumps. The columbines are well budded, but Jack-in-the-pulpit has scarcely broken ground. On the top of the bank the dogwood stands unchanged, and the pinxter flower seems lifeless.

A brown bird, with reddish tail and buff, arrow-speckled breast, runs shyly through the underbrush, and perching on a low bush, begins a haunting, flute-like song. It is the hermit thrush. Its notes have been translated into syllables thus: "Oh speral, speral! Oh holy, holy! Oh clear away, clear away; clear up, clear up!"—again and again he repeats and reiterates, until seeing us he slips into the bushes. Over the spring in the open is the thrush's kinsman, the brown thrasher, a large bird of muscular build, with speckled breast and rust-brown back, who thrashes the air with his tail held erect. He is a mocking thrush, allied to the southern mocking-bird, and like him is a vociferous singer.

Beyond the meadow a heavy belt of maples marks the course of the river; the gray, misty hue of winter has gone from their tops and they are flushed with red; the willows are yellow, and here and there show signs of leaf, but the white birches loom grim and chilling, with their tassels only ex- panded, and the anatomy of tree, bush, and brier is as clearly defined as in January. Bluebirds are very rare this spring; some chipmunks invaded their house last year, an intrusion which they sorely resented; but a number of warblers are flitting about, and feeding on young twigs or bark insects. The war- blers, though insignificant singers, have the most varied and beautiful plumage; for a week, a flock of the black-throated green species has haunted a group of hemlocks, lighting the dark branches with glints of their gold and green feathers. The swallows are skimming over the meadow, and yesterday a belted kingfisher sat high in a dead maple by the river, with a flock of jays screaming and quarrelling near him. The snow- birds, buntings, nuthatches, and kinglets have passed to the north, as well as most of the owl tribe; but the little screech- owl remains to blink in the summer woods. Yonder black cloud, settling on the great chestnut, is an army of purple grackles, our crow blackbirds, and their glossy kin with the scarlet shoulders, whose cry is a shrill "Quank-a-ree," is the red-winged swamp blackbird.

Far down the meadow, where the grass is coarse and sedgy, and dry tussocks offer a shelter, the meadow lark is weaving its nest, working so deftly that its home is practically safe from human invaders. See him there, striding along in the full splendour of his plumage, dark brown above, with speckled sides, wings barred transversely, with brown, yellow breast, black throat-crescent, and yellow legs; while his mate is hardly less brilliant.

We must turn homeward now, for the birds are hurrying to shelter, the wind is rising, and the sound of the waves on the bar, two miles distant, is growing distinct and rhythmic. Big drops of rain are rustling in the dry beech leaves, the smoke of burning brush has enveloped the spring and shut off the meadow. The logs blazing on the hearth will give us a cheery welcome, for the mercury in the porch registers only ten degrees above freezing. Is it November? No, surely, but one of the twelve months has slept, and so wrought all this strange contradiction. This is the first of the Moon of Leaves, the May-day of Old England, and we have gathered violets and daffodils, and we have heard the hermit thrush singing in the lane:—

"The word of the sun to the sky,
    The word of the wind to the sea,
The word of the moon to the night,
    What may it be?"

12

MARY HUNTER
AUSTIN

1868–1934

Mary Hunter Austin was born in 1868 in Carlinville, Illinois, and received a Bachelor of Science degree from Blackburn College in her hometown in 1888. After Mary's graduation her widowed mother decided to relocate at a desert homestead in California's San Joaquin Valley, where the oldest son was pioneering. Mary accompanied the family to this desolate outpost. The desert landscape quickly took hold of Mary, an oddly sensitive and intellectual young woman whose rapid mood swings and uncontrolled curiosity irritated the already overburdened Hunters. Seeking independence for herself and relief for her mother, Mary began providing private school lessons to ranch children scattered over the valley. Various tutoring jobs continued until 1891, when she married Stafford Wallace Austin, a young aesthete from a Hawaiian missionary family. Wallace Austin failed continuously in any attempt to earn a living for himself or his wife. Scheme after scheme fell through

Mary Austin, photographed by Charles Lummis.
Courtesy of The Southwest Museum, Los Angeles.

until Mary, by then with a severely retarded daughter born in 1892, decided to support herself teaching in larger towns where medical care might be more readily available for her child.

For ten years Mary Austin vacillated between reconciliation with her husband and subsequent enslavement to his impecunity and the difficult life of a single working parent with a child requiring constant custodial care. Throughout this traumatic decade Austin tried writing and slowly began to sell essays to the *Overland Review*, a Los Angeles based regional journal. She established contact with the intelligentsia of California, especially the group of artists and writers gathered around the poet Charles Lummis, who was working as a journalist in Los Angeles.

In 1903 Austin, beset with emotional and financial difficulties, published fourteen sketches about the desert of California called *The Land of Little Rain*. This slim book, a classic of American nature writing, won her immediate fame and enough money to break with her husband for good. After placing her child in an institution where she could be adequately tended, Austin built a small cottage in Carmel, where a colony of California artists and writers including Jack London and Ambrose Bierce had settled.

In Carmel, Austin finally found an environment where she could give free expression to her remarkable artistic and intellectual powers. Among the bohemians of Carmel, she began to feel herself integrated with the intensely spiritual and emotional sides of her nature, long held in check by bourgeois convention. Although under constant financial pressure and often in ill health, after the publication of *The Land of Little Rain* Mary Austin produced thirty books, many of them novels, and more than two hundred essays. After 1912 she divided her time between Carmel and Manhattan, where she associated with the artists and writers in the circle of Mabel Dodge and served often as a publicist for the suffrage and birth control movements. Frequent lecture tours were squeezed in between feverish bouts of writing.

While visiting London in 1910 Austin discovered that she had become famous. H. G. Wells, with whom she met several times, called her the most intelligent woman in America. His judgment may well have been correct.

Among other activities, Austin took up the study of American aboriginal language. Her poem play *The Arrow Maker*, which was based on her research, was produced in New York in 1911. Her intense interest in Indian culture as well as in Spanish colonial culture led her to resettle in Santa Fe, New Mexico, where she built a Spanish-style adobe house in 1924. There she continued to study aboriginal culture and campaign for Indian rights. Writers and artists frequently stayed with her; Willa Cather wrote *Death Comes for the Archbishop* while Austin's houseguest. Mary Austin died at her home in Santa Fe in 1934.

Many of the facts about Mary Austin's life come to us from her autobiography *Earth Horizon*, published in 1932. In this ruthlessly analytical self-portrait she revealed much of the suffering that had colored her existence. She was one of the most intellectual of the early feminists in the United States. Her analyses of female roles in the midwestern society which formed her are sophisticated and pungent. Mary Austin was a huge personality, moody and irascible, opinionated and aggressively self-confident. The literary corpus she left as a record of her life is only slightly less impressive than the personality which created it.

The selection reprinted here, a sketch from her recognized masterpiece, *The Land of Little Rain*, demonstrates Austin's poetic descriptive style. She wrote about birds with a unique spiritual intensity. Her prose style, suave and polished, is nonetheless redolent of nature's mysteries. Although Mary Austin achieved enormous fame in her own lifetime, her reputation has waned considerably. But *The Land of Little Rain* deserves to be viewed again as a classic of American nature writing, and *Earth Horizon*, her autobiography, as one of the great feminist documents of our century.

The Scavengers

Fifty-seven buzzards, one on each of fifty-seven fence posts at the rancho El Tejon, on a mirage-breeding September morning, sat solemnly while the white tilted travelers' vans lumbered down the Canada de los Uvas. After three hours they had only clapped their wings, or exchanged posts. The season's end in the vast dim valley of the San Joaquin is palpitatingly hot, and the air breathes like cotton wool. Through it all the buzzards sit on the fences and low hummocks, with wings spread fanwise for air. There is no end to them, and they smell to heaven. Their heads droop, and all their communication is a rare, horrid croak.

The increase of wild creatures is in proportion to the things they feed upon: the more carrion the more buzzards. The end of the third successive dry year bred them beyond belief. The first year quail mated sparingly; the second year the wild oats matured no seed; the third, cattle died in their tracks with their heads towards the stopped watercourses. And that year the scavengers were as black as the plague all across the mesa and up the treeless, tumbled hills. On clear days they betook themselves to the upper air, where they hung motionless for hours. That year there were vultures among them, distin-

guished by the white patches under the wings. All their offensiveness notwithstanding, they have a stately flight. They
must also have what pass for good qualities among themselves,
for they are social, not to say clannish.

It is a very squalid tragedy—that of the dying brutes and
the scavenger birds. Death by starvation is slow. The heavy-
headed, rack-boned cattle totter in the fruitless trails; they
stand for long, patient intervals; they lie down and do not
rise. There is fear in their eyes when they are first stricken,
but afterward only intolerable weariness. I suppose the dumb
creatures know nearly as much of death as do their betters,
who have only the more imagination. Their even-breathing
submission after the first agony is their tribute to its inevita-
bleness. It needs a nice discrimination to say which of the
basket-ribbed cattle is likeliest to afford the next meal, but
the scavengers make few mistakes. One stoops to the quarry
and the flock follows.

Cattle once down may be days in dying. They stretch out
their necks along the ground, and roll up their slow eyes at
longer intervals. The buzzards have all the time, and no beak
is dropped or talon struck until the breath is wholly passed.
It is doubtless the economy of nature to have the scavengers
by to clean up the carrion, but a wolf at the throat would be
a shorter agony than the long stalking and sometime perchings
of these loathsome watchers. Suppose now it were a man in
this long-drawn, hungrily spied upon distress! When Timmie
O'Shea was lost on Armogosa Flat for three days without
water, Long Tom Basset found him, not by any trail, but by
making straight away for the points where he saw buzzards
stooping. He could hear the beat of their wings, Tom said,
and trod on their shadows, but O'Shea was past recalling what
he thought about things after the second day. My friend Ewan
told me, among other things, when he came back from San

Juan Hill, that not all the carnage of battle turned his bowels as the sight of slant black wings rising flockwise before the burial squad.

There are three kinds of noises buzzards make—it is impossible to call them notes—raucous, and elemental. There is a short croak of alarm, and the same syllable in a modified tone to serve all the purposes of ordinary conversation. The old birds make a kind of throaty chuckling to their young, but if they have any love song I have not heard it. The young yawp in the nest a little, with more breath than noise. It is seldom one finds a buzzard's nest, seldom that grown-ups find a nest of any sort; it is only children to whom these things happen by right. But by making a business of it one may come upon them in wide, quiet cañons, or on the lookouts of lonely, table-topped mountains, three or four together, in the tops of stubby trees or on rotten cliffs well open to the sky.

It is probable that the buzzard is gregarious, but it seems unlikely from the small number of young noted at any time that every female incubates each year. The young birds are easily distinguished by their size when feeding, and high up in air by the worn primaries of the older birds. It is when the young go out of the nest on their first foraging that the parents, full of a crass and simple pride, make their indescribable chucklings of gobbling, gluttonous delight. The little ones would be amusing as they tug and tussle, if one could forget what it is they feed upon.

One never comes any nearer to the vulture's nest or nestlings than hearsay. They keep to the southerly Sierras, and are bold enough, it seems, to do killing on their own account when no carrion is at hand. They dog the shepherd from camp to camp, the hunter home from the hill, and will even carry away offal from under his hand.

The vulture merits respect for his bigness and for his bandit airs, but he is a sombre bird, with none of the buzzard's frank satisfaction in his offensiveness.

The least objectionable of the inland scavengers is the raven, frequenter of the desert ranges, the same called locally "carrion crow." He is handsomer and has such an air. He is nice in his habits and is said to have likable traits. A tame one in a Shoshone camp was the butt of much sport and enjoyed it. He could all but talk and was another with the children, but an arrant thief. The raven will eat most things that come his way—eggs and young of ground-nesting birds, seeds even, lizards and grasshoppers, which he catches cleverly; and whatever he is about, let a coyote trot never so softly by, the raven flaps up and after; for whatever the coyote can pull down or nose out is meat also for the carrion crow.

And never a coyote comes out of his lair for killing, in the country of the carrion crows, but looks up first to see where they may be gathering. It is a sufficient occupation for a windy morning, on the lineless, level mesa, to watch the pair of them eying each other furtively, with a tolerable assumption of unconcern, but no doubt with a certain amount of good understanding about it. Once at Red Rock, in a year of green pasture, which is a bad time for the scavengers, we saw two buzzards, five ravens, and a coyote feeding on the same carrion, and only the coyote seemed ashamed of the company.

Probably we never fully credit the interdependence of wild creatures, and their cognizance of the affairs of their own kind. When the five coyotes that range the Tejon from Pasteria to Tunawai planned a relay race to bring down an antelope strayed from the band, beside myself to watch, an eagle swung down from Mt. Pinos, buzzards materialized out of invisible ether, and hawks came trooping like small boys to a street fight. Rabbits sat up in the chaparral and cocked their ears, feeling themselves quite safe for the once as the hunt swung near them. Nothing happens in the deep wood that the blue jays are not all agog to tell. The hawk follows the badger, the coyote the carrion crow, and from their aerial stations the buzzards watch each other. What would be worth knowing is how much of their neighbor's affairs the new generation learn for themselves, and how much they are taught of their elders.

So wide is the range of the scavengers that it is never safe to say, eyewitness to the contrary, that there are few or many in such a place. Where the carrion is, there will the buzzards be gathered together, and in three days' journey you will not sight another one. The way up from Mojave to Red Butte is all desertness, affording no pasture and scarcely a rill of water. In a year of little rain in the south, flocks and herds were driven to the number of thousands along this road to the perennial pastures of the high ranges. It is a long, slow trail, ankle deep in bitter dust that gets up in the slow wind and moves along the backs of the crawling cattle. In the worst of times one in three will pine and fall out by the way. In the defiles of Red Rock, the sheep piled up a stinking lane; it was the sun smiting by day. To these shambles came buzzards, vultures, and coyotes from all the country round, so that on the Tejon, the Ceriso, and the Little Antelope there were not scavengers enough to keep the country clean. All that summer the dead mummified in the open or dropped slowly back to earth in the quagmires of the bitter springs. Meanwhile from Red Rock to Coyote Holes, and from Coyote Holes to Haiwai the scavengers gorged and gorged.

The coyote is not a scavenger by choice, preferring his own kill, but being on the whole a lazy dog, is apt to fall into carrion eating because it is easier. The red fox and bobcat, a litttle pressed by hunger, will eat of any other animal's kill, but will not ordinarily touch what dies of itself, and are exceedingly shy of food that has been man-handled.

Very clean and handsome, quite belying his relationship

in appearance, is Clark's crow, that scavenger and plunderer of mountain camps. It is permissible to call him by his common name, "Camp Robber:" he has earned it. Not content with refuse, he pecks open meal sacks, filches whole potatoes, is a gourmand for bacon, drills holes in packing cases, and is daunted by nothing short of tin. All the while he does not neglect to vituperate the chipmunks and sparrows that whisk off crumbs of comfort from under the camper's feet. The Camp Robber's gray coat, black and white barred wings, and slender bill, with certain tricks of perching, accuse him of attempts to pass himself off among woodpeckers; but his behavior is all crow. He frequents the higher pine belts, and has a noisy strident call like a jay's, and how clean he and the frisk-tailed chipmunks keep the camp! No crumb or paring or bit of eggshell goes amiss.

High as the camp may be, so it is not above timberline, it is not too high for the coyote, the bobocat, or the wolf. It is the complaint of the ordinary camper that the woods are too still, depleted of wild life. But what dead body of wild thing, or neglected game untouched by its kind, do you find? And put out offal away from camp overnight, and look next day at the foot tracks where it lay.

Man is a great blunderer going about in the woods, and there is no other except the bear makes so much noise. Being so well warned beforehand, it is a very stupid animal, or a very bold one, that cannot keep safely hid. The cunningest hunter is hunted in turn, and what he leaves of his kill is meat for some other. That is the economy of nature, but with it all there is not sufficient account taken of the works of man. There is no scavenger that eats tin cans, and no wild thing leaves a like disfigurement on the forest floor.

· 13 ·

MARGARET MORSE
NICE

1883–1974

Margaret Morse Nice was one of the world's foremost ornithologists. Almost entirely self-educated, working without an
academic position or access to research funds, Nice, in the
words of noted ornithologist Ernst Mayr, "almost single-hand-
edly initiated a new era in American ornithology. . . . She
early recognized the importance of a study of bird individuals
because this is the only method to get reliable life history
data." Margaret Nice achieved this prominence while raising
five daughters on the modest earnings of her husband, Leonard
Blaine Nice, a professor of physiology. Her achievements can
be viewed as, among other things, an extraordinary triumph
of the will.

Margaret Morse Nice was born in 1883 in Amherst, Massachusetts, where her father was a professor of history at Amherst College. In 1901 she entered Mount Holyoke College;
five years later she earned a Bachelor of Science degree. While

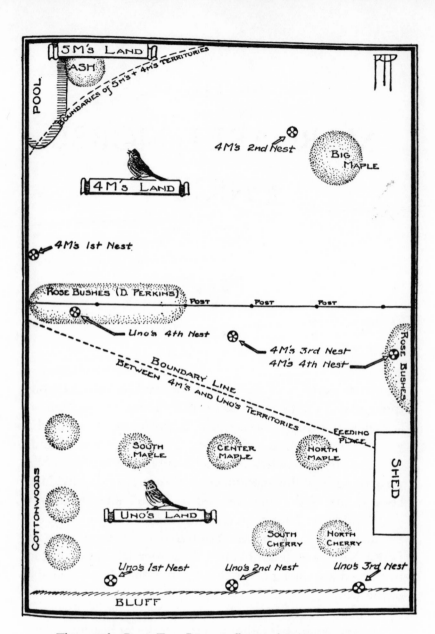

*This map by Roger Tory Peterson illustrated sparrow territories
in* The Watcher at the Nest *by Margaret Morse Nice.
Courtesy of Roger Tory Peterson.*

a graduate student in zoology at Clark Institute in Worcester, Massachusetts, Nice met her future husband, a fellow student. The couple were married in 1909. After studying medicine at Harvard, Blaine Nice accepted a teaching position at the University of Oklahoma in 1913. By 1923 Margaret had given birth to five daughters. Sandwiched between childbearing and rearing, she had published a few ornithological articles based on the results of her graduate research into bobwhite feeding habits. During this decade, remarkably, Nice also studied child psychology and in 1915 received a master's degree in that field from Clark. She subsequently published eighteen papers on child psychology based upon observations of her own children. Nice was from the start primarily interested in animal behavior, hence her devotion to child psychology while observing the development of her own family.

During the 1920s, as her children grew older, Nice turned increasingly to nature for stimulation and succor. Birds returned to her life in Oklahoma, where the out-of-doors was easily accessible. Althea Sherman, who met Nice at an ornithological conference, encouraged Nice, a woman half her age, to pursue ornithological research more seriously. Taking this advice to heart, Nice with the help of her husband began a survey of Oklahoma birds, a five-year project. The survey led to the publication in 1924 of *The Birds of Oklahoma*. But Nice had yet to reach her true stride.

In 1927 the Nices moved to Columbus, Ohio, where Blaine would teach at the University of Ohio, and acquired a house on the Olentangy River. Sixty acres of scrub land led from their yard to its banks. Dubbed Interpont by Margaret Nice because it was bordered by two bridges spanning the river, this tangled wasteland became her outdoor laboratory. Conspicuous among the birds frequenting Interpont were dozens of nesting song sparrows, and it was this noisy species which captured Nice, taking over her waking and sleeping hours. She began to study in depth the life cycle of these birds, particularly their breeding behavior. The results of her years of research startled the ornithological world.

Nice developed new methods of identification so that she could actually trace the life cycle of individual song sparrows who resided at Interpont for several years in succession. Fortunately for us today, the scientific publication in 1937 and 1943 of her research, *Studies in the Life History of the Song Sparrow* was supplemented in 1939 by a popularized account of the study, *The Watcher at the Nest*, which was the first book illustrated by bird artist Roger Tory Peterson.

Nice's research was revolutionary in two important ways— one methodological, the other theoretical. By banding individual birds and observing them closely in the wild over several years' time, she was able to gather data profoundly rich in detail. Her theories were based not on surmise but on observations gathered in thousands of hours of watching and waiting at Interpont. Equipped with an extraordinarily synthetic mind, Nice was able to construct general principles of bird behavior based upon the solid evidence she had so painstakingly amassed. The most important avian behavioral phenomenon that she identified and defined in detail was the principle of territoriality in song sparrow breeding, which she described clearly in *The Watcher at the Nest*. This was a tremendous contribution toward future ornithological research.

Margaret Morse Nice did not achieve immediate fame in the United States. It was in Europe that the revolutionary nature of her research was first recognized. While on an extended European tour with her family in 1932, she met noted Berlin ornithologist Erwin Stresemann, who arranged for her long song sparrow study, "Zur Naturgeschichte des Singammers," to appear in the *Journal für Ornithologie* in 1933 and 1934. Nice had been unable to place the study in any American ornithological journal. (It finally appeared in English in 1937 and 1943 as a publication of the Linnaean Society in New York.) European scientists were more open to the principles of animal behavior adumbrated in the song sparrow study. Ethologists such as Konrad Lorenz and Oskar Heinroth were receptive to the possibilities inherent in Nice's methodology. Subsequently in 1938 she spent two months studying captive bird breeding with Lorenz at his research estate outside Vienna. Margaret Morse Nice died in 1974, leaving behind a legacy of research still profitable to scientists.

Now recognized as one of the pioneers of behavioral ornithology, Margaret Morse Nice was a woman of ardent feeling and sympathy. During World War II she struggled with her husband to assist European scientist refugees, arranging their relocation in England and the United States, and often hosting exiles in her own home for months at a time. Her belief in the importance of nature study for the average person was as strong as her commitment to serious scientific research.

In her autobiography, *Research Is a Passion with Me*, which was published posthumously, in 1979, Nice provided a reticent portrait of a life-long struggle for recognition and an equally intense search for scientific truth. In the passages from *The Watcher at the Nest* reprinted here, she demonstrated her clarity of mind with a simplicity of expression which belies the complexities of the methodology she describes.

The Way of a Song Sparrow

It was the rose hedge that formed the boundary between the domains of the two Song Sparrows that shared our garden. Uno claimed all the land around the house, the steep bluff directly west of it, and the three Norway maples in the garden proper, while 4M was owner of the ground beyond, starting with the hedge and including a box elder and a great silver maple on a meadow of blue grass. That this ownership was no mere figure of speech will be evident in the course of the narrative; the land was defended and won by age-old ceremonies and fierce battle, as definitely as in our courts of law, a piece of ground being released and quitclaimed by one bird and lawfully seized by the other.

These two birds, Uno and 4M, are the heroes of my story. Their conflicts with each other and their other neighbors, their luck with their wives and devotion to their babies, the exuberance of their glorious singing—not to mention the fortunes of their sons and daughters, grandchildren and great-grandchildren—all these were watched season in and season out until tragedy overtook them. Uno lived in our garden for three years, while 4M by the greatest good fortune escaped the perils that beset his kind for nearly three times as long. Uno was my first love among the Song Sparrows, but 4M, because of his long life and notable character, was to become, as an eminent German ornithologist put it, "world-famous."

It might be well to remind those of my readers who are not bird students that the Song Sparrow's colors are brown and grey; back and breast are heavily streaked, and in the middle of the breast there is a characteristic dark spot.

When in the fall of 1927 we came to Columbus, Ohio, we settled near the banks of the Olentangy because of the great weed tangle that stretched between our house and the river. The sixty acres of land which I called Interpont offered a bit of wilderness to the birds and me. Great cottonwoods and sycamores lined the banks of the stream, while a row of elms and hackberries had sprung up along an old fence. Patches of elders stood white in the late spring, and a deserted vineyard was overrun with briars. Weeds were everywhere—jungles of giant ragweed along the dikes that led to the river and along its sides, inhospitable nettles in the shade of the cottonwoods, thickets of burdocks, spectacular cow parsnips, and hosts of others. In short, Interpont was a tangled waste, despised by the conventional, but a place of happiness to the boys of the neighborhood, carp fishermen, an ornithologist, and the wild creatures.

It was on March 26, 1928, that I made an important capture in my trap on the feeding shelf—the first Song Sparrow that I had ever banded. Later I was glad to note that he had taken up his territory next to us. I called him Uno, while the male nesting to the south was 2M, the one to the north 3M, and the bird to the west 4M. The last-named individual attracted my attention by his fine and varied singing, and four of his songs I recorded in my notebook.

One morning a robbery occurred in our garden. I was sitting quietly near the north rosebush when a male Cowbird alighted on the woodshed, giving his high double note; a minute later, much to the distress of a Field Sparrow and a pair of Indigo Buntings, a female appeared. She vanished into the weeds and shortly returned, carrying in her bill an egg which she leisurely ate, contents and shell, while poor 4M and his mate protested.

A few days later I found Uno's nest well concealed under a large dandelion on the bluff. When the eggs hatched, I settled down to watch the parents, Uno being distinguished by a band on each leg, and his mate by a dark crescent on her side, evidently the result of some injury. She was an efficient mother, knowing exactly what to do with babies, for, although she had the task of brooding them, she fed them more often than Uno did during the first two days. This may well have been his first experience with fatherhood. He soon woke up to his responsibilities, however, and outdid his mate not only in the number of meals brought, but particularly in their size, for some of the insects he carried looked nearly as large as his offspring.

Unfortunately some predator carried off Uno's babies. 4M had even worse luck, for he lost not only his nest but his mate as well. We left Columbus in early June and knew nothing further of the happenings in our garden that season.

To my unbounded delight Uno entered my trap on March 9, 1929, giving me 100 per cent "return" for this species. My return percentages with Song Sparrows have always been high, but never again did they reach perfection.

To those of my readers who have not heard of the great game of bird banding let me briefly explain that hundreds of thousands of birds each year in Europe, India, Japan, and North America are being provided with aluminum anklets, each bearing a number and an address to which a report should be made in case the bird is found. In our country it is the United States Biological Survey that supplies the bands and serves as the clearing house. Many of the birds are banded as nestlings, but others are adults, captured in a variety of traps that lure the subjects within by means of bait, and take them unharmed by tripping devices, funnels, or the pulling of a string by the eager watcher. So little does the experience of banding seem to frighten most birds that some enter the traps many times a day. This is called "repeating"; "return" is used in connection with the recapture of a bird at or near the place of banding after the migration.

The object of banding is to individualize the birds, to enable one to know he is observing a particular subject and not another that looks just like him. Aluminum bands have afforded rich stores of information on migration, even though recoveries of marked birds do not ordinarily run above three to four per cent. For life-history studies, however, colored celluloid rings need to be used in addition to the official band of aluminum, for by means of different colors and different arrangements a large number of birds can be individually marked and readily distinguished in the wild with the aid of field glasses. Some students glue colored feathers to the tails of their subjects, but I feared that such conspicuous badges might jeopardize my birds.

Although Uno received the warmest of welcomes from me, the situation was vastly different in the garden. Ever since February 26th I had been studying with great interest 4M's splendid singing from the big silver maple in the west end of our land and the box elder in the middle of the garden. But on the day of Uno's capture I noted:

"4M is spreading himself over two territories and seems to take special delight today in singing right next to our house, over land that belonged to Uno last year. Poor Uno—he always was a mild-mannered Song Sparrow. I don't know what he will do."

Early the next morning I found out. I quote from my notebook:

"Uno and 4M are in Uno's southeast corner, down on the ground and in the weeds; Uno sings quite steadily from these low positions—rapidly and not loudly. They pay no attention to me, although I am very near. Both are very much puffed out, and even fly in this odd shape. 4M says nothing, but follows Uno, going for him or after him every minute or so, but not fiercely; Uno merely flies a few feet. This keeps up for perhaps ten minutes. Then 4M grows more belligerent, chases Uno around and about, and at last they come to blows, falling to the ground and fighting furiously. They separate and Uno sings in the Norway maple, while 4M goes to his box elder. Each sings and sings and sings."

Apparently the battle is won and the territory apportioned.

The witnessing of this "territory establishment" sealed my fate for the next seven years. I was so fascinated by this glimpse behind the scenes with my Song Sparrows, that I then and there determined to watch Uno for several hours every day, so as to follow the daily course of his life, to find out the meaning of his notes and postures, in short, to discover exactly what he did and how he did it. In particular I wanted to study the matter of "territory," which has been a burning question with ornithologists ever since the appearance of H. Eliot Howard's *Territory in Bird Life* in England in 1920, although the basal facts had been pointed out fifty years earlier in Germany by Barnard Altum. "Territory," as Ernst Mayr defines it, "is an area occupied by one male of a species which it defends against intrusions of other males of the same species and in which it makes itself conspicuous." Although it was obvious, once it had been pointed out, that many birds were territorial, yet hardly a beginning had been made in determining details with various species.

Incredible as it may seem, almost complete ignorance reigned as to the life history of this abundant, friendly, and well-nigh universally distributed bird. I went to the books and read that this species has two notes besides the song, and that incubation lasted ten to fourteen days and was performed by both sexes— meager enough information and all of it wrong. The men at the State Museum, fine field naturalists and well acquainted with the local birds, could not answer my questions; they did not know whether 4M's singing in late February meant that he had taken up his territory, nor could they tell me when the nesting Song Sparrows arrived. None of us suspected that some of our breeding birds were permanently resident, for we believed that all our wintering Song Sparrows nested farther to the north. Indeed, I have never had a subject of research in which I had so little idea what to expect as these Song

Sparrows. It was an unknown world, and each day I made fresh discoveries.

The main business of 4M and Uno at first was song. And what was its significance? Was it "a sweet and sincere little petition," a "little prayer of thankfulness" sent "straight up to heaven by the shortest route"? I fear we will have to discard this pious fancy. As Bernard Altum stated nearly seventy years ago, the song of a territorial bird at the beginning of the season is a warning and an invitation—in short, an advertisement that this particular bit of land is preempted by a certain male, that other males must keep their distance, but that a mate will be heartily welcomed.

From dawn on through the morning each male spent most of his time on high points over his territory singing steadily at the rate of some seven songs a minute; the chief interruptions, besides brief meals, being sallies to clear the land of trespassers of his own or other species. By the middle of March the migration of transient Song Sparrows was in full swing and all owners of territories busied themselves chasing these unfortunate travelers. I thought a tourist camp was sorely needed.

I began to wonder how Uno would recognize a possible mate, since both sexes are dressed alike. And I looked forward eagerly to learning what form of courtship display and special song he would use to win the lady.

Then all at once both Song Sparrows stopped singing. Instead of two hundred and sixty songs an hour, perhaps three were given. The change was nothing short of startling. It seemed as if Uno *must* sing as he alighted on one favorite singing perch after another.

My notes at this time are full of puzzling situations as the following excerpts will show.

"Mar. 15. Uno approaches a new Song Sparrow; it flips its

wings, then opens its bill and says *eee eee eee* in a high nasal tone. Uno retires; it flies into a small tree; Uno dashes for it and attacks it.

"Uno has a short fierce fight with a stranger, after which he stands with crest raised and bill open. Stranger doesn't leave. As if Uno didn't have troubles enough this morning, 4M is back again, hunched up, threatening him.

"Mar. 17. Uno flies down near the stranger; 4M appears in the shape of a balloon. Uno spreads out his tail, but little else. He always keeps between 4M and Stranger. Why *don't* Uno and 4M sing any more?

"Mar. 18. Uno hops on lawn, Stranger keeps behind. He goes up the road a way, is chased by some other Song Sparrow, tries to get back to his land, but is driven off by a cross scold from Stranger who is perched on the corner burdock. (Think this must have been a migrating male of considerable courage.) If Uno were not banded, I should be perfectly distracted by this multiplicity of birds that all look practically alike."

It was not until the next day that the truth began to dawn upon me. I noted: "Stranger starts working up the bank as if hunting for a nesting site; at one hollow she twitches her wings."

So Stranger was Uno's mate! But still I had seen no courting.

"I think I have solved the problem as to how males tell females," I wrote. "When the owner of the land dashes at a strange bird, a male either flees or fights; a female shouts *eee eee eee*, and he at once desists from any exhibition of hostility."

But Uno behaved very oddly at times.

"Una flies down from the south end, Uno rushes at her, hits her, and leaves singing triumphantly. She crouches there, saying *eee eee eee*. This must have been a mistake on Uno's part."

A *drawing from* The Watcher at the Nest, *the first book illustrated by Roger Tory Peterson.*
Courtesy of Roger Tory Peterson.

At length I realized that this "pouncing" *is* Song Sparrow Courtship, that and the sudden cessation of song. Uno guarded Una from attentions of 4M and other males, and he gave the excited *tit tit tit tit* of fear when a cat or hawk appeared, thus showing his concern for her safety. And although he dominated her by his pouncing, yet in many little everyday encounters, *she* dominated *him*, and the net result was that they were the best of friends.

By the study and interpretation of my notes in the light of experience, I discovered that 4M's mate—Quarta—had arrived the day before Una did. The two pairs met many times a day at the feeding station I maintained on the boundary between the two territories. Sometimes my conscience pricked me about this arrangement; two feeding stations would have meant fewer quarrels, but how much less exciting life would have been! I will describe a meeting:

"4M balloons at Uno who is somewhat puffed up with tail spread. 4M goes near Quarta who pecks at him. Una balloons at Quarta who retires. Males threaten back and forth, coming within three inches of each other. Suddenly a real fight is staged, the males springing into the air, the females seizing each other with bill and claw, then an indiscriminate melee."

Perhaps two-thirds of the encounters passed off with mere bluffing, but fights occurred several times a day. Besides these boundary quarrels, the birds often deliberately trespassed on each other's territories. The rose hedge held a fascination for Uno and Una, and every now and then they foraged beneath it, sometimes returning home without the knowledge of the owner, but at other times being driven back in a hurry! 4M made his excursions alone, sometimes boldly on the wing, again stealthily on foot; but, whatever the method, the result was always dramatic.

While the presence of another Song Sparrow on the territory was not tolerated for an instant, other birds were also treated with conspicuous lack of hospitality. Eighteen species, ranging in size from the tiny Ruby-crowned Kinglet to the imposing Chewink, that weighs twice as much as a Song Sparrow, are recorded in my notes as being hustled off by Uno, and eleven of them by Una. Most of these were migrating sparrows and thrushes, over half of them larger than the birds that drove them. As to the birds nesting in the garden later in the season, the Song Sparrows seldom paid any attention to species larger than they—Robins, Cardinals, Catbirds, Brown Thrashers, and Mourning Doves, while smaller species— Maryland Yellowthroat, Indigo Buntings, and House Wrens— ducked into cover momentarily and proceeded with their several occupations. Two species, however, often failed to give way before the hostile approach of the owners of the territory; English Sparrows and Goldfinches as a rule took no notice of the threatened attack and continued to eat dandelion seeds or to sit placidly wherever they had alighted; with their bluff called, the only thing the Song Sparrows could do was to ignore these visitors.

One morning a curious thing happened: contrary to the feminine custom of keeping to low situations, Una flew to the top of a small tree and delivered a song. And *what* a song— a squeaky, unmusical affair of some six or seven notes, yet given with all the aplomb that Uno employed with his lovely melodies. On seven occasions during the last week of March I noted Una singing one or two of these foolish little ditties from a tree or the top of a weed, and the impression I gained was of something vestigial, something that had no meaning nowadays. Was this a relic of the earliest form of Melospizan song, existing before the sexes had differentiated their roles, the male developing it as an indispensable tool and a work of art into a thing of beauty, the female almost forgetting it?

For five days the south wind blew, and late March became balmier than May. This strange weather stirred the birds to a new activity:

"Mar. 21. To my astonishment Una has a long piece of dead grass. She flies east of the shed, Uno following her.

"Uno gets a double piece of grass. Flips wings. Goes into a tunnel in some rocks. Later gets an immense piece of grape-vine bark.

"Mar. 25. Uno's zeal in getting nesting material was the outstanding feature of today's session. He got several large loads, flying with them dangling from his bill. One he carried into a cavity in the rock pile, Una following him. He takes stuff to two places at opposite ends of his territory.

"Mar. 27. Uno and 4M are both occupied with nesting material, but their mates are mere spectators. Today I see coition for the first time, Una fluttering her wings beforehand, and saying *eee eee eee* directly after, but Uno makes no sound.

"Mar. 29. Una, as well as Uno, is now busy manipulating dead leaves, grass and bits of bark, but this interest has not crystallized into the definite project of nest building. Uno got six big loads and dropped them all. Una dropped most of hers."

March had seen stirring drama in our garden: the return of Uno from the South and the winning of his territory from the grasp of 4M; the tireless singing of both birds until the coming of their mates; the resolute defence of territories; and the symbolic nesting activities. Yet all of this was but the first act in the age-old drama of the renewal of life upon the earth.

· 14 ·

LOUISE DE KIRILINE LAWRENCE

born 1894

Louise de Kiriline Lawrence was born in Sweden in 1894. After qualifying as a registered nurse, she traveled extensively with various international service agencies. She married for the first time in 1918, but her husband, Oleg de Kiriline, a White Russian, died two years later in the Russian Civil War. A posting to Ontario with the Canadian Red Cross in 1927 brought her to this continent where she still lives today. She married Leonard Lawrence in 1939, and they settled in the watery wilderness of southeast Ontario on a lake about 180 miles north of Toronto.

Lawrence's first book, *The Quintuplets' First Year*, appeared in 1936. It was followed in 1945 by *The Log House Nests*. Her mature writings appeared much later. At the urging of her friend Margaret Morse Nice, Lawrence undertook a serious ornithological study. *A Comparative Life History of Four Species of Wood Peckers* was published in 1967 by the American Or-

Louise de Kiriline Lawrence.
Courtesy of the author.

nithologists' Union. It is totally scientific and tedious reading for the amateur bird enthusiast. Lawrence's acknowledged masterpiece, *The Lovely and the Wild,* appeared in 1968 and was awarded the John Burroughs Medal for outstanding nature writing by the American Ornithologists' Union. A later book, *Another Winter, Another Spring,* recalls her years as a Swedish Red Cross volunteer in Russia while married to the White Russian de Kiriline. This book, which tells of the Russian Civil War, is powerful and tragic as well as gripping.

In the selection from *The Lovely and the Wild* reprinted here, Lawrence tells how transformations in her attitudes toward birds and their study came about from living in the wilderness. Her description is especially effective in juxtaposing factual information with recalled impressions and conversations. The reader learns something new about the author, and something new about the relationship of any person to the world of nature.

Lawrence discovered the continuity between her own universe and the universe of wild creatures after the continuity of her existence had been shattered by the advent of World War II. For a European and a nurse, this bloody conflict was all the more acutely disturbing. Lawrence's reaffirmation of life's meaning through nature is central to the transcendental tradition of American thought. Her compelling description of this discovery is absorbing and immediate. Her achievement is even more impressive when one considers that she writes in English, which is for her a foreign language.

The Lovely

"I just saw a robin at the spring," Len announced as he came in with two pails of sparkling water. Tiny drops trickled down the outside of the pails and dripped on the floor. He filled the little tank by the door with the day's supply.

At first his words did not register with me because I was busy with breakfast. He took off his mitts and rubbed his hands. His eyes glistened in the dim light of our small kitchen.

"Louise," he went on, "Spring's here!"

But still I did not catch on to his exciting message. Only a few days ago the house was sitting in snow to the eaves, and with the cold frosty nights spring seemed very far away.

Our first winter at Pimisi Bay had been hard. It had been full of trials and errors and all kinds of unknown conditions.

The snowfall had been heavy and the problem of keeping the traffic lanes open out to the road and up to the spring turned out to be a major task demanding a great deal of energy. The snow had been banked high on each side of the paths, in places level with our shoulders. We had tried just trampling the snow down, but with the first thaw we discovered the disadvantages of this method. It made of the paths hard rounded ridges that were fine to walk on in cold weather when the snow gripped. But when the weather was mild these ridges became so slippery as to defy progress even with snowshoes. This was the lazy man's way and soon the snow shovels and we became great friends.

A fire in the fireplace is a wonderfully pleasant and cosy thing and a wood fire is fine to cook on. But during the coldest part of the long northern winter to keep the house warm, only moderately warm, with wood as fuel, wood fetched directly from the forest, is quite another matter. Before winter started, inexperienced as we were, we had no qualm whatever about the heating question. The forest was full of trees. All there was to do was to chop the tree down, cut up the trunk with the crosscut saw, and carry or drag the pieces down to the house in deep snow. During the coldest weeks to get enough wood to keep us warm took the whole day. Len became as hard as nails and as lean as the trees he cut down.

Then there was the difference between dry and green wood. All our wood was green. We had never thought of that. The green wood had to be coaxed to burn, but once aflame it lasted longer than dry wood though it gave less heat. It also gummed up the stove pipes and the chimneys. When the black tarlike substance accumulated too thickly, it oozed from the joints of the pipes and dripped on the floor, smelled acrid and strong, and would not wash off, had to be scraped away. Once it caught fire and the chimney belched forth thick black smoke.

We stood watching with our hearts in our throats. But the chimney withstood the heat of that fire.

We had a heater-type cookstove with a large round fire box down to the floor which held a lot more wood than an ordinary range. We counted on it to do more heating than cooking, which also it did. But it was no miracle burner. Of course it warmed only so long as the wood lasted, no more than two or three hours when stacked full in the evening. As the fire died down the frost bit into the roof and the logs and the wood contracted with loud reports. But it hardly disturbed us; we never slept more soundly than under the warm blankets in our freezing house.

Outside in the night the temperature stood at below zero. An icily cold full moon lavished its silvered reflections upon the snow, the stars sparkled. The night was eerie. Three deer came out of the shadows and meandered slowly down the southeastern slope, plowing narrow tracks like ribands behind them. The shadows cast by the trees absorbed them, then again released them to the moonlight. There was no sound, not even the crunch of the snow as the deer carefully lifted and set down their dainty cloven hoofs in the soft white stuff. Nothing—except the frost cracking in the trees with the effect of a sudden minor explosion.

Today had dawned mild. During the past week there had indeed been a feeling in the air of an impending change. The snow had shrunk, bare patches were showing, and with the wind blowing from the south the forest smelled different. As the snow melted, seeds, leaves, and other debris of the forest, accumulated and buried during the winter, came to light and now rode on top of the shrinking snow mass. In odd places a collection of light footprints suggested a bird's opportune looting of this well-preserved residue.

"A robin at the spring, did you say? Are you sure? Let's

go and see it, do you think it's still there? Come on!" I was outside in the clear fresh air.

It smelled of thaw, warm sunshine, and humidity. We ran up the path toward the spring. The dead leaves were soft and wet underfoot, the snow in the remaining patches was coarse as gravel and glided away as we stepped on it. The chickadees were singing, one higher, two lower notes, bell-clear. We got to the spring and looked for the robin. We looked at each other disappointed; it must have gone. No, there it was, just a bit farther up past the spring on a branch, resplendent, its breast appearing never so rust-red as today when seen for the first time, the first robin in the obscurity of the tall trees.

The bird scanned us questioningly with its left eye. It uttered a soft note, *que-wit-wit.* Did it mean who are they? It flapped its wings softly against its flanks. It flew farther in amongst the trees, sat for a while, then flew out of sight down on a spot of bare ground. We could hear the very light rustle of the leaves as the bird turned them over in search of food. Beautiful bird! Beautiful springtime!

I turned and danced down the path in front of Len, two hops on each foot. My heart was light and gay with a wonderful feeling of release, the sun, the air, the lovely reawakening world. "Spring's here, spring's here!" I chanted.

"There's a song sparrow down by the lake," Len volunteered, to make me feel still happier.

I was overwhelmed by all these signs of spring crowding in upon us all at once. "Where, where? What does it sound like? I've never heard a song sparrow."

"Listen!" We stopped. "I love the song of the song sparrow," Len said, "it's my favorite bird. When I was a child . . ."

Faintly, because the song came through the trees from a distance, but distinctly, first the introductory notes, then the warble dropped upon the air liquid and clear. Cautiously we approached a little closer. There the bird was, in its modest brown plumage, the dark breast spot, the streaks, the buff-colored edges of the feathers on wings and tail, drawn sharply in the bright light of the sun. It sat on a small twig above the slushy ice with its head tilted backward, and the short bill, pointing skyward, opened and closed, opened and closed. The tail hung down slack and trembled with the effort of the bird's vocal performance.

"When I was a child . . ." Len's words struck an echo from my own past of long ago. Birds and the things of nature had the same meaning to him as to me. This was a new and wonderful realization. So far we had neither had time nor opportunity to test our individual reactions to the new life. But these things are inborn. His favorite bird was the song sparrow, mine had been the crested tit.

Suddenly a glimmer of better understanding came to me about the real meaning of this land that we had striven to possess for the realization of a dream rather than an end. It was real and this was the main point. The things in it were real. The situations in it developed accurately according to a logical design. The stars that penetrated the darkness of space were real, not just a distant glitter. The shimmering snow sparkle was real, not tinsel. The bird was real, not an imitation or a falsehood. The winter's hard labor we had just experienced was performed for a real purpose, not just for gain, and it had a salubrious effect upon our bodies and our minds. It had to do with life, real life; it had to do with survival.

Nature is a deep reality and whether we understand it or not it is true and elemental. Here in our own wilderness with its essence of actuality we had a marvelous chance to probe into the meanings of this saner kind of life with its purer values.

The way I started to walk when I was very young but had abandoned, the threads lost by the death of my father, I could now pick up again under circumstances and in an environment which at least in their most essential parts bore a likeness to the old life at Svensksund. And from this day I began to look and to listen in a new way. I began to see and to hear things I had never seen or heard before, because I became gradually more sensitive to everything that existed and lived beside us.

To learn how to identify a bird by its general outline, markings, and behavior as a species belonging to a certain family or order was a new and thrilling occupation, and so it remains, I think, forever new, forever thrilling throughout life with every watcher of birds.

I began to make interesting discoveries. For instance, until a brown-headed chickadee arrived upon the scene and by its brownish tints and raspy voice proclaimed itself as obviously distinct from the common black-capped chickadee, I did not know there were two kinds of this engaging little bird. The confusions I worked through learning to tell the thrushes apart before I realized the meaning of a rust-red tail, or a reddish head, or a cream-colored eye-ring, or a gray cheek, or the absence of all four, were stumbling blocks not the less real because recognition is now automatic and I can laugh at my early difficulties.

Having reached this stage, I began to take notes, naively written as if I were speaking to the birds directly—you did this, you did that, sort of thing, This seemed to lead us, the birds and me, into a more intimate relationship. It also led me into an entirely anthropomorphic appreciation of the birds and their behavior. But for a long time I remained blissfully ignorant of even the existence of that long word and certainly of its meaning and of the impediments it posed to the art of objective observation.

LOUISE DE KIRILINE LAWRENCE

The great horned owl was one of the first birds to appear on my written pages. The magnificent secretive bird made a strong impression upon me; it was the wilderness incarnate and it was much more common in those days than it is today.

"Going up the river in the canoe," I wrote, "on this beautiful late summer day of August, we saw you again. In broad daylight you sat in full view in the very top of a distorted gray chicot.[1] Gravely you turned upon us your facial disk. The rusty brown coloring margined by black of each cheek and the fringe of fluffy white feathers around your hooked beak appeared very distinctly and beautifully drawn as you sat against a backdrop of shaded rock and evergreens. At deliberate intervals gray membranes worked across your yellow orbs, shutting their light off and on as you observed our stealthy approach to get a closer look at you. There was, we thought, immense dignity and aloofness in your pose and in your slow motions, as if you alone belonged to this wild and enchanting scenery—and we did not. Presently your soft feathered wings lifted and spread, hooked talons disengaged themselves from the perch, and as a speckled shadow, borne on a breath of wind, you vanished among the trees."

During the years that followed this impressive encounter, the owl showed itself again many times. Once, after a series of unearthly screams and hiccups had called me out in the gathering dusk to identify the originator, I came face to face with the large bird sitting on a low branch in a tree beyond the spring, blinking and smacking its bill. Undoubtedly, a pair nested somewhere along the river between Talon Lake and Pimisi Bay for many years, but we never found the nest. Then evidences of the owl's presence became scarcer, dwindled to a few occasions when in the morning we found a small collection of furry tails under one of the feeders, all that remained

1. French term for a dead tree stub.

of an engaging crowd of flying squirrels after the owl's nightly visit. Then nothing more. The wide-eyed flying squirrels were relieved from one of their most deadly enemies, at least temporarily.

One day in May sunny climes seemed magically to enter the Pimisi Bay with an exotic-looking bird we had never seen before. At that time all my ornithological research was conducted with the help of Chester A. Reed's modest but within its limits excellent *Bird Guide*. Frantically, lest it vanish, I searched for an explanation of the extraordinary apparition. There I found it, orange and black matching the warm deep yellow color of the bird in the cherry tree, beautifully offset by the shining black head, neck, wings, and tail. It could not be anything else, the bird sampling our suet was, of all things, a Baltimore oriole, an amazing sight, for in my ignorance of the local avifauna I had not expected to see so colorful a bird so far north.

The next day the female, lovely in her softly demure greenish-yellow coloring, introduced herself. A few minutes later she engaged in a fight with a hairy woodpecker over domination of the feeding tray. Soon after I came upon the male battling a red squirrel in the top of a pine.

Nothing of this registered in my mind as other than detached events without any particular meaning. My discovery of the orioles' nest hanging beautifully bulbous from a branch in one of the twin birches on the southeastern slope did not even suggest to me at that time any significant connection between the birds' occupation of the land and their pugnacity. Quite another observation, actually more sophisticated than this first instance of territorial defense I had witnessed but not understood, carried the probing of my curiosity a step further. The following year I was pretty sure the same pair returned to our forest to nest again. Both birds behaved as if they were quite familiar with the premises. But now the male's loud whistled song was much more varied and elaborate than it had been the year before. I listened with delight to the lovely notes and wondered about the reason for this. Did the bird's innate ability to sing gradually develop in skill from year to year? Or was his more elaborate phrasing acquired through imitation? The question was unanswerable, but of course the important thing was the question itself.

Later I learned that Baltimore orioles are by no means uncommon in this region, and they are also to be found much farther north. But their preference is for open parklands and gardens where the broad-leaved trees predominate. Just by chance, then, one pair, possibly in the first year of their adulthood, found within our closed-in mixed forest a limited area on the southeastern slope that answered to their requirements. And so there they nested and to this place they returned to nest again another year.

The deeper I became involved in my preoccupation with birds and nature, the more irksome I found my ignorance of the most elemental things about them. For my own satisfaction I needed some kind of purpose to which my curiosity and interest could be geared.

This was particularly important just at this time, because Len had enlisted at the start of the war and I was alone. For how long nobody knew; I was prepared to be without him for months certainly, probably for years. It was therefore necessary to fill my days with pursuits that were absorbing and worthwhile and, from that viewpoint, this was the chance of a lifetime to concentrate on the serious study of the life around me.

The actual turning-point came unexpectedly when a friend presented me with P. A. Taverner's book, *Birds of Canada.* I sat down and read it from cover to cover.

Mr. Taverner was curator of birds at the National Museum

of Canada and knew his subject. But this was not what prompted me to write to him. What impressed me was Mr. Taverner's talent of turning what could have been a dry annotated list of birds, a description of species by species, what they look like, what they do, what they eat into a tale of astonishing fascination and vividness. And this I told him.

The effect of that letter was beyond all expectations. The author's acknowledgment came as complete surprise. It was richly colored with the enthusiasm and insightful humility which I later learned so characterized his gentle spirit. From this first contact a friendship developed between us, I do not recall exactly how, that turned out to be of great significance to me in my new role of serious nature student, and endured until Mr. Taverner's death six years later.

We never met and personal acquaintance did not seem necessary. By letter we discussed many things from past and present events to politics and philosophy, war and peace, always with birds and natural history as the central theme from which the digressions emanated and expanded. This was my first real contact with somebody who represented the scientific attitude, somebody with the larger vision. The way he challenged my ways of thinking without ever seeming to do so, the spur of canny encouragement he applied to urge me on, the fine realism with which he expressed his ideas always elicited my immediate and eager response. To be linked to such a giver as the fortunate recipient of gifts was a wonderful experience. Rather miraculously I had acquired a companion and a co-observer who could see the things I saw and *explain them,* even though he was not there in the flesh.

One spring day I identified a mysterious bird, so like a thrush, that sang loudly and almost without interruption back in the forest. It was an ovenbird and a flock of them had arrived from the south that morning. Their loud seesawing notes, in force and expression mounting toward the end of the song, came from several parts of Green Woods, from the southeastern slope, from the thickets around the spring and in the ravines, from the escarpment farther back. One ovenbird answered another, a third one chimed in, the voices of a fourth and a fifth blended with each other.

On this particular spring morning the ovenbirds appeared to have descended from the skies for no other purpose than to burst into song. And so perhaps they had. And having sung, they moved on "surface-hopping" from one place to the other, along the shore, inland, always northward. In those early days the ovenbirds were numerous in these parts. Throughout the breeding season their voices were heard from at least as many micro-locations as they occupied on this day of their first arrival from the south. Their boldly striped breasts, their cute strutting walk, their broad-legged singing pose assuring the maintenance of needed equilibrium during the forceful delivery of their outpourings, all this was continually in evidence from the day they arrived to their departure and made this water-thrush one of the most familiar summer residents of our forest.

All that summer I listened to the loveliest flight-songs without being able to discover their author. I heard them most often at dusk, more seldom in the daytime, sometimes at night, and in the hours just before dawn they seemed to be performed with particular ardor and élan. Often the mysterious bird startled me by beginning its performance from somewhere else, bursting forth with those loud spaced introductory notes announcing that the main aria was about to begin. And then came the song proper, delivered as if each warbled note were fetched with tremendous effort from the singer's innermost reaches, poured from the heart, until the bird fell from the skies as if exhausted. In vain I searched for the singer returned to earth without ever spotting the trace of even an escaping shadow.

One day in July, in the role of a father with a young one in tow, one of the ovenbirds appeared at the feeding station. In the sun the feathers on his back acquired a lovely greenish sheen and the orange stripe along the crown reflected the sunbeam. By contrast, the coloring of the fledgling was all dullness and suffusion with a counter-shaded effect that blended beautifully with the milieu, designed to safeguard the survival of the young one through the period of its immaturity. The father was silent and intensely preoccupied with picking from the ground tiny specks of suet dropped by the other birds. High-stepping out front, he led the two-bird procession across the dappled shadows. Every so often he turned in his tracks to pop a morsel of food into the mouth, hastily agape, of his begging child.

A few days later the ovenbird came walking past my door, this time alone. I stood on the threshold watching him. The next instant he disappeared. At the same moment the sharp introductory notes of the flight-song came to me from right overhead, followed by the remarkable warbled sequence. At the end of this performance my astonished eyes perceived the ovenbird the very second he touched ground, almost in the identical spot whence he had vanished. Thereupon he stepped out of sight as if entirely innocent of ever having left the earth or uttered a note. And the riddle of the flight-song was solved at last.

This was a year of many new discoveries and one thrilling event followed upon the other in my world of nature. My capacity for observation improved markedly. New sounds impinged upon my ears with greater intensity and selectivity. I began to detect movement and form belonging to the creatures of the forest where in earlier days I would have heard or seen nothing. A new bird, correctly identified, added itself to the last one on my list. And so it went.

However, with the loss of novelty I found myself inclined to lose interest in the new bird. I concentrated all my attention on looking for the next unknown bird that might be lurking in the bushy entanglements, just waiting for me to record it. This is the great danger of "listing." It is a pitfall quite common to the novice bird-watcher. One is greedy for the sensational at the expense of experience in depth. One forgets that the less spectacular is often the more significant detail of birdlore, which provides the knowledge that makes the expert out of the watcher. But in spite of these beginner's failings that afflicted me, each new experience added, almost unnoticed and not without lasting gain, its golden coin to my collection.

On the last day of May I heard a soft clicking, tuck—tuck-tucktuck—tuck, uneven in rhythm, a sound I had never heard before. As I crossed over to Green Woods whence it came, the sun was getting low and its beams seeped through the trees, making the smooth white bark of the birches shine golden. Dusk coming on and these strange notes from a strange bird gave me a feeling of mystery and subdued excitement.

I caught sight of the bird almost at once. I pursued it as it flew into a tree, stumbled over rocks and undergrowth with eyes glued to the slim form, hoping not to scare it away before I had time to note all its markings. The bird was as large as a blue jay, brownish-gray in color with a faint wash of green on the back, white underneath. Its long flirting tail was as straight and wide as an ordinary footrule, and marked every inch or so on the underside with a penciled bar in black and white. It had a finely curved bill, all black.

The sight, especially the form of the bill pulled forth a memory from long ago. I knew this kind of bird, I had seen it before, although I remembered something of a darker color and barred markings, a cuckoo. Could this be a cuckoo? But there was at the moment no time to check with the books.

From somewhere else in the distance came the same clucking notes, sharper and louder as a second bird approached. There it was, another cuckoolike bird, perhaps the mate of the first one. With soft languid movements it advanced toward the first bird, remarkable movements I thought they were, whose meaning I could not rightly assess. At that moment the first bird flew out as if to meet the second one, but halfway across the distance that separated them it changed direction abruptly and flew off, giving very soft *tuck-tuck* notes. Come on, come on—was this the meaning this plausible maneuver suggested? The next instant the two birds came together on a horizontal branch, the briefest airiest meeting of their light, faintly greenish bodies, then they separated, flew apart, vanished among the trees. I stood entranced looking at the spot where they had just been. Color, form, setting—simplicity, harmony, beauty!

The books said that two species of cuckoos may be found in these latitudes of Pimisi Bay and that the black-billed is the more common of the two.

Summer passed, and autumn, filled with arduous birding. The first snow came and at dawn one day in early December my ear once again caught an unfamiliar note, this time a grosbeaklike bird vanishing among the trees. It was too dark to go after it and the sighting of the ghost slipped my mind until, in broad daylight, my eyes fastened upon an incredible sight.

The broom I held in my hand clattered to the floor. Scarcely more than ten feet away out there on the ground was a brilliant red bird, its head adorned with an elegant pointed crest. A velvety jet-black area around the large pink bill, extending to the twinkling dark-brown eyes and forming a bib under the chin, was the only divergence from the bird's overall scarlet plumage. There was no need to consult the books on this one. I had looked at its picture many times, envying those who might count it among their common birds, never dreaming that so exotic an apparition would ever sit in the midst of the snow of this northern landscape.

The next day, to my surprise and delight the cardinal was still there. From then on, every new day with this red bird in our inhospitable white world was a gift of grace. Could it possibly survive the rigors of our northern climate? On days when the temperature sank to below zero the cardinal emerged from its roost in a small dense spruce with a patch of frozen breath stuck to its back where its head had been buried among the feathers of the shoulder. It sat on its feet to keep warm and nibbled nuts with the other birds, but otherwise it showed no sign of being uncomfortable or affected by the cold. When at Christmas time I had the house gaily decorated with red wreaths in the windows and the red bird was perched on the peak of the roof or sprawled bathing in the deep snow, one motif in red matched the other.

On a mild day in late February the cardinal sang for the first time. In the top of a tall pine he sat framed in green with his breast aflame in a beam of sunshine and his full throat bubbled with these new mellow whistled notes; and the harsh northern environment put its own stamp of distinction upon their delicious clarity and modulations. Every day for a month and a half the cardinal sang, and I was the only one who heard him and listened to his song. At the end of this time he was still alone without a partner of his own. One day he vanished and for a while the sun went out and the silence lay stark and oppressive over these woods where the cardinal had been but was no more.

Naturally I shared the whole history of the cardinal's stay at Pimisi Bay with Mr. Taverner. He was particularly interested because that winter saw an unprecedented invasion of cardinals eastward and northward. My bird had come some two hundred miles farther north than the main body of this incursion. After this, reports of cardinals being seen or visiting feeding stations began to come in more frequently from this part of Ontario, even from as far north as Kirkland Lake, two hundred and fifty miles north of Pimisi Bay.

Sixteen years later a cardinal once again appeared at Pimisi Bay. This was a lone female arriving from the north on a dark November evening. She stayed three days and then vanished. Several years later, in late June, another male cardinal, singing as he passed through our area northward, provided a rare summer record. But, so far as I know, no nestings have been reported, and thus the presence of the cardinal in our latitudes must still be considered only accidental.

The war went on and on interminably. Len went overseas with his regiment and the prospect of our reunion and his happy homecoming appeared inordinately remote.

With every new discovery my desire increased to turn my bird-watching into something more meaningful. Real bird-watching—when you sit and watch every move and detail in the behavior and the activities of certain birds known personally and then record all you see and hear—was beyond my ken. It did not even occur to me. Finally I turned to my friend and asked, "What can I do?" Certainly the opportunity was mine, all I needed was a purpose, a channeling of current activities into a definite direction.

Mr. Taverner's answer came back promptly: "Why not take up bird-banding?" He also told me where and how to apply for a license. He proposed himself as one of the two sponsors who are required to vouch for the applicant's ability to identify birds. The other was Hugh Halliday, the well-known writer and bird photographer, with whom I had recently come in contact by correspondence. With these two names on my application form, I was soon in business as a full-fledged bird-bander.

My relationship with the birds changed dramatically. Personal recognition became a thrilling possibility. The bird was no longer just a member of a certain species but a special individual of unique character, whose life history could be followed from stage to stage.

As banding activities go, I can claim no spectacular achievements of any kind. One or two foreign birds, banded elsewhere, and less than a dozen of my own birds recovered abroad out of a total of slightly more than twenty-five thousand birds banded are on record in my files. This adds very little to our general knowledge about, for instance, their migration, their mortality and ages. But for my own close-range study of bird behavior, into which my bird-watching finally led me, banding proved to be a significant accessory. This is, indeed, one of the most profitable ends of bird-banding.

Three of the most interesting recoveries of my own birds ought to be mentioned here. One of these was a young pigeon hawk hatched in a tall pine on the slope of Brule Hill. We rescued it from starvation after its parents had disappeared and raised it to adulthood on beef liver and dog food. Early in September the young hawk migrated, and the next summer it was killed at Deer River, Stasca County, Minnesota, in the same latitude as its birthplace but about a thousand miles farther west.

Few house wrens come to nest in our forest. The environment is not particularly to their taste. They favor fairly open places where a cavity of some kind is available. One year, nevertheless, an unmated male wren arrived and established his territory around the house with a birdbox in the cherry tree as the main attraction. Being alone, he filled the place with his singing from morning until night, full loud lovely songs. Even from a distance a passing female could not have missed hearing him. But no prospective mate appeared to put the feminine touch to any of his many cocknests, constructed in every conceivable niche. In early July he departed as unmated as he had arrived, and in September four years later the sweet bird was killed against a power line at Walker, West Virginia, about seven hundred fifty miles south of Pimisi Bay.

Most of the blue jays of this region are permanent residents, provided they can find enough food to see them through the winter. Early one January I banded one of them, a bird of the year as shown by its plumage which lacked the black barring on certain wing feathers. It stayed around the feeding station all that winter and in the spring nested not far away. At Christmas time, almost a year later, it was shot at Henderson, Tennessee. Thus, in the fall of its second year, this blue jay migrated in a slightly south-southwesterly direction and was caught by death about a thousand miles from its birthplace.

A year before Len finally returned home safely after five long years, two naturalists and bird-watchers, Doris and Murray Speirs, found their way to Pimisi Bay.

Perhaps it was symbolic that on this particular day the rose-breasted grosbeak should greet them with a full-voiced concert of mellifluous notes; that the ruby-throated hummingbird, first for the season, should have chosen just this day for its return; that a flock of pine siskins, hitherto unknown to me, should flit about in the top of a tall tree so that I could learn to recognize their raspy twitter. This was the first time I came in personal contact with people with whom I could share exciting experiences, who knew how to look at birds and nature with the discerning and objective eye. And in the years of fruitful association and friendship that followed I learned from them the best and proper ways to study birds. I learned how to appreciate the richness of my untouched forest and to draw therefrom the knowledge and understanding that would eventually surpass my earlier highly unsophisticated efforts.

Through them I was to be introduced into a new intellectual environment which culminated in my first meeting with Margaret Nice. World famous as a student of bird behavior, this remarkable and gifted friend took hold of my purpose, and my work, and the whole of my thought life in fact, and as gently as the wind blowing from the south in the spring, as gently and as surely, changed all of it.

· 15 ·

FLORENCE PAGE
JAQUES
1890–1972

Florence Page Jaques was born in Decatur, Illinois, in 1890. After attending Millikin University she remained at home, occasionally writing poetry and children's stories, some of which were published. In 1923 she moved to New York City to study literature at Columbia University. She met Francis Lee Jaques, a naturalist/illustrator on the staff of the American Museum of Natural History, in 1925. They were married two years later. Jaques said of her husband, "I had never known anybody who liked to stay outdoors as long as I did, and here was one who liked to stay out longer." Thus started a long and successful career for the couple—he as diorama painter and book illustrator, she as author of natural history travelogs illustrated by her husband.

Eventually Lee Jaques became discontented with his life at the museum and was able to give up full-time employment. The couple moved permanently to the wilderness of Minne-

sota, where Lee free-lanced as a natural history illustrator and
Florence wrote books about their wilderness experiences. Their
first collaboration, *Canoe country*, appeared in 1938, followed
in quick succession by *The Geese Fly High* (1939), *Birds Across
the Sky* (1942), and *Snow Shoe Country*, which in 1944 won
the John Burroughs Medal of the American Ornithologists'
Union for distinguished natural history writing. Two more
books followed—*Canadian Spring* in 1947 and *As Far as the
Yukon* in 1951. Lee Jaques died in 1969, Florence Jaques three
years later. At the time of her death she had all but completed
a biography of her husband. It was subsequently published by
their friends as a combined biography, anthology, and catalog
of both Jaqueses' lifework.

Lee Jaques's fame as a bird artist is growing rapidly. A show
devoted to his art mounted by the Natural History Museum
in Minneapolis toured the country in 1983 and has done much
to enhance his reputation. The work of Florence Jaques, on
the other hand, remains obscure, a fate she ill deserves. Her
books are frank and humorous. They are pleasantly, if unpre-
tentiously, written. Her husband's obsession with birdwatching became the source of her subject matter. Apart from stimulating some of the best natural history book illustrations of
our time, her writings communicate an open enthusiasm for
the out-of-doors. Her modesty of expectation makes for a prose
style which in its simplicity does not dominate the world of
nature. Theirs was a happy partnership, from all accounts,
and Florence Jaques clearly did not resent the path her life
took as a result of her husband's career and way of life. Lee
Jaques made the choices for the couple, but is would seem
that Florence Jaques was delighted with them.

In the selection from *Birds Across the Sky* reprinted here,
Jaques describes her personal awakening to the pleasures of
birdwatching. Through the device of relating conversations

between her husband and herself, she manages in an entertaining way to instruct the reader on basic points of bird
behavior and identification. Above all she communicates an
utterly sincere enthusiasm for the wilderness and its creatures.
Jaques wrote the poem "There Once was a Puffin" for *Child
Life Magazine* in 1930. It is still very funny.

There Once Was a Puffin

Oh, there once was a puffin
Just the shape of a muffin,
And he lived on an island
In the
   deep
     Blue
       Sea.

He ate little fishes
Which were most delicious
And he had them for breakfast
And he had
    them
      for
       tea.

But the poor little puffin
He couldn't play nothin',
For he hadn't anybody
To play
    with
     at
      all.

So he sat on his island
And he cried for a while, and
He felt very lonesome
And he
    felt
        very
            small.

Then along came the fishes
And they said, "If you wishes
You can have us for playmates
Instead
    of
        for
            tea."

So they all play together
In all sorts of weather,
And the puffin eats pancakes
Like you
    and
        like
            me.

Birds Across the Sky

The green witch-color of ferns and moss was all around me,
as I perched on a triangle of granite ledge which jutted out
into the rapids. The frothing white water, tumbling past, was
dangerous with molten curves of clear black, swinging into
fans of vivid jade. The green of the cedars on the shores was

Puffin, by Francis Lee Jaques.

clouded with dim purple and bronze, and the scent of pine
was strong in the sunny air.

We were in the wilderness. A real wilderness; no halfway
solitude! The wonder I had felt on a May afternoon in Rhine-
beck, as to how it would seem for Lee and me to have days
alone with clouds and grass and fluttering things—that wonder
was now being answered. For our first extended holiday together Lee and I had taken to the wilds.

His long-beloved canoe country was on the border between
Minnesota and Canada. It was entirely savage; there were no
settlements, not even cabins, except one or two for forest
rangers. Hundreds of lakes lay solitary, with rivers lacing them
together and dense forest separating them; here was a last

stronghold of our primeval continent. No roads, and few paths except the portages which remained from the time of the fur traders. You traversed this country only by its waterways.

Lee had traveled it by canoe in many summers, and now he was showing it to me. We had come out from Duluth to the little town of Winton, and there from a casual dock we had set out into these solitudes.

I looked up the rock to our property. A light canoe lay on the stony shore. On a pinestraw carpet between two huge pines was our seven-by-seven tent, looking ludicrously small, and inside its doorway lay three packsacks, one of food, one of clothing and one of miscellaneous items. These were our sole possessions for three weeks. And how I hoped that nothing in Lee's carefully prepared lists had been overlooked! For there was no one here we could buy or borrow from.

Before we started, I had wondered a little how I would react to gypsy living, for I had never camped out overnight in my life, and my canoeing had been only desultory. I knew I liked outdoor life for stray hours; how about whole weeks of it?

But I had fallen in love with this northern wilderness the moment I entered it, and even on the first night of sleeping outdoors, I hadn't had a qualm.

In the morning I had waked to weird whoops of laughter which came through the walls of white fog surrounding our small white tent. Lee had described these cries of the loons, as untamed as the lakes themselves, now I heard them. Eerie, fantastic, exultant, they forever after meant this country to me, no matter where I heard them.

All day I gloried in the long passages down the sapphire lakes, and in the discovery of winding streams. Tramping across the portages, shadowy green or sun bright, with our packsacks on our backs, made me feel as adventurous as any early explorer. I even reveled in the fact that we had to retrace our paths for second loads, since that gave us a chance to become well acquainted with each portage, whether it was a small one all in a frenzy of vines and thickets, or an extended vista magnificent in ferny slopes of towering pines. I discovered fresh pleasures, such as treading on various surfaces, rough granite, sandy loam, smooth mats of pine needles or springy depths of moss.

When in mid-afternoon we had come to this opening in the forest, with white water rushing down past it, Lee suggested that we make camp; fishing was always good below rapids like these, he said. Having put up the tent, he got out his fishing gear, and now he was on a great rock in the midst of the foam. I meant to pick blueberries for our supper.

They made an untamed garden all around our tent, their green sprays jeweled with berries of deep blue. Such enormous berries, almost too lustrous to eat. But when I tasted them and found no insipid half-taste, but a real berry flavor, tart and sweet, my reluctance to destroy such beauty seemed to melt away.

I soon found that if I picked them by the spray, instead of berry by berry, dessert for supper was easily provided. Then I began to gather dead wood and pinecones for the campfire. A high windfall behind the tent barring me from the great hill back of us, I took my way along the river's edge.

Around the bend the water lost its headlong rush and spread out gently into ruffles of blue and bronze. The tall pines murmured almost unheard. For miles around us there was no one else to see this afternoon. Those hills were untrodden and beyond them lay lake after lake in utter and exquisite loneliness. What peace there was in that knowledge!

And we were as free as if we were in paradise—no claims, no duties; all we had to do, I thought, as I gave a long sigh

Kingfisher by Francis Lee Jaques.

of gratitude, was to wander blissfully about through blue water or blueberries! I sat down on a flat boulder, letting serenity flood through me.

Then I noticed a blue kingfisher on a cedar bough near me. He was hunting for his supper, but he seemed a novice at searching for his own fish and rather overwrought with it. His silly crest, which looked more like hair than feathers, stood up as if he had had a permanent scare, his head was too big and his tail too small and he had no feet worth mentioning. The white collar around his neck made him look as if he had an ambition to be well-groomed and immaculate, but he'd made a mistake in the size so that it half swallowed him.

He really was very small to be out fishing alone. Watching him, I had a sudden pang of sympathy and liking.

This moment was one of those we have at intervals through our lives, small moments of revelation which widen our vision, so that the world has one more facet for us, ever after. Before this, I had been looking at birds because Lee did, but they had seemed only decorations in the landscape. But suddenly, I really *saw* this bird, as I had always seen animals, as an individual and a reality.

It was partly finding him myself, I suppose, that gave me the personal interest in him. I had become used to having birds pointed out to me; this was my own discovery. Like the Ancient Mariner, I looked at this happy living thing and I "blessed him unaware."

As I watched him proudly, he dashed off down the stream, making an excited arrow of himself. His farewell cry was not worthy of him—it sounded rusty, as if it had been left out in the rain—but probably he was inexperienced at that too.

That night, as we lay full length on the tilted rocks, listening to the roar of the rapids and watching the stars climb through the great horizontal boughs above us, I found myself wondering about my kingfisher as I would have wondered about any friend who had gone farther on down the river. Where was he now? Had he caught his fish? Where had he camped for the night?

I surprised myself, next day, as our canoe raced along the sunny morning, by begging for information about the birds we encountered, instead of accepting facts in a placid coma.

I advise anyone who is just beginning to look at birds for themselves, to choose a place like this for their first trial identifications. Here were relatively few species and all of them large or striking, very distinctive—I could hardly have mixed them if I'd tried. Summer and winter, too, are simpler than spring or fall, for only resident birds are about, not the hordes of feathered tourists migrating north or south. I could always find one individual to watch, and there were not too many species; I was not overwhelmed with them as I had been in the spring.

And now it was not a fleeting glimpse of a bird on the wing that I caught; I had time to watch it leading its own life in its own way. This made the most enormous difference in my feeling toward birds. They were no longer mere bothersome patterns of feathers that I was forced to name correctly, but as the days went on they became persons of importance in our lives. For they gave us a feeling of real comradeship.

There are some people who are so weighed down and oppressed by a feeling of complete solitude in this wilderness that they cannot bear it; they are impelled to rush back for some contact with civilization. Not long ago in reading John Buchan's account of his boyhood in Scotland, I found he had that panic on the Scottish moors, if there were no sheep or heather about him. Heather seemed half-human to him, he said, and so it companioned him; if neither sheep nor heather were in sight, he had to run!

But in this country all its inhabitants seemed our companions. It was not odd to feel this concord with the animals, but to have aerial playmates seemed rather like living in folklore. It amazed me a little.

One great advantage that a rank amateur has, however, is that everything *is* amazing. The most well-known facts made me stand open-eyed and I went through our unpeopled days with surprise accompanying me.

For instance, the mere sight of herring gulls startled me. I had always thought of gulls as sea birds. To see a gull standing composedly in the middle of an immense expanse of sky-blue water, on a minute island of bare stone, never ceased to seem strange, especially as when we were floating low in our heavily laden canoe the bird loomed up above eye level and looked as unbelievable as a dodo.

And the great pileated woodpeckers which flashed through the woods with black and snowy feathers, and scarlet crests brilliant in the sun, fascinated me by their enormous energy. Lee showed me trees where they had ripped off great strips of bark and flung chips around like mad. And when I heard how they danced wild courtship dances, tiptoe in the treetops, hurling themselves into the sky in joy flights and then tumbling back to dance in the branches again, I was entranced. I had heard of strange nesting habits, but the fact that birds danced in their courting days was headline news to me.

Now bird observation came naturally into our daily life. As we paddled leisurely back to our tent, after an evening stroll in the canoe to look for beavers, and the black and gold of the ripples in a serene afterglow changed to the black and silver of night, we would be accompanied by the far-off hootings of a great horned owl, deep-toned, solemnly melodious.

And if the owls sounded the curfew for us, reveille was announced by loon laughter. We would be wakened to morning shafts of gold-gray light slanting down misted branches, by their cries of elation, which, without the savagery of beasts, are yet as wild as anything in nature.

When we ran down to bathe from a sandy perch, gilded freshly by the first touch of the sun, we would see a pair of loons outside the cove in shining water, and they would shame us by the astounding length of their dives. These birds, because their legs are set far back, can only toddle slowly on land, upright like penguins, but less expert; if they hurry they fall on their stomachs and crawl with their wings. But in the water they are so completely at home that in their long dives, using wings and feet to propel themselves through the water, they overtake even trout. Water seems to be their true element; though they are adequate fliers they seem to be reluctant to leave the surface of the lake and stride along splashing for a long time before they take off. They made me wonder,

> O diver! shall I call thee bird,
> Or but a wandering fish?

Later, as we breakfasted hilariously on the flat rocks, with the morning world so childishly innocent around us, we might have an eagle soaring above our drooping canopy of jack pines. One morning I said to Lee, as we watched a bald eagle looking noble on a dead pine, "Which is the fiercer bird, a bald eagle or a golden one?"

"You can't call birds fierce," he answered. "They just go around getting enough to eat."

"Of course you can call them fierce," I said argumenta-tively. "You always hear of the fierceness of hawks and eagles."

"Well, when you see hell chased out of them by some indignant scrap of a bird, it disillusions you," Lee said. "I think," he went on after pondering, "the fiercest bird is a humming bird."

I broke into helpless laughter. "You'll *never* let me keep any conventional traditions!"

"Well, kingbirds chase eagles; humming birds chase the kingbirds. Doesn't that prove my case?"

It did seem to me that the eagles, and the ospreys too, looked especially magjestic and supercilious as they soared above me when I was scouring the breakfast plates and pans with sand. But I always felt their equal as soon as the packing was done and we launched our green canoe and started forth once more. Surely there is no way of traveling as completely delightful as canoeing! A canoe has a buoyant gaiety, a way-wardness held in check by skill (Lee's skill, not mine!) that makes paddling as gallant a pleasure as riding a thoroughbred—and on a thoroughbred you can never vary your delight by drifting lazily in a dreamy calm.

So completely different from the everyday habit of finding my way about the land, this wandering along liquid lanes was something I had longed to do, all my life. I never ceased to marvel at the strange good fortune, as we sped down a lake of clematis blue, guarded by dark spikes of spruce, while great tumbles of lavender and faint rose and creamy clouds flew by in the early morning wind.

We would get out our map and look at it with the joyful knowledge that it did not matter where we chose to go—we could not find a way that was not utterly beautiful. If we tramped that short portage to the north we might get wilder forest with ancient pines and huge cliffs; by paddling west down the lake we might find bare hills and spruce bogs with moose in them, and if we floated down that river's current to the south there might be beaver and bear mixed in with reeds and waterlilies—it was only hard to choose because we didn't want to miss *anything*. At first I had thought there were a few regions where I might get a rest from enjoying the scenery—the burned-over hills, for example, stark and desolate. But Lee, sketching charred pine trunks and the sharp outlines of abrupt slopes, taught me to appreciate even these.

Folding our map and starting out purposefully (a paddle feels so alive and exhilarated in the morning air!) we would rush along immaculate shores. But ahead of us might be a flotilla of mergansers—these were ducks old enough to be feeling very capable but not old enough to fly. Lee said they seemed to fly by the calendar and not by their size. Here it was September, however, and they were still waterlogged. There might be twenty or thirty youngsters together (evidently various broods united), and they usually traveled in long lines, single or double file, though they would break ranks to feed on the schools of little fish which were unlucky enough to come by.

Then we would forget our plan to make a portage by nine o'clock and give chase down the lake, around a jade island, into a quiet bay, laughing to see them speed full steam ahead. They would rise to their feet in the excitement of the moment and run madly along the surface of the lake, all those webbed feet making a tremendous splashing. We splashed equally wildly as we dug our paddles furiously into the waves, trying to head them off. It was like playing tag again.

And on our portages, though it was September, we might be accompanied by the song of a phoebe or the lovely notes of a white-throated sparrow. Only once, on our most faraway and magical island, did we hear the hermit thrush, but its gold-dark song was the perfect melody for the forest light and shadow and I still long to hear it there.

It was glorious, through these days, to have no set plans to follow. We took our way as chance directed, and reveled in this freedom so absolute that we forgot completely the chaos of the modern world we had left behind. Here there were no clashes. Every bit of time and space was filled with lucid beauty.

I had wondered a little, before we left New York, if such isolation might sometimes grow monotonous. It never was. I was never bored an instant. Sometimes I was tired out, some-times uncomfortable, too hot or too drenched or too chilled. Sometimes I was frightened momentarily, as when I thought I heard a bear eating blueberries at midnight, just outside our tent, and we had no weapon except a small ax; or when a sudden squall made it impossible for us to make headway against plunging waves. But it would have been a shame not to have been touched, at least, by primal terror.—No, I was never bored.

In general, I had such a feeling of harmony with our forest environment that I might have slept in a wolf den as a child, like Mowgli himself. The creatures around us seemed such adequate companions that I did not even realize we were without human society.

In our whole three weeks, we met only five or six people, and our contact with them was only casual. The whole land was a sanctuary for animals and birds and I rejoiced in the knowledge that this country belonged to the deer we often met face to face, the bear we glimpsed occasionally, the wolves we never saw, thank heaven, though we heard them in the night, and the porcupines sticking around persistently. I liked the watery fields to be held in common by ducks and loons and herons, and the treetops to be supervised by eagles.

As the days went by, the birds seemed more and more intimate associates. Often on the winding rivers, a kingfisher flew before us, curve after curve, till we felt as if we had a flying puppy darting ahead of our canoe, waiting for us, then dashing on again. We almost always camped on islands, and each one seemed to have its special bird for us. The hermit thrush was hidden on one, a richly colored sparrow hawk guarded another and a third was polka-dotted with chickadees.

Chickadees are special favorites of Lee's, though he likes them best in winter. I liked them too, for though they were small they were easy to remember and even I could not mistake their *chick-a-dee-dee*—like icicles in the grass, Thoreau said. Their quaint habit of not paying attention to whether they were right side up or upside down and the way they could curl around a pine cone when they were so round themselves, was enough to win the most indifferent observer. They ranked with chipmunks for charm, but they did not know they had it as the chipmunks did. You never caught a chickadee definitely posing, prune seed in hand!

It was the chickadees that first made me wonder about birds at night. On our stormiest midnight, when our tent, perched high on a rocky island, almost took wing, and we sprawled full length clutching its corners, while thunder crashed about us, waves lashed the rocks and the wind clamored in the trees, I bean to wonder about our chickadees.

Where were they—where did they sleep all night, at any time? Where *did* birds sleep? "Birds in their little nests agree"— but that was when they were young. Dignified adults did not sleep in nests. Where, then? Did any sleep in holes, except owls, if they did? Or on the ground? Did they lean drowsily against friendly trunks or swing cradled in leaves, or what? I grew fonder of birds, that night of thunderstorms, because I didn't know how they slept. And still don't.

Sometimes, but not as often as we wished, the moosebirds (or Canada jays) visited us. They look like gigantic chickadees, but they have far more curiosity about human beings than their small counterparts. However, though they certainly earn a reputation for impudence, I welcomed them around our campfires. Their large eyes had a gentle look—not at all calculating or shrewd, like really impudent birds—parrots, for instance.

But they could be troublesome in their friendliness, as children are, with the disadvantage that you could not suggest with any tact that they go away and play. One breezy night their added breeziness was almost too much for me. It was cool and we were hungry after a long afternoon of paddling and portaging. I wanted my supper—coffee, especially. But the wind hindered me, flapping any loose end it could find, blowing my hair in my eyes, and encouraging the fire to be unruly, though I had tucked it down in a cleft of rock where it should have been docile and steady.

And then a pair of moosebirds took it into their heads to help with the party. I had made the mistake of taking out the rye crisp and I had to guard it from their eager snatches while mixing flapjacks and broiling fish. The birds grew more and more mischievous, getting into my precious George Washington coffee and flying about my ears, till I ended by spilling the powdered milk and mistaking the sack of salt for the sack of sugar. The coffee was far from the delicious brew we had counted on and the fact that I liked moosebirds even after that is a real tribute to them.

Once we went fishing with a fish hawk. It was raining that day, a gentle rain that fell like mercy on the broad lily pads and us. The osprey swooped from a dead cedar, we floated less fiercely in our canoe near by. He was a beautiful bird, larger than the other hawks we had seen but smaller than an eagle, and from beneath he looked almost pure white. Sometimes he sat with great dignity on his perch, looking thoughtfully into the water, sometimes he flew slowly about the lake. When he saw a fish he stopped sailing an instant, then plunged strongly down so that when he struck the water he sent a great fountain of spray into the rainy air. The fish he brought up quite impressed me.

"I don't see how he holds the slippery thing," I cried. "It's impossible. Look, he shifted it as he flew: I couldn't do it."

"I could if I had those long curved claws," Lee said, "and sharp stiff spikes in the palms of my hands. The fish simply can't slip."

One evening as we approached an island to make camp, we frightened some young mallards into flying off while their mother, who had been in the wood, was left behind. That night she was still looking for her lost children, swimming through the moonlit water past our island and calling to them reassuringly.

She made me realize again, as I had with the inexperienced kingfisher, the *actuality* of a bird's life. As the duck's small silhouette was engulfed by deep shadow, my thoughts tried to follow her through the night, in an existence as complete as our own, although so different. These immensities of land and water—we were sharing them equally, if they were not more hers than ours. A poignant sense of the relationship between living things touched me. "Feathered friends" was no longer a teasing phrase, and my growing kinship with winged creatures gave a deeper tone to my joy in the unsullied perfection about us.

Our last evening in the real wilderness, before we turned toward Winton, was one of the most memorable. We had been paddling all day through country with shores of smooth-washed stones, backed by small jack pines, but now we came again to the densest forest, darkly-lichened rocks with twisted pines about them.

We decided to make camp early, on a smooth semicircle of sand beach, and prepared to land there. As we slid up to the shore Lee was saying, "I stopped here four years ago and found bear tracks in the sand." Stepping out of the canoe, there we saw bear tracks on the beach before us!

"I'm not going to stay here," I said. "This beach still belongs to your bear. He's old by now—I don't intend to cross him."

Lee argued vainly that bears are always more anxious to avoid us than we are to miss them. I took a high moral stand. This was the bear's cove by right of seniority and I did not care to intrude.

Around the next point we found another small bay, its shore set with delicate birches. We had not camped before in a birch wood and the slim whiteness of the trunks made such clean colonnades about us that I was glad we had deserted that beach. The water in the bay was dark, and reflected the pale yellow birch leaves and the silver trunks with pure precision. Then migrating warblers, lemon-colored, whirled down along the frail branches till I could hardly tell which were leaves and which were birds.

I sat down on roughened ivory grass to follow the warblers with my field glasses. Scores of tiny birds, gay and quaint, making evanescent compositions among the laced twigs. I remembered my despair in May, my inability to see small birds with binoculars or without—really, I'd made amazing progress since then! I could follow one now—oh, for half a minute! After a sunset supper, Lee found from our map that a hidden stream led from this bay to another lake, and he thought we might find moose there. This was our last chance to see them and we took it.

It was a mild September evening. There was no wind. As we went down the lake in the light of a pale afterglow, there was no slightest ripple in the water. It was as if we floated in the colorless air.

The reflections of the trees and hills were exact. Every twig, every leaf and pine needle was so perfectly duplicated that the one below us seemed as real as the one above. This illusion was especially strong as we moved past the cliffs whose vertical lines seemed to extend far below us to break off in an abyss of air. It was impossible to tell where the water met the shore; we drifted in midair as if we were in an Indian legend.

Even when we came to the marshy river, and the canoe curved through clotted grass into its shallows, the illusion held. The water was transparent, the reeds and bulrushes extended slim dark rods below us and above on either side—we floated in a channel of pale light between suspended grasses. As we hung in this curving airy path, the silence around us was unbroken.

But the light was leaving us, the blue dusk was flooding up from the east. We came to a drift of poplars on a secret shore, and our canoe slipped out into a silvered circle of lake, ringed with tall pines that were blurred and gauzy in the twilight. Here the bulrushes still held the curved lines into which a vanished wind had slanted them.

This liquid space looked more solitary, more remote somehow, than any forest had. It had an atmosphere of mystery, as if it were awaiting the unknown. Then as we floated out upon the still circle, a great blue heron flew up before us.

He looked like a huge legendary bird, appropriate to the windless way we'd come. His wings were vast pinions as he rose into the night, his long neck and long legs making him a fantastic figure against the gray shore. Circling like some great mythical creature about us, his wings seeming to obliterate the sky, he made me experience a real awe as he disappeared in silence. I felt as if I had come upon the Thunder Bird.

Mystery seemed to fill the evening to overflowing, as the water filled the brimming lake. And the great heron was the symbol, the embodiment of this solitude. But he was a reality. He was life.

As we took our way back through the river channel, floating now with stars below and above us, I thought I understood why Lee liked to paint birds in his landscapes. Here, in a living thing, was expressed the spirit of the place in which it lived.

I thought of the kingfisher and the mallard—the kinship I had felt with them. Now here was a great heron and his mystery which I could never fathom. This must be the secret of the fascination which birds hold for human beings, I told myself. To know them, but never completely to understand.

· 16 ·

HELEN GERE CRUICKSHANK

born 1907

Helen Gere Cruickshank is one of several women in this anthology who accompanied a naturalist husband on a life long adventure with birds. Born in 1907, she received a Bachelor of Science degree from Pennsylvania State University in 1927. Cruickshank taught school in Rye, New York, until her marriage in 1939 to Allan Cruickshank, a staff member of the National Audubon Society. Allan was primarily a nature educator but achieved his greatest distinction as a bird photographer. He eventually became the official photographer of the National Audubon Society and left a legacy of bird images unsurpassed in the history of the genre. Helen Cruickshank joined in her husband's lifework with complete enthusiasm, becoming a master bird student and photographer in her own right and a major bird educator through her several books about birdwatching.

The Cruickshanks were particularly knowledgeable about

the birds of Florida and Maine, especially shore and oceanic birds. For many summers in succession, Allan taught bird study at the National Audubon Society's nature camp on Hog Island in Muscongus Bay near Rockland, Maine. From these experiences came Helen Cruickshank's first book in 1941, *Bird Islands Down East*. This book, like many subsequent publications, was produced in partnership with Allan, whose glorious bird photographs form the centerpiece for Helen's birdwatching descriptions. Along with a second book about Florida birding, *Flight into Sunshine* of 1948, which won the John Burroughs Medal for nature writing, it is an excellent example of a kind of travelog which serves to gently educate the reader without the burden of scientific complexities. Cruickshank's forthright style and spritely wit engage the reader immediately. The birding travelog has never been more effortlessly informative.

Other books followed. Most distinguished among them are two historical volumes, *John and William Bartram's America* of 1957 and *Thoreau on Birds* of 1964. Both are useful introductions to the documentation of natural history in America and are especially helpful for the serious amateur seeking entry into the scholarly field of Americana.

The Cruickshanks lived and breathed birds. Their large circle of colleagues and friends included most of the prominent naturalists of their day. In fact, it was Florence Page Jaques, wife of bird illustrator Francis Lee Jaques and herself the author of numerous books on birdwatching, who first suggested to Helen Cruickshank that she write about her adventures with Allan. Roger Tory Peterson was on staff at the National Audubon Society during the same years as Allan Cruickshank. A Peterson drawing hangs today in the Cruickshank home in Rockledge, a Florida town on the Indian River across from the Kennedy Space Center and Merritt Island National Wild-

Helen Cruickshank banding gulls with two colleagues.
Courtesy of Helen Cruickshank.

life Refuge, which Allan Cruickshank helped to establish before he died in 1974.

Although Helen Cruickshank, a lively septuagenarian, still lives in Rockledge, she spends summers in the Southwest photographing birds. Her unassuming manner and simplicity of style belie a keen intelligence and gargantuan knowledge of American birds. At the Merritt Island sanctuary she delights in the crowds which visit on fine weekends.

In the chapter about a cormorant nesting island from *Bird Islands Down East,* selected for this anthology, Helen Cruickshank's dry wit and determination are evident. The day on Cormorant Island was a ghastly experience, but it was no less educational for all its impossibilities. From this chapter one learns about the obsessive nature of bird photographers and of the trying moments any partner in adventure experiences. A great deal about cormorants is learned along the way.

Double-Crested Cormorants

From the very first time I saw a cormorant posed on a spar buoy with its wings outstretched and its bill pointed haughtily toward the sky, I wanted to get close enough so that I could see the curling tufts of feathers on its head which gave it its first name. When that wish was born I did not dream how long nor how intimate an acquaintance I should have with cormorants before it was granted. Artists always showed those feathers erected but no matter how many cormorants I studied through the binoculars not one of them had the crest standing upright.

We watched great skeins of migrating cormorants laced across the sky over Long Island, skeins which lengthened, wavered and flowed overhead with heart-lifting beauty. We watched lines of them, all carefully following the leader, swoop down from the sky to skim over the water with undulating scallops, just out of reach of the waves. We visited colony after colony of nesting cormorants on the Maine coast but summers passed and for us the species seemed to have completely lost their crests. Even dead birds showed no indication of the decoration when we examined them.

Forbush tells us that, in 1923, the only cormorant colony on the coast of Maine was on Black Horse Ledge, a great, bald rock rising out of the ocean like half of a gigantic ball, near Isle au Haut. Since then the birds have spread rapidly down the coast until, in the summer of 1940, they were found nesting just outside Boston Harbor. This phenomenal increase is due not only to legal protection but also to the fact that fishermen, who for many years carried on an illicit warfare against them, have discovered cormorants to be really useful. Analysis of the stomach contents of many specimens has proved conclusively that their food is mostly useless fish which prey upon food fish of commercial value.

Upon our return to the mainland after our first trip to Machias Seal, Allan said that we had time to spend one day on Old Man Island, southeast of Cutler, provided we could go the next day. On Old Man there is a large cormorant colony. I was delighted that we were to make the acquaintance of another island so soon, particularly since there we might observe closely one of the most characteristic birds of the coast.

The alarm clock whirred at half past four the following morning. We saw that our lobsterman was already aboard his boat. That meant he considered it possible to make a landing on Old Man. The sky was clear except for a few wisps of the omnipresent mist. Shortly we were once more moving down Cutler harbor and out into the ocean. We sailed along a high, rocky coast on which the sea pounded with a thundering roar. The waves would rush in, throw themselves high on the cliffs and then recoil, leaving great cavities between the cliffs and the water, revealing ugly, jagged and hitherto concealed rocks. Back the waves would rush with tremendous force making the air quiver with the violence of the impact. I was glad that we kept well away from the frothing, angry shoreline.

South we went and finally east to where Old Man juts abruptly out of the ocean. The fog had deepened swiftly after we left Cutler and was creeping closer and closer upon the island as we approached. Most forbidding was our first fog-shrouded glimpse of it. Though less than a mile in circumference, Old Man rose sharply like a partially submerged mountain peak, as it well may be for Maine has a sinking coast. Somber and bleak in the dull light, above its rocky border it was covered with the standing skeletons of spruces. In the dead trees perched the motionless, misshapen, black figures of the island's inhabitants. Overhead screamed a multitude of gulls. On that dreary, noisy island we were to spend the day. As I looked at it and the surf beating upon it, my enthusiasm for bird islands temporarily weakened.

At one place a channel pierced far into the rocky body of the island almost cutting it into two unequal parts. We were landed on one side of the channel. If landing on Machias Seal appeared risky to landsmen unaccustomed to ocean islands, landing on Old Man was really precarious. There are few days when it is possible to land there safely. Only by the most skillful handling of the dory was the lobsterman able to hold it still long enough for us to leap out on the slippery rocks, without pitching us into the racing sea, and keep it from being shattered on the rocks. One person was landed on a wave, then the dory was hurriedly withdrawn until another opportunity was presented.

At last we were deposited on the rocks with the cameras and blinds and no casualties other than the inevitable scratches made on our persons by the rocks as we scrambled over them. Our lobsterman, perturbed by the rising surf, said he would not try to take us off until high tide that evening a little after seven o'clock. He hoped he could get us off then. And so did I.

We hauled our equipment out of reach of the waves and then surveyed the island from which we could not escape before evening.

It rose abruptly from a rocky shore to a considerable height for so small an island. Covered with dead trees, long since killed by the strong excrement of nesting birds, it presented a repellant appearance. Broken, bare and ugly, the trees were in all stages of decrepitude. The dead trees held the untidy, dusky masses of cormorant nests in their arms. Some cormorant nests were built on the broken-off stubs of tree trunks and others were on the ground. Out of the nests waved the snaky, grotesque necks and heads of the young birds. Perched on all available projections were the adult cormorants, looking for all the world like the fantasy of a bad dream.

It was a sight to make us pause but there was work ahead. As we toiled up the steep slope it was difficult to find firm footholds. We dug our fingers into the soft, crumbly soil and used great care lest we lose our grip and roll back upon the rocks below. Nowhere was there a living tree whose roots or trunk might offer us support. Only dead trees were in our path and they, instead of lending aid, threatened to topple upon us.

The adult cormorants took wing as we climbed. In trepidation they wheeled and circled overhead, finally taking refuge in a compact mass on the ocean where they floated half concealed by the fog. The young cormorants, upset by our invasion, uttered weird grunts and moans and coughed up half-digested fish. Care had to be taken not to walk too close to the nests on the ground or under any of the nests in the dead trees. Allan said coughing up fish was the birds' mode of defense. Certainly it was effective as far as I was concerned. I had no bloodthirsty designs toward them but their defense appeared effective enough to deter even a starving creature.

The cormorants had left their nests unguarded and the Herring Gulls took possession of the trees. Others flew overhead, chattering and mewling. Some of the gulls began to settle on the deserted nests. Allan assured me that they were eating the coughed-up fish but I was not consoled. I regarded

Double-crested cormorants photographed by Allan Cruickshank for Bird Islands Downeast. *Courtesy of* Helen Cruickshank.

his assurances as another of those masculine attempts to conceal the harsher facts of life from the weaker sex. I saw unhatched eggs and one writhing young bird swallowed by the gulls which surveyed us with glassy stares. The cormorants made no attempt to defend their nests.

Sometime later in Texas I saw Great-tailed Grackles eat egret eggs while the egrets stood patiently on one side of their nests until the grackles had finished their meal. But by that time I had become more accustomed to the food habits of wild birds and could accept the grackle's appetite as quite as natural as our enjoyment of the turkey on our Thanksgiving table. Nature is extremely bountiful in order that all may eat. Then, however, the fact that birds ate other birds and their eggs seemed to me incredibly cruel. Even today when a gull flies over a sandy beach in bright sunlight and the light reflected upward turns the bird into a creature of ethereal radiance, a vision of that horrid sight on Old Man returns and I can think only of the shallow coldness of their eyes.

The waving necks of the cormorants in the ragged, long-dead trees, the mists weaving around them, the wild screams of the gulls and the crashing surf made a deep impression upon my memory. Mingled with the sights and sounds was the vile odor of decaying fish and dead birds.

We discovered that the cormorants had all their nesting sites on the summit of the island. The Great Black-backed Gulls and the Herring Gulls nested on the rocky border. The Black-backed Gulls' nests were empty and the young birds were on the wing. Some of the Herring Gulls were flying but many were still in the downy stage and in some nests eggs were still being incubated. We found one eider-duck nest but it was empty and we saw, in the channel, a female eider with five young eiders following her. We also found two Savannah Sparrow nests, such tiny, frail structures to exist on that austere island.

The young cormorants were a ridiculous sight. The very young birds that had just been out of the egg for a day or two were a repulsive, gun-metal grey, entirely naked with swollen, closed eyes and too big heads that lay weakly on the ends of long, helpless necks. They made feeble, fruitless attempts to raise themselves from the nests and only succeeded in placing themselves in more awkward and grotesque postures. Those a week and more old were covered with very dense, black, woolly down. They had large, orange-yellow cheek pouches which were puffed out like balloons and then vibrated rapidly as they waved their sinuous necks about, chattering all the time with monotonous, wailing moans.

The nauseating odor which rose from the dead birds, regurgitated fish and excrement was appalling. Suddenly I became conscious of an uncomfortable feeling about my ankles. Putting down the light meter which I had been holding helpfully, I was dismayed to find that the bird lice that infested the island were actually crawling on me. Now it was my turn to wail and moan. I refused to be consoled by any assurances from Allan that bird lice would not bite me, since they had no mouth parts with which to bite even if they wanted to and that they might scurry around my ankles and tickle a bit but could do nothing worse and would soon crawl off again. I beat a hasty retreat to the shore, leaving him to arrange his blind and to work alone.

Lunchtime came and we sat by the waves for a few half-hearted nibbles at our sandwiches. Too much food had been packed for once, too much when we usually seemed to have too little. Now Allan did not regard the island in the ugly light with which I saw it. On the contrary, he liked the strangeness and the opportunities for unusual pictures of these primitive-looking birds. Very few bird men had spent much time on Old Man due to its inaccessibility. Yet even Allan, who usually could completely shut out every distracting influence when he was watching and photographing birds, found the odor of the island not conducive to an appetite. Our attempts at conversation also did little to cheer us.

"Adult cormorants have bad cases of adenoids," I remarked to Allan.

"It wouldn't do them any good to have an adenoid operation," he returned. "The young breathe through their nostrils which close up as the birds near maturity. A bone structure grows completely over them so henceforth they must breathe through their mouths. Did you know that cormorants, another species than this one though, are trained by the Chinese to catch fish for them?"

"From the way these cormorants gulp up fish," I said, "I don't see how the Chinese gain anything by harboring them. I should think they would begrudge the cormorants their food since fish is most important in a Chinaman's diet."

"But the Chinese take care of that. They put rings around the necks of trained cormorants so they can't swallow the bigger fish they catch. Of course some small ones may slip down. But in order that the cormorants won't become discouraged and stop work, the ring is removed and they are permitted to fish for themselves after they have made a sufficient catch for their owners."

But as we ate lunch we realized it was growing too dark for photographing those black birds even with the fastest film. Besides the dullness of the light, moisture kept condensing on the lenses. The fog no longer had that luminous quality that it has when the sun shines above it. Allan must be content with his morning's work as far as pictures were concerned. At least he was sure that he had some unusual studies of the cormorants.

As we piled our now useless cameras near the place where we had landed, we could see a Herring Gull that had had the misfortune to alight on the top of a broken tree with a narrow slit in it. In some way, one foot had slid into the crack and when the bird attempted to fly it had been thrown off balance and was held as if by a trap. There it hung, struggling desperately and fruitlessly. The more it struggled, the more firmly its foot became wedged in the crack.

On such a grim island where survival of the fittest was the rule of life it was absurd to feel concern for one bird. Indeed the accident to the gull may have saved the nest full of cormorant eggs in the next tree. Yet such inconsistent creatures are human beings that they can cause bloodshed and revel in it but when cataclysms of nature occur, or the strong attack the weak, the forces of civilization are rushed to succor the suffering.

Old Man was predominantly a cormorant island. We had watched the gulls destroy many of the cormorant nests. Yet we wanted to rescue that gull trapped by an accident. In spite of our wish to aid it, there was apparently nothing we could do but leave the bird to a very horrible death. The tree was very rotten, far too rotten to climb, and the top was at least twenty feet from the ground. But Allan, in looking over the situation discovered he had a solution.

Taking a thick stick, as strong as he could find in that land of dead wood, he hurled it with all his strength, aiming at a point about five feet below the top of the trunk. His aim was accurate. He had not thrown the javelin at college for nothing. The stick caused the top of the trunk to snap off and the gull, its leg released, fluttered off wildly and, I am sure, with considerable astonishment. With never a glance at the nearby cormorant nest and its three eggs, the bird disappeared in the fog, too subdued for once to utter one scream.

Not until high tide could we leave the island. The late afternoon hours dragged by with the leaden interminableness of a nightmare. The day grew steadily darker. The dense fog chilled us. For a long time I sat just out of reach of the waves. There the air was fresh and untainted by the decay behind me. As the tide advanced, I retreated, giving way only when the waves threatened to engulf me. At last Allan gave up watching the cormorants and joined me.

We wondered if we could be taken off the island when the boat came. The waves were rushing in with much greater force than in the morning. We huddled dejectedly together, our slickers drawn closely about us and considered the dismal possibility of having to remain all night in that dreary place. We remembered that it was unsafe for even the master boat-men of the Maine coast to land on Old Man much of the time. The light grew dim. Sullen skies and dense fog would bring an early darkness. Now and then a spurt of rain fell through the murky air. Just as we were giving up hope, the boat appeared out of the fog. It was anchored and the lob-sterman came toward the island in the dory. How relieved we were in spite of the ordeal immediately before us. Getting off the island would not be a light undertaking.

The lobsterman came cautiously toward us and at last brought the dory close to the rocks. He leaped out and held it firmly against his landing place. The blinds were put in it when the wave was at its crest. It receded leaving the dory at an awesome tilt, an almost ninety-degree angle with one gunwale awash. He told me to jump in on the next wave. Never did I like the prospect of getting in a dory less, but I gathered up my courage and jumped in at the proper time. No sooner was I in than the water rushed away leaving the dory at the same hazardous incline as before. But I did not fall out. I clutched the rock from which I had just jumped with a viselike grip while the offside gunwale of the dory bumped painfully against my ribs.

In came another wave and into the dory jumped the lobsterman. He, too, was anxious to get away and there could be no heavy loading of the dory in that sea. As for me, I was terrified in spite of the fact that we were riding the waves lightly. Allan was still on that hideous island. What if the dory were wrecked on its return for him? The cameras were on the island with him. Even without them, he could not possibly swim out to the lobster boat. The surf breaking on the rocks would pick him up and hurl him upon them before he could get through it. I was most unhappy as I watched the dory career over the waves on its return trip for my husband.

This time the lobsterman chose a different rock by which to make a landing. Perhaps it was a better choice or perhaps it was because Allan was a better gymnast, but it looked from the lobster boat as if the loading took place more smoothly. As the dory came alongside, the lobsterman grinned.

"You sure left your mark on that island. Your fingerprints are pressed permanently into the rock you gripped."

We realized that our first visit to a cormorant colony had netted us little beyond an exciting experience, a few photographs and a very superficial acquaintance with the birds. Not seeing any cormorant crest raised had been a real disappointment to me. However we had learned a valuable lesson. If one really wants to enjoy the islands of Maine, it is necessary to be unhurried.

In Maine they say, "If you don't like the weather, wait an hour or so." Actually, one must have more patience. It is never safe to say, "Tomorrow I will go to Old Man or to Matinicus or to Eastern Egg." The weather rules one's actions and seldom reveals its intentions more than a few hours in advance. But allowing nature plenty of time, the perfect days for visiting island bird colonies come with surprising frequency even near the stormy Bay of Fundy. There are days when the sea is smooth, when there is little surf breaking on even the most exposed rocks, when the sun is bright enough to gladden the heart of the most fastidious photographer and landing on outlying islands presents no problem at all.

Old Man remains in my memory as a dark, fearsome island populated by unpleasant creatures. In this new and strange place I was too timid thoroughly to enjoy my experiences.

On Old Hump Ledge in Muscongus Bay is another cormorant colony. It holds a place in my thoughts unlike those aroused by Old Man Island. Old Hump is a small heap of great, tumbled rocks rising out of the ocean and culminating in a double peak, a most appropriate place for Double-crested Cormorants to nest. As it happens, I have only been there on fine days. The excrement of the birds makes a glittering whiteness on the top of the island which may be seen for miles. As one approaches it on a bright day, the reflection is so brilliant it dazzles the eyes. The guano, unlike that of the cormorant's close relatives on the arid islands off the coast of Peru, does not accumulate. On Old Hump each summer's deposit of excrement is washed away by the winter storms. The ice and snow polish the rocks before the next nesting season.

There is a tiny cove on the northeast side of the island which forms a fine anchorage for our boat when we visit the colony. Four pairs of birds nested there, in 1931, and formed at that time the most southern colony on the coast. The number has increased with great rapidity as the cormorants have spread farther and farther south. Now hundreds of pairs nest there. They are so accustomed to human visitors that they pay little attention to them, the adult birds grudgingly giving way as observers climb up the rocks. Before the dory has left the island on its way back to the anchored boat, they begin returning to their nests.

For several years we have made repeated visits to Old Hump, over a dozen of them each summer. Sometimes we go to photograph the cormorants, sometimes to count them, to study them or to put government bands on their legs. Every time we visited a cormorant colony, I looked at the heads of the adults, hoping to see the crests which have given them their names. One day early in June, five years after my first visit to a cormorant colony, I was bending over a nest on Old Hump Ledge. In it were eggs not only showing definite variation in size but ranging in color from the lovely blue of a cormorant egg when it is first laid to chalky white and dirty brown. These changes in color were due to the sun and dirt. I decided it was worth a picture in color. Just then Allan called,

"Look behind you."

Twenty feet from me was an adult cormorant. It stood upright on a dazzlingly white rock with the sun making iridescent its usually dull-black feathers. Silhouetted against a deep-blue sky, it pointed its orange-yellow bill at me and erected its two curling clusters of feathers.

17

HELEN BLACKBURN HOOVER

1910–1984

Helen Blackburn Hoover, our best-known nature writer, was born in 1910 in Greenfield, Ohio, the daughter of a factory manager. After attending Ohio State University from 1927 to 1929, she left Columbus to settle in Chicago. There she worked as a proofreader until, having acquired a scientific education in night school, she obtained work in 1943 as an analytical chemist. She married the artist–illustrator Adrian Everett Hoover in 1937. The couple renounced city life for good in 1954 and took up residence in the wooded, watery wilderness of northern Minnesota. From a remote outpost consisting of log cabin and summer house came Helen Hoover's formidable achievements in nature writing. *The Long-Shadowed Forest* appeared in 1963 and was followed by *The Gift of the Deer* in 1966, *A Place in the Woods* in 1969, and *The Years of the Forest* in 1977. All Hoover's books, including several for children, were ably illustrated with her husband's drawings. She wrote women's fiction, also, under the pseudonym of Jennifer Price. She died in 1984.

Hoover's books about life in the backwoods are best when read as a series, for it is the saga of the couple's entire experience from early years as greenhorns to later years as seasoned woodsmen that emerges when the books are read chronologically. Hoover writes about the intense physical hardships she and her husband experienced as near penniless pioneers struggling to survive winters in northern Minnesota. These passages are hair-raising and demonstrate that the pioneer spirit lived on, along with the Man in the Gray Flannel Suit, in the 1950s. Pioneering was not fashionable in the era of Eisenhower and the cold war. In fact, the Hoovers were somewhat ostracized by their neighbors, who thought them all but deranged. They persevered nonetheless.

Hoover's descriptions of physical hardships, colorful to read and exciting to imagine, contrast admirably with the beauties of nature that enriched their venture and gave it profound meaning for the authors and ultimately their readers. An owl at the frozen suet feeder in the still of a winter night, a starving deer in the icy woodlot, intrepid chickadees at the birdfeeder are the protagonists which enliven and soften Hoover's dramas. Eventually, as book followed book, the Hoovers became more experienced in wilderness life and less desperate financially. They acquired an automobile, an oil stove, a typewriter, and a printing press for producing note paper to be sold as Christmas cards and gifts.

Through all of Hoover's writing there is a strong thread of optimism and humor. The Hoovers' love for one another and their patience with each other are clear. Her books have a true harmony of purpose and unity of spirit which is as touching as it is unusual. The Hoovers conducted a difficult life they had chosen with free will; that choice led to the

Helen and Adrian Hoover.

The Hoovers' cabin, below, in the Minnesota woods.
Courtesy of Adrian Hoover.

appreciation of nature so eloquently expressed in Helen Hoover's books. They were pioneers in the old nineteenth-century sense, seeking out a life in one of the last untouched wildernesses.

In the chapter from *The Long-Shadowed Forest* included here, Hoover demonstrates her lively appreciation of the least beloved family of American birds, the raptors. This chapter was chosen specifically to demonstrate her enlightened point of view about birds of prey. Unlike such writers as Neltje Blanchan Doubleday and Anna Botsford Comstock, Hoover is unprejudiced about predation, recognizing its logical place in the ecological chain. This chapter, pleasant to read, is no less a lesson in ecology and the role of birds in maintaining the balance of nature. Hoover neatly juxtaposes factual information with apposite personal anecdote, leaving the reader better informed and with a greater understanding of birds of prey. Hoover's keen eye for description and her positivistic world view combine to form a kind of nature writing exclusively American in its flavor.

The Air Hunters

The whistling roar of a jet plane broke the stillness of an autumn afternoon and I looked up, to watch a silver spangle draw its white ice trail across the clear sky. Far below, a bald eagle crossed the spreading streak at a right angle. Its white head and tail seemed one with the great wings that steadily raised and lowered, driving powerfully ahead. Behind came a second eagle, wingbeats timed with those of its mate, and, following, their dark-feathered, immature young one. As the contrail drifted away in the upper air, the migrating family flew out of sight beyond the southern hills.

In the past, the bald eagle's six- to eight-foot wingspread and its carnivorous feeding fostered ridiculous tales of its stealing half-grown sheep and even children. This, combined with the fact that so large a bird makes a splendid target, encouraged widespread shooting. Many others were accidentally destroyed when they tried to steal fish or meat bait from spring traps. Although the bald eagle was chosen as the national emblem of the United States in 1782, it was not given protection until 1940 and, in Alaska, 1952.

The apparent decline of the species has led to the Continental Bald Eagle Project of the National Audubon Society. The Audubon staff have been assisted by federal and state conservation agencies, private conservation organizations, and many interested individuals. At the end of two years of a five-year study much has been learned about eagle numbers and movements. A nationwide count in January, 1962, showed 3,807 bald eagles in the United States (exclusive of Alaska whose population will be studied later). Fifty-seven per cent of these wintering eagles were seen in the Midwest, mostly along the Mississippi River from southern Illinois to Minnesota. Dams in this area help to keep the water open in winter and the associated generating plants supply injured fish as food for the eagles. Florida reported 529 birds (fourteen per cent); the majority were nesting. The Northwest accounted for ten per cent and the mid-Atlantic states for six per cent of the total. The remaining thirteen per cent were scattered throughout other areas of the United States. Only twenty-four per cent of all eagles counted were reported to be immature birds, but not enough is known at present to indicate whether this is abnormal or not. (Anyone wishing to aid in the "eagle count" or to report eagle nests may obtain information from: National Audubon Society, Box 231, Tavernier, Florida.)

The bald eagles that I saw migrating nest on the Canadian

shore, probably at the top of the tall pine stubs left after a fire in 1936. The young birds might have been from a pair of eggs laid the previous year, because it may take three years for an eagle to grow its mature plumage.

Although the bald eagle's beak is designed for tearing flesh, its feet are too weak to permit it to lift much weight. It picks up dead fish and crippled small mammals near water; it bullies the osprey into dropping freshly caught fish which the eagle then devours; and sometimes it catches waterfowl. In the winter I have seen bald eagles driving ravens away from wolf-killed deer carcasses on the lake ice. Scavenging may not be an elegant way of making a living, but it is harmless and useful.

Any bald eagle in flight is something to remember and the sight of a youngster brings a flare of hope for the future, but a close-up view of an unconfined adult is awesome.

In January, 1958, an enormous, wide-winged shadow slid across the snow in the clearing as an eagle glided down to light on a small storage shed twelve feet from the log cabin. It gripped the edge of the roof with its taloned yellow feet and sat, brown body tense, brown wings half-lifted, tail folded into a white strip, and snowy head thrust forward. The heavy yellow beak, with a powerful hook on the upper mandible, was almost as long as the head. Feathers grew low and straight across, like a scowling brow, above the fierce, golden eye. The mighty bird perched for some minutes, looking right and left, then sprang out and up on huge, lifting wings. It rose in a great spiral. Gradually it diminished in size until it seemed black and headless, then only a dot. Then, so high that it was a pinpoint, it disappeared in the sea of light.

I thought of the men who selected the high-flying eagle as our national emblem, and of later critics who suggested that the wild turkey would have been a better choice. I wondered if these critics had considered the present status of the two birds. The bald eagles, though not so numerous as they once were, still fly free. Wild turkeys have largely lost their identity through interbreeding with domestic stocks and their small numbers are recovering in some areas only because they are being bred and stocked by men; their destiny seems to be the oven. My vote goes to the eagle.

The shrikes are present here in two hard-to-distinguish species. The loggerhead shrike breeds throughout temperate North America, laying four to eight eggs in a nest located in a bush or tree, usually in farming country. It appears here occasionally in late summer or when migrating. The northern shrike lays the same number of eggs, but breeds in openings of the farthest limits of the boreal forests. Individuals winter here, but they are not common.

Although they have the hooked beaks of flesh eaters, shrikes have weak feet and no talons. The loggerhead feeds largely on insects, which do not have to be gripped firmly while being eaten. The northern shrike consumes small birds and mammals, snakes, and insects, with a frog now and then. It may grip the prey with one foot, the leg lying across its perch and the food hanging from the foot, or it may impale its victim on a sharp thorn or twig, as an aid to holding it while tearing it with the beak. A thorn bush, decorated with this bird's accumulated food, is a gruesome sight, and the custom has given the northern shrike the unpleasant name of butcherbird.

A friend once told me that she had seen a gray jay attack a chickadee that had been stunned when it flew against a windowpane. The attacker was surely a northern shrike, whose gray and black and white markings are somewhat like those of the gray jay. The jay, although a carrion eater, never attacks a living bird or mammal, even though it be lying motionless.

We have never seen a northern shrike in our feeding yard.

I have little doubt that such a visitor would be promptly driven away by our cooperative battalion of blue and gray jays, with embattled chickadees bringing up the rear. But I am not sure, and I do not like to think of one of those fat chickadees, today sitting on my finger and picking crumbs from my palm, tomorrow perhaps impaled on a twig for a shrike's dinner.

On the other hand, I am downright fond of owls, although they do not kill gently. We are well supplied with them, particularly with barred owls, which find many tree cavities and old squirrels' nests that may be used for the rearing of their two or three young. Mother owl lays her eggs on the accumulated rubbish in the nest and does little by way of improvement. These owls stay for years at one location, and the nesting cavity gradually becomes lined with downy feathers shed by the young as they grow adult plumage.

The barred owls are so much a part of our background that we wonder what has happened when we do not hear them for a week or two. "Hoo-waaah!" booms from the dark woods. "Hoo-hoo-hoohoo, hoo-hoo-hoohoo-wah!" comes the answer in a melodious treble. Sometimes these owls gather near the cabin and hold long conversations. They chuckle and hiss, whisper and grunt, cackle and hoot, in such a variety of sound that hearing them is like listening to a newscast in an unfamiliar language; one strains his ears on the chance of hearing a familiar word. One of these owls had a favorite hooting perch in the big pine west of the log cabin. One night, in the midst of a series of gentle hoo-hoo's, it stopped, presumably took a deep breath, and screamed—a long, horrifying shriek that ended in a bubbling gurgle as of something with its throat cut. It twice repeated its ghastly cadenza. Then, as though satisfied with its performance, went back to its pleasant hoo-hooing.

Barred owls see very well in the light and do much of their

hunting by day. There was an October afternoon when an eighteen-inch individual settled on a branch overlooking the feeding yard and prepared to select its dinner from the small visitors. Its brown eyes, encircled by pale feather disks, and its sweeping feather moustache gave it a look of amazed good-nature. The cross-barring of its breast extended upward to surround its head, which appeared as a large feather ball. As it leaned forward to watch the ground, its brown-and-white streaked belly feathers covered its downy white feet. The brown and gray and white patterning of its back blended perfectly into the tangle beyond.

To my surprise, neither the other birds nor the mammals paid any attention to the owl. It looked around in a leisurely fashion, then concentrated on the earth beneath, where some-thing tasty might run out from under the woodpile. Then I noticed that, although most of the birds were still feeding, all the blue jays but one had withdrawn to high branches. This remaining jay flew from low branch to low branch, always keeping the owl in view. Abruptly the hunter launched itself toward an unwary young squirrel. As easily as though it had been rehearsed, the blue jay flew in an arc that just intersected the owl's flight and spoiled its aim. The squirrel hopped away, the jay preened on a branch, and the disgruntled owl stood flat-footed on the ground. It whirled its head around in that way which almost convinces one that owl heads are screwed on, looked at the jay as though thinking the woods would be a pleasanter place without such interfering creatures, and flew off to a less-policed hunting ground.

Several people have asked me if this move was planned by the jay and, if so, why. There are no satisfactory answers. Planning and reasoning, in the human sense, do not apply to birds. The group behavior of the blue jays was uncommon, as they usually gather in a noisy flock and pester an owl or hawk until it retreats. The single jay's interception of the owl's flight was so perfectly timed that it *appeared* to be deliberate. Beyond that, anything I might say would be guesswork.

In almost ridiculous contrast to the twenty-four inches of a large female barred owl is the seven- to eight-and-a-half inch saw-whet owl, about the size of a white-throated sparrow. This woods has many old woodpecker holes where the little owls may lay their three to seven eggs. We knew they were present because on February and March nights we heard what sounded like the filing of a saw when no one was near who might actually be doing so. Although these owls, especially in remote areas, are quite tame, we had little hope of seeing them because they are largely nocturnal, but a suet feeder, forgotten at night, attracted one.

I was looking at the moonlight that turned falling frost into blue and white sparks when I saw the little owl, standing on a horizontal limb just above the suet cage. It considered the suet gravely, turning its head from side to side, then flew to perch on top of the cage. It worked patiently with its beak but could not extract the food through the wire mesh. Nothing daunted, it flew back to the branch, where it paced one way and then the other, bobbing its head and giving the impression of having its wings folded like arms behind its back. After due consideration, it tried to cling to the tree trunk and thus attack the food, but had to give up and go back to branch-pacing. I opened the door a crack and tossed a small chunk of suet to the base of the tree. The owl halted with half-lifted wings, then sidled to the trunk and leaned so far forward to watch the door that I thought it would tumble off its perch. Satisfied, it drifted to the ground and circled the suet on foot, beak open and ready to return any attack. Then it flew up, circled once, and pounced successfully on its "prey."

Since owls are thought to have only a rudimentary sense

of smell, I wondered how it discovered the suet, which was surely unfamiliar and in no way resembled a mouse or other ordinary owl food. We have often seen birds perching and watching the regulars feed, after which the newcomers ventured to approach. Perhaps the saw-whet had done the same during the daylight hours and had come in to see what the attraction was.

It visited regularly for several weeks, and, on a night bright enough for good owl-watching, I set a large ham bone, with fragments of meat and rich marrow, on the shelf by the door. The little owl soon arrived, clutched the bone with one foot, and tore the meat away in strips. After it removed each morsel, it leaned far back to peer at the bone in the strained manner of one who needs, but will not break down and buy, reading glasses. (This is not so far-fetched as it sounds. Although owls have unusually sharp distance vision, they cannot adjust their eyes to see well at close range.) It was undergoing one of these farsighted stretches when it saw me inside the glass of the door, not two feet away. It stretched a wing protectively in front of the precious bone and puffed up to twice its usual size, snapping its beak and making a hissing squeak. The miniature mouser looked very fierce indeed; I "fled" from the door and in the morning the bone was cleaned.

Although I have not seen any screech owls here, I have infrequently heard ululating calls that might be theirs, and that probably were made by transients, for these owls prefer more open nesting sites. The idea that they screech may have originated when the fearsome shriek of the barred owl, or other creature, was heard by someone who saw screech owls in the vicinity.

A pair of these owls nested in the basement of my childhood home. They were gray (although there is also a rufous phase), and could not be mistaken for any other bird, because screech owls are the only small owls with "horns." My father, appreciating their value as mousers, left a window open for them and they reared three young. The parent birds protected the furnace room very effectively against attempts to pry into their domestic affairs. Sometimes they called in the night and the soft notes crept up in ghostly echoes through the hot-air ducts. When the winter coal was delivered, the owl family moved out and I last saw them sitting in a row on the telephone wire that was strung on poles along the street curbing.

The boreal, or Richardson's owl, which rears four to six young in coniferous forest like this, but farther north, visits us irregularly in very cold weather. One of them once spent an afternoon hour on a branch near the cabin. It looked much like an enlarged saw-whet, wearing big, black, horn-rimmed glasses. Its forehead was spotted whereas that of the saw-whet is striped vertically, but this distinction may be obscured by windblown or other otherwise ruffled feathers. It seemed restless and displeased with the other birds and, when the blue jays began to pester it, went off without delay.

Another winter visitor, and one of the most beautiful, is the snowy owl that comes from the Artic in search of food about every fourth year. These owls nest on hummocks in the open northern barrens. The nest is a mere hollow, often surrounded by snow. The mother begins incubating the first egg as soon as it is laid and, at irregular intervals, lays more until the clutch reaches from three to thirteen. The eggs hatch in the order laid and the unhatched later ones are often partially covered by downy nestlings while the mother procures food for the eldest of the brood, which may be fully fledged when the last egg hatches.

The females and immature birds are heavily barred and patterned and are not so easily recognized as the white, lightly barred male. We had a fine view of a male, sitting on a fence post by the road to town as we were driving in for supplies four months after we moved here. Ade stopped and we exchanged curious glances with the owl, which was side-lighted and had squinted the eye on the brighter side so that it wore a most dissolute and tipsy expression. We could even see what appeared to be short horns, almost hidden by other head feathers. It did not seem large until it spread wings like white triangles and sailed away, legs swept back and swaying in a negligent manner.

Ade came in one night last December, looking shaken, and asked me if I thought we just might have ghosts around the place. Something white and silent had flown past his face, almost brushing his nose. Two nights later the ghost flew up from a stump as I opened the door, a burst of white that looked like a clump of snow, exploding upward and disintegrating as it reached the level of the lower branches. An owl it had to be, because of its soundless flight, and probably a snowy, although I sometimes think wistfully that it *might* have been the rare pale arctic horned owl.

We have been told that the more usual brown great horned owl is resident here, but have never heard its booming. This two-foot fellow, with tall feather horns, white chin ruff, and round golden eyes looks like no other bird. However, several times we have heard the hooting of the barred owl misidentified as that of the great horned. There is a question, too, as to whether the screams attributed to the great horned owl are not those of the barred owl.

The great horned usually lays only two eggs in thick woods. It is the largest common owl in North America. Its appetite for rodents makes it beneficial, except when food shortage forces it to raid poultry yards. There are a number of races of horned owls and, cumulatively, they nest over the Americas from the Artic Archipelago to the Strait of Magellan, excepting the Caribbean Islands.

I dream of seeing the great gray owl that nests in the boreal forests as far north as the tree limit, as far south as the northern rim of the United States. Its nests, containing three eggs, have been found not far from our location, and the owl occasionally migrates somewhat south and east of here in winter. I know what it looks like: a three-foot, smoky version of the barred owl, with yellow eyes, breast and belly striped and faintly barred from throat to tail, and a six-foot wingspread. I also know that if I am ever granted a sight of this bird, no photograph or painting or stretch of my imagination will have attained its mysterious beauty and dark dignity.

The best reminder I have ever had of keeping an unprejudiced mind toward wild things came from a lady visitor. She was feeding young gray jays when I called her attention to a goshawk, maneuvering its forty-inch wingspread through the brush with not-quite-credible speed and dexterity. "Goodness!" exclaimed my visitor. "You ought to shoot that hawk. You wouldn't want anything around here that would kill a *bird!*"

The goshawk is one of the accipiters, along with the sharp-shinned and Cooper's hawks. These birds have a distinctive shape when flying, with a long slender tail and stubby wings that aid their headlong flight through the forest. They do feed on other birds, but not exclusively. All three of them are present off and on in our yard in summer, and the goshawks nest here, but our bird population remains stable. If the hawks were not here, the other birds would increase, but this would lead to starvation for some of the resident birds if we were not here to feed the overpopulation in winter.

All three accipiters nest in thick woods, usually laying from three to four eggs. The goshawk finds either coniferous or mixed growth suitable, and the very large nest on our property is placed some sixty feet up in the crotch of an old birch. Cooper's hawk prefers coniferous forest, and the sharp-shin likes coniferous edges. Probably those individuals of the last two species that we see are rearing their young in nearby seclusion.

The twenty-one- to twenty-five-inch goshawk is the largest of the three and, when mature, is gray, with a lightly barred gray-and-white breast and a strong white line above the eye. A young one once took up a waiting position atop a stone pile which protects the entrance to a chipmunk burrow. In common with the other immature accipiters, its back was dark brown and its vest striped in brown and white. It held its smooth head, with strongly hooked beak, fiery golden eye, and white "eyebrow," as proudly as a king, but gradually it began to shift uncertainly from one big yellow foot to the other as the jays dived and circled and said unpleasant things in bird language. It held its ground until I stepped outside and sent it elsewhere for breakfast.

Ranging down in size from the goshawk are the fourteen- to twenty-inch Cooper's hawk and the ten- to fourteen-inch sharp-shinned hawk. When mature, both have slate-gray backs and tails and lack the white eyeline that identifies the goshawk. Their white breasts are barred with rusty-red instead of the goshawk's gray. At the middle of the size range they are hard to separate, although the Cooper's tailtip is rounded and the sharp-shin's is notched.

A lifetime observer of birds could probably separate these hawks at a glance, as one recognizes close friends at a distance. In eight years here, I have come to know some of our birds so well that a passing shadow identifies them. Others I recognize when I see them clearly. Still others remain disembodied voices. There are many that I have glimpsed or briefly heard; I *think* I have placed them, but I am not sure. These are not yet on my life list. I prefer a small, sure list to a large one of glimpse-and-guess species.

There was no doubt of the identity of the sharp-shinned hawk that shot across the yard to perch on a stump last spring. It was not much larger than a robin and the sun brought out blue lights in its slaty head and back and tail and brightened its red-barred breast. It flashed from the stump to the doorstep in a way that justified its name of "little blue darter." It clutched the step edge with its yellow feet and bent down, trying to peer under the woodshed, first with one eye and then the other. I could hear, from beneath the shed, the tremulous *squeak-squeak* of a chipmunk that had narrowly escaped disaster. The hawk, effectively separated from the chippy, looked almost wistful. Then, with a blur of wings, it rose, whirled, dipped, and lifted from the ground only a few feet from Ade with another chipmunk in its talons.

When the sharp-shin arrived, our chipmunk population was so large and hungry that the ground vegetation was in danger. I saw nineteen chippies nipping off new green sprouts at one time. The little hawk hunted for four weeks. I found a gray jay's tail feathers, and a warbler ceased to buzz in the trees, but the chipmunk population was reduced to a safe level for the growing things and for the vegetarians that would feed on them. The hawk drifted on, leaving its gift of vegetables and flowers.

In late winter I saw, against the white sky glare, the silhouette of a falcon, made of straight lines and obtuse angles, with triangular slender, pointed wings, and a long slim tail. A shape without detail, it circled slowly, not very high. I held my breath.

Was this the American representative of the peregrine falcons, those fabulous wandering hunters that drop on their prey like bolts from Olympus and have been timed at one hundred and eighty miles per hour? Even when called by so prosaic a name as "duck hawk" these birds move in an aura of romance, sprung not only from the days when falconry was a sport of European nobles, but also from their extraordinary swiftness, strength, and courage.

The bird broke out of its pattern and swooped to the top of a smallish cedar twenty feet from where I stood. It looked at me as though it might never have a seen a human before, and well it might not have, because this was not the peregrine, but the rarest of all visitors from the Arctic, the king of the royal family of raptors, the white gyrfalcon.

It had honored our clearing with its presence because even a royal bird must preen wind-ruffled feathers. Carefully it tended its wings and breast, then fluffed and settled and posed on the treetop. Its broad, heavy breast testified to its great flight power. Its feathers were like fresh snow. Even its beak and feet were pale. Its pupils were circles of black fire, and the dark dotted lines on its back and wings, the chevron marks on its primaries, were like ermine tails on the coronation robes of nobility.

It stayed long enough for me to store the memory of its beauty, then lanced upward and turned straight into the north, toward the open spaces over which there is room for a king to fly, toward the rugged northern cliffs of Greenland or Ungava, where it would rear its young by the light of the midnight sun.

A pair of broad-winged hawks nest somewhere between our two cabins, but I have had no sight of them so clear as that of the accidental gyrfalcon. They reared three young last summer and Ade called me to see the family's broad-winged, fan-tailed silhouettes overhead. Their high-pitched whistling brings consternation to the feeding yard, as only the gray jays have their own chosen paths, through and under concealing branches, by which they avoid all hunting birds and arrive safely on the woodshed roof for food. The broad-wings have never hunted within sight of the house and seem even to avoid other birds. This bears out the sometimes questioned statement that these and other hawks of the Buteo family are enormously valuable because they feed on rodents and large insects by preference.

I have seen one other Buteo here, and that for a few minutes only, while it sailed high across the clearing. It was a red-tailed hawk, and I recognized it even before, banking, it poured the sunlight from the bronze upper surface of its tail. For a red-tailed hawk taught me a lesson, bitter but without price.

During one of my childhood summers a family of five red-tails lived in the belfry of a church near my home. I used to watch one of them every morning as it soared above the branches of a great elm that had survived from Ohio's primeval forest. I had been told about hawks—wicked birds that killed robins and stole chickens and generally were a mistake of the Almighty, according to my adult informants. But I thought that hawk beautiful and, although I was too young to under-stand, I found it encouraging and inspiring.

Then a neighbor's grandson bragged about his ability with an air gun. My father, wisely deciding that the familiar is not dangerous, had taught me to shoot when I was hardly big enough to rest his .22 rifle on a support and aim it. The next morning I took the .22, called the boy to witness, and shot the hawk out of the sky.

Much puffed up, I took the hawk's head to the proper county office and collected a $2.00 bounty. This, added to the praises of my parents, made me quite insufferable.

The next morning I looked from the window. The emp-tiness of the sky was a shock. I had forgotten that the hawk was gone. Nothing was left but a pile of bloody feathers and two dirty dollar bills. I hated myself, the rifle, the money, and struggled painfully to grasp the meaning of my unhappiness. Slowly I realized that out of selfishness I had destroyed something of great beauty that had brought me only delight. Being sorry could not help. Nothing could help. A killed thing is forever dead.

18

ELEANOR RICE PETTINGILL

1908–1977

These selections end with a chapter from Eleanor Rice Pettingill's *Penguin Summer* of 1960, an account of the photographic expedition she and her husband, ornithologist Olin Sewall Pettingill, undertook to the Falkland Islands from 1953 to 1954. Their purpose was to film for Walt Disney Productions footage of the vast colonies of penguins that live on these rocky islands.

In many ways Eleanor Pettingill epitomizes the qualities of loyalty and élan so necessary for the ornithologist's wife and companion. Friend and ally of such other women as Helen Cruickshank, she was born in 1908 in Salem, Massachusetts, and graduated from Wheaton College in 1929. Although she taught school for seven years both before and after marriage to Pettingill in 1932, she left teaching to raise two daughters and assist her husband, who was on the faculty of Carleton College in Northfield, Minnesota, from 1936 to 1953.

The couple devoted themselves to free-lance ornithology and photography until 1960, when Sewall Pettingill became director of the prestigious Laboratory of Ornithology at Cornell University. In 1973 they retired to Wayne, Maine. Eleanor died there in 1977.

Olin Sewall Pettingill, one of America's foremost ornithologists, bird photographers, and birdwatchers, made several photographic expeditions to far-off places during his wife's lifetime; she often accompained him as assistant and companion. Their travels took them to northern Canada, Iceland, New Zealand, and Antarctica as well as to the Falkland Islands, which they visited once in 1953 and again in 1971.

Eleanor Pettingill is remembered by her longtime friend Helen Cruickshank as a competent editor and critic of her husband's numerous books, both popular birdwatching guides and more serious ornithological studies. She was greatly esteemed by the group of wives in professional ornithological and natural history circles for her dedication to Sewall's research expeditions and for her great style as hostess to visiting scientists and students.

Penguin Summer is Eleanor Pettingill's only book. In it she reveals, more openly than do any of her contemporaries, the extraordinary difficulties of bird study in the field. Often broadly humorous, Pettingill's tale of this sometimes disastrous and dangerous photographic expedition remains a remarkable document of companionship, dedication, and loyalty. Without her contribution the expedition would have been impossible. This was a woman of quiet strength who imparted to her harrowing tale some of her enthusiasm for adventure as well as some of her fears. With a keen eye for bird description and a sharp sense of personality, Pettingill gives us a penetrating look into the life of the obsessed birdwatcher and student.

Kidney Island

"You'll live comfortably on Kidney Island," Edwin said, after I had described some of the inconveniences of Charles Point. "It's a good hut, with a good stove. Plenty of birds, and sea lions too. They sleep in the tussock grass."

But when the day came for us to leave, Edwin was distraught. The *Philomel*, the government ship he had engaged to take us, was not in Stanley and might not be in for a week. The *Stockfish* was not insured to leave the harbor, and even if we could get permission, he doubted that it could make the short trip over the rough water off Mengeary Point. The only other possibility was the *Protector*, a cargo vessel now loading to go around the camp. The captain was willing to take us to Kidney Island—for a price: seventy dollars.

I winced. But Sewall said we'd take it.

I went shopping for supplies, including one hundred pounds of coal for the stove. When I ordered it, I knew why everyone burned peat. Coal was ninety dollars a ton.

Then I went to the spic and span Kelper store to engage Tommy Goodwin and the Land-Rover to take us to the jetty. A pleasant woman stood behind a counter of rings and bracelets set with Falkland Island pebbles—very hard agates—and I made a note to buy some. "Tommy Goodwin is in the next building working with the minerals," the woman said. I hadn't known that it was Tommy who set these stones in silver.

I went next door to find him. He was busy filling bottles with soda pop from large tanks. Minerals? Agates? Mineral water, of course.

Mr. Goodwin was delighted to be asked to drive us to the jetty at four—and would we mind if he came along on the trip?

"Of course not," I said. "It's a big ship. Bring someone else too if you like."

On the way back, I met Mr. Rowe, the banker, who asked me what arrangements we had made for emergencies. When I said none, he advised us to take a walkie-talkie so we could report to Stanley once a day. But we already had too much gear; and Edwin said that when he went to Kidney Island he always phoned the lighthouse keeper and told him he was going and would build a fire if he got in trouble. We could do the same.

"Everybody knows you're going," he added. "Some of them will be at the jetty to see you off."

"And some are coming with us," I told him.

He glowered. "None of them is going ashore. If they think they're going out there to collect penguin eggs, they're just dead wrong."

I felt like Mrs. Astor when I walked up the gangplank of the *Protector*, Mrs. Astor boarding her yacht in blue jeans, Mrs. Astor greeting her guests and hovering over a bag of coal more precious than gold. Mr. Goodwin was there with several strange gentlemen. Rowan came right from school, and there were other youngsters, children of the crew and friends. Mary, Edwin, Sewall, and I had tea in the tiny saloon. It was quite jolly, like a holiday outing, and after we passed Mengeary Point, quite rough. Of course there was no sun. We hadn't seen the sun for more than five minutes at a time since we arrived, and by the time we dropped anchor in the kelp-enclosed harbor of Kidney Island it was raining.

There was a path up the steep thirty-foot rise to the hut, but we couldn't find it. With the crew of the ship hauling the supplies and equipment, we forced our way through dense grass higher than our heads, pulling ourselves up by grasping the blades, then sliding back on the wet slippery ground.

Finally we emerged on a level open area and hurried toward the hut.

Edwin looked in and stood speechless. I looked in, and felt nausea coming on. This was the hut where we were going to live so comfortably. There were broken bottles, smashed dishes, overturned lamps, scattered playing cards, torn clothing, greasy pans, and everywhere the unmistakable signs of birds—big birds. Newspapers were ripped to shreds, bits of linoleum chewed up, a nest started here, a pile of ashes there, hunks of coal everywhere.

"Someone left the door open," Mary said weakly.

Edwin looked so stricken that I felt sorry for him.

At that moment, several sharp toots came from the *Protector*. Her captain, like all captains in the Falklands, felt a storm coming. The crew put down their load. They must go. The Cawkells must go. In a matter of seconds we were alone on Kidney Island.

I didn't think we could do it, but we did. Starting at the stove in the far end of the hut, we pushed north through the door—shoveled, swept, and finally scrubbed. Everything in the hut was either washed or tossed into the tussock. The odor of birds remained—it probably always will—but otherwise the hut was as clean as human hands and cold water could make it.

The hut had been built by the government to house the tussock cutters who came yearly, if small boats were available, to harvest tussock grass for the Stanley cattle. It had built-in bunks, tables, benches, and shelves to make housekeeping convenient, and a real stove to warm it. From the wreckage we salvaged dishes, pans, a ship's teakettle, and even a scrap of carpet—all donations, no doubt, of previous occupants. Now it was in order. At ten-thirty we sat down to dinner cooked over a coal fire in the stove. Then with the last of our strength blew up our rubber mattresses, and crawled into our sleeping bags.

We were awakened at dawn by something big landing smack on the tin roof, then scratching and clawing its way to the ridge pole.

"Bird," Sewall said, and was out the door with me after him. A turkey vulture sailed off into the wind, then returned with three more, circling over us hopefully again and again.

At breakfast we studied a map that Edwin had drawn of the small island. Directly north of the hut the land rose to a high ridge running east and west to form a sort of backbone of the island. Beyond that the terrain dipped down abruptly and leveled off to the edge of the cliffs where the rockhopper penguins lived. It did not seem far from the hut, up over the ridge and down to the penguin colony—or so we thought until we learned about tussock bogs.

The early settlers in the Falklands found tussock grass covering all the small islands and ringing the larger ones. In order to grow, they said, tussock grass must "feel" salt spray on its blades. Their livestock, emaciated after the long voyage from England, grew fat on the tussock, but wherever sheep were pastured, tussock disappeared. Now tussock is limited to the smaller islands and headlands from which sheep have been barred. Kidney Island was completely covered by it; because of the shortage of boats, it had not been cut for two years.

We set out for the northern cliffs. Only a short distance from the hut we found ourselves enveloped in tussock. Numberless tussock plants with waving blades five or six feet long sprouted from pedestals composed of the tough entwined roots and stems of former plants. A single pedestal, often as high as my head, together with its fountain of green, is called a tussock bog. Where the old blades were broken off, I could walk between the chunky, irregular bases beneath a canopy of green; but more often the canopy was just at eye level, and I could not walk under it or see over it.

The bogs were just far enough apart to prevent our hopping from one to another, but close enough for their blades to entwine to form an impenetrable wall. Along with the physical exertion required to make our way in the tussock I had an intense feeling of claustrophobia that came over me in waves as we pushed, climbed, crawled, or stumbled, getting nowhere. Sewall, six inches taller than I, fared better, and went ahead to break the path. After we crossed the ridge the ground became wetter and before we reached the cliffs we were wallowing in a filthy morass.

We smelled and heard the rockhopper penguins long before we saw them. I had sniffed at the slight odor from the gentoo colony, which was washed clean by constant showers and dried by brisk winds; but I nearly gagged at the stench that rose from the rockhoppers' premises, damp, shaded, and surrounded by tussock. Old tussock bogs served as nest sites; dried blades of grass were heaped around dirty eggs. Little creatures with mud-stained plumage peered at us around every bog and vigorously protested our passage through their colony.

I was so intent on trying to find a solid place to put my foot that I did not notice an angry little penguin that shot like a fox terrier from behind a tussock bog, latched onto my leg just above my high boot, and beat me viciously with its flippers. I screamed, kicked, and stamped to shake it off, and clawed at the tussock bog to keep from falling into the mire. The bird fled as Sewall crashed back through the tussock.

I looked from my bleeding leg to his laughing face. "It hurt," I cried angrily.

"Stop groaning," he said, "after all there aren't many women in the world lucky enough to be bitten by a penguin."

After that I carried a stick to ward off attacking penguins,

Eleanor Pettingill with a colony of gentoo penguins.
Courtesy of Oliver Sewall Pettingill, Jr.

but none ever came near me again, and although they made a lot of noise, most of them paid no more attention to us than the gentoos had.

On the cliffs we had our first good look at rockhopper penguins. Here clean little birds guarded eggs or worked on nests of pebbles and tussock grass in crevices all up and down the steep rocks, a precarious location for a colony of flightless birds. They were small, about half the size of gentoos, and their distinguishing feature, a streak of yellow feathers that slanted upward above each red eye and formed a tuft above each ear, gave them an oriental look. When they were disturbed the black feathers on their heads stood straight up, turning them into fierce little monsters. The din was terrific. At first we thought that our invading their cliffs was the cause; later we discovered that rockhoppers are just plain noisy all the time.

To avoid the tussock, we returned to the hut along the shore, circling the eastern end of the island. As Edwin had said, it was an ornithologist's dream. The rockhopper penguin colony blended into the colony of king shags. They waggled their heads at us but never left their enormous nests of tussock and seaweed that dotted the face of the cliff.

King shags, also called blue-eyed shags, are extraordinary creatures with black backs, white fronts, orange caruncles at the base of the bill and several curly black plumes on the top of the head. Their brown eyes are circled by a hand of vivid violet-blue skin.

At the eastern end of the island where the cliffs broke down into a boulder beach, we found a pair of black oyster-catchers. They were the same size and shape as the black and white variety but they were totally black except for red bills and eyelids, yellow eyes, and pale beige feet and legs that looked nude, untanned, slightly unfinished. The birds screamed at us but did not fly from their beach. Sewall, studying the ecological niches of the oystercatchers, noted that the black ones inhabited boulder beaches, while the black and white ones were found on sand beaches.

We became aware of some small birds that followed our footsteps across the kelp-strewn, rock beach. There were Falk-land robins, wrens, and several dark birds, a little smaller than the robins but much bolder. Sewall identified the wren as Cobb's wren, a subspecies of the Neotropical house wren, found only in the Falklands. The brown bird was a tussockbird, belonging to the family of South American ovenbirds. One came right up to the toe of my boot and turned over bits of rotted kelp with quick flips of its bill. They were supposed to be so tame that they would light on a man's shoulder and tug at the hairs on the back of his neck.

But we forgot them when we saw, on the next promontory, a pure white goose, a large one, so striking against the dark water that I caught my breath. It was a kelp goose. It held its ground while we came close to see its black eyes, bill, and feet. We found its nest easily right on the edge of the tussock. An enormous bog leaned over it, the blades of grass forming a curtain that concealed the female. Black, barred with white, she sat calmly until we pushed her off the nest to count the eggs—seven—then slid back on.

Logger ducks yammered at us when we reached the sand beach where we had landed the previous day. I waved at them. This was ornithology as I liked it—not too many birds, all tame and easy to see, a far cry from chasing wood warblers in dense forests. This was fun. I was not yet aware of the thousands of petrels, fairy-like birds of the dusky twilight, that were at that very moment incubating thousands of eggs in thousands of burrows on Kidney Island.

As I charged down the beach I roused a sea lion from his nap on a bed of tussock. He rose up, puffed out his neck with its shaggy yellow mane, and gave out a terrific roar. At the same time he spouted steam, his breath condensing in the cold air. Then another roar, and another, as I froze in my tracks not six feet away.

I shrieked. "That's a dragon breathing fire!"

Sewall came up behind me laughing. "Don't go near him."

He picked up a small rock and tossed it at the dragon. The beast slid from his bed and down along the worn rocks to the water. After sticking his head up and looking us over once more, he disappeared beneath the maze of kelp in the harbor.

"That, my pet, was a male sea lion," Sewall informed me. Male sea lions, or bulls, are dangerous only during the rutting season, September. This was October. They would not attack us. However, we must be careful not to be in the way when the huge, six hundred pound animals decided to take to the water.

From that moment on, the tussock, already unpleasant, held real terror. Every time I came to a place where the grass was matted down, I moved warily for fear of stepping on a sleeping sea lion.

All afternoon a storm raged across the island. The wind went down with the sun and night came on starlit and clear. Standing in the doorway of the hut we watched the beams of Pembroke Light sweep across the sky, and listened to the bellowing of the sea lions. It was cold, the air was crisp, but inside the hut it was warm and cozy.

The next morning we set out to make a trail through the tussock so that we could transport the cameras to the penguin cliffs. Hacking and chopping with a hatchet and saw (what they were doing on a treeless island I'll never know), we made our way to the top of the ridge, marking the trail with stakes cut from the ruins of an old shanty, and laying the freshly cut grass in the path.

When we advanced downhill into the filthy swamp, the rockhopper penguins were furious. They resented our approach as if we were a slum-clearance committee. We trimmed off the tops of bogs and sunlight poured into their odoriferous hollows. By lunchtime we had a trail we could follow, if we were careful.

A storm made photography impossible that afternoon. As I lay on my bunk listening to the sounds of the wind whipping the tussock against the tin walls of the hut and driving showers of rain in spasms on the roof, I fell asleep. Sometime during my nap Sewell took his Graflex and left the hut.

I slept on until the door burst open and Sewall said, "Hold everything. I've broken my arm!" I jumped to my feet. Sewall was leaning against the door jamb.

"That's all right," I heard myself saying, calmness struggling with utter confusion, "I'll splint it."

He sat down on a low bench and leaned on the upright that supported the bunks. His left arm hung limp. Slowly, inch by inch, I worked off his coat, and cut the sleeve from his sweater. I was about to cut through his flannel shirt when I remembered what I had learned in a wartime first-aid course: keep the patient warm, no stimulants, watch for shock, above all, keep him warm.

It was cold in the hut and he was already shivering. If I cut off the wool shirt and the underwear, how would I keep him warm? And the fire—I had no idea how to run a coal stove. He was frightfully pale.

"Let's look at that arm," I said, "then I'll splint it."

When I looked at it I forgot about splints: there was a huge swelling around the shoulder. The break was very far up.

"It's the humerus, near the head," Sewall said. I let it go at that. I was helpless. He was in great pain.

"Maybe I can fix a sling to take the pull off the shoulder?" I suggested without conviction. The first-aid course had recommended substituting a pillow case for a proper sling. Where would I find a pillow case on Kidney Island? I fashioned a sling from a blouse and a scarf, wrapped the heavy coat around him, and fastened it securely with a belt.

He was paler now and shivering even more. What to do for shock? Whisky? No, not until all danger of shock had passed. Coffee? Aspirin? Tea? Tea was safe enough. Waiting for the water to boil on the primus, I poked at the stove, added coal, and chatted endlessly—to myself. Sewall said not a word. Only the desperation in his eyes told me what he was thinking. Here we were, ready to go; all the time, energy, and thought—and now this. Never in all our years together had life looked so black.

With the hot, strong tea the color slowly returned to his lips and the shivering lessened. He told me what had happened: he thought he'd get one more picture of the kelp goose; then he slipped on a bit of spray-dampened lichen. As he bent his arm to save a camera, all the weight crashed down on his elbow. And now would I please just leave him alone. Would I go for the camera on the ledge just opposite the kelp goose's nest on the eastern end of the island.

"And while you're there," he added, "you might as well finish off the film. It's probably ruined anyway." Then he said gently, "I'm sorry I had to leave it. I tried. . . ."

"I don't mind," I said quickly. Suddenly I was anxious to escape the hut and leave him alone. "I'm sorry I had to leave it. . . ." If only he had yelled at me so that I could have yelled back and burst into tears.

Considering the steep bank of tussock and the high rocky ledges he had to climb over, it was a wonder he'd been able to get himself back, let alone the camera. The Graflex, sprayed by the surf, sat high on a rock in plain view. Although I'd had no intention of doing so, I couldn't resist using up the last four exposures on the black and white female kelp goose standing beside her nest, and the pure white male close by. But as I snapped the final picture, a huge wave—the seventh, I suppose—crashed against the ledge and drenched the camera and me.

"To hell with kelp geese," I screamed at the innocent birds, and started struggling back over the rocks.

Now I began to worry about getting help. The *Protector* would not call for us for a week. Somehow I must get in touch with Stanley. But how? I knew from our experience on Charles Point that I couldn't hope to hail a passing ship. I looked across the channel to Kidney Cove where we had lunched that first day. If only I were a good swimmer—but even if I could swim it, there would be too long a hike in icy clothes through snow and wind.

Edwin had mentioned lighting a fire, but the thought of it terrified me. A fire fanned by that driving wind would sweep across the whole island. No, that would only be a last resort. When I got back to the hut, I still had no solution.

Sewall had finished a second cup of tea. He managed a twisted smile when I showed him the water-soaked camera. "Looked bad enough before," he said, "but I don't think it'll be hurt if you take it apart and dry it right away."

This was a dangerous suggestion to make to anyone as unmechanical as I, but under his directions I took the camera apart and dried it carefully. Then I broached the subject of getting help.

"I think you can see the lighthouse from the top of the island," he said. "I'm quite sure I saw it this morning when I climbed one of the bogs to drive a stake."

"And. . .?"

"Simple. You can signal from there tonight with the big flashlight and the Stroboflash."

My hands went rigid. I nearly dropped the camera. I could not. I would not go into the tussock alone by day, let alone by night, for a broken arm, a camera, Walt Disney Productions, or anything else. I wouldn't.

All this I never said. Yes, I would. Just as soon as I finished drying the camera, I would go look for the lighthouse.

Even in daylight it was hard enough to follow the five stakes that marked the trail to the top of the ridge. I got lost several times before I reached the top and climbed on a bog higher than my head. I could see the lighthouse just over

Mengeary Point. I shivered to think of coming back at night. I would need a wider path, much wider; a turnpike, in fact.

For the rest of the daylight hours I sawed tussock to widen the trail. As I cut, the blades left standing leaned over and twined together as if to compensate for their lost members and obscure the trail. At dusk I walked up and down again and again until I was sure I could follow the path with a flashlight. On one trip up I met a jackass penguin, the first I had seen on Kidney Island. Both surprised, we stopped and stared at each other. I kept my eyes on his vicious bill and waved my saw at him, saying "Shoo!" He stood his ground, wagged his head from side to side, and went on staring. I stepped aside and he waddled on by. After all, it was his path.

By this time Sewall was wretched with pain. The danger of shock seemed to have passed, so I gave him an iceless Scotch highball and looked in the carefully packed medicine kit for aspirin. The shock was mine. There were only four tablets left in the bottle. I concealed my chagrin at having neglected to check the kit, and gave him only one.

By the time we had eaten our gloomy dinner and I had learned to use the Stroboflash, a black night had closed over Kidney Island. Armed with the flashlight equipment and precious little courage, I started for the ridge. There was a strong, gusty wind; the sky was clear, the stars very far away and unfamiliar. The sounds of the surf crashing on the beach, the incessant clamor of rockhoppers on the cliffs, the roaring of the sea lions did not bother me; they were distant and identifiable. But there were sounds that were closer—moans and groans and cries from the tussock—that were frightening. Under my feet things scurried and rattled the dry grass. Something with big wings crossed the beam of the flashlight and was quickly gone. Looking back now, I do not see how I forced myself to climb that hill.

On the high bog, with the wind beating my back, I began

to flash at regular intervals toward the lighthouse. Then I tried the Stroboflash, which went off with a brilliance that seemed to light up the entire island. After a few minutes my gloved hands were so numb with cold that I had to return to the hut.

"Any reply from the lighthouse?" Sewall asked.

"Of course not," I said scornfully. My grandfather had been a sea captain and had rounded the Horn any number of times in a sailing vessel. I was an authority on the sea. "They *never* change the rhythm of the light." I held my hands over the stove. "But Sewall, the noises in the tussock—they're horrible. It's crawling with groaning things. Sounds as though people were being murdered."

He tried to smile. "Probably just jackass penguins in their burrows, or maybe sooty shearwaters." I poked the stubborn fire in the stove. "The scurrying things in the path," he added, "may have been small gray-backed petrels, and the big flying birds were probably short-eared owls."

Every half hour until well after midnight I trudged to the ridge and flashed, but there was no response. Somehow I managed to help Sewall into his bunk, where he sat propped up with rubber mattresses, camera cases, and duffle bags. All through the long night I tended the fire and tried to read by the light of one candle. At dawn when Sewall seemed to be dozing, I fell onto my bunk still dressed. I had nearly gone to sleep when a turkey vulture arrived on the roof.

Disgusted, I got up and made coffee on the primus, and kicked angrily at the coal stove. The fire was completely dead. Then I went outside to scan the harbor for some sign of a ship.

About midmorning I nailed one of Sewall's whitest T shirts to a stick and set out for the signaling post. The path was broad and easy to follow by day; but now it was littered with dozens of soft, blue-gray wings—all that was left of the petrels killed during the night. My cutting the tussock had exposed their trails and burrows and made them easy prey for owls.

I tied the white flag to the stake on the highest bog with only a faint hope that it might be seen from a ship, a plane, or perhaps the lighthouse. If only the frigate would choose this clear, beautiful day for a reconnaissance of the coast, or the *John Biscoe* would leave for South Georgia.

As I ran downhill toward the hut I saw three turkey vultures, with wings spread, sunning themselves on the roof. This was too much. Breaking off chunks of tussock bog I rushed at them throwing wildly and screaming, "You get off this house!" They left in a huff and circled me sullenly. I was almost in tears. I had enough trouble without turkey vultures on the roof.

By afternoon I had more. Sewall had a fever. The wind rose steadily; the clouds closed in. It was colder than ever, 30° F., and I couldn't make the stove burn properly.

Long before dark I was on the signaling bog, ready to begin flashing as soon as the first beams appeared from Pembroke Light. Suddenly, while I waited, birds, big birds, circled silently over me, coming closer and closer until I shrunk from them. In a moment they were gone and the air seemed to fill with smaller birds whirling about. They too were gone quickly; and from the tussock came groans and cries.

Just then a beam of light passed over the island, and I flashed toward the lighthouse. Soon it seemed that the steady, rhythmic flashing of the light from across the water had changed. Was the pause between flashes longer than usual, or were my eyes playing tricks on me? I waited, but there were no more pauses.

I said nothing about the light when I went back to the hut; I did not want to raise false hopes in Sewall. But when I returned to the bog in fifteen minutes my first flash brought a definite reply. The light stopped turning and trained its beam straight on me. Before I was down off the bog, a searchlight cut the clouds in the direction of Stanley. The signal had been seen.

I ran to tell Sewall. "They can't come tonight," he said. "Not on a night like this." The wind was howling again.

I went to the ridge several more times and flashed, just in case. At ten-thirty I saw the lights of a ship off Mengeary Point.

Bursting into the hut, I cried, "They're coming," and started to pack. I gave Sewall the last two aspirin and a strong drink of whisky. Every movement caused him such pain I wondered how I would get him to the beach.

When I had finished packing I went out to check the progress of the ship. It had passed Kidney Island and was far out at sea.

I had to tell Sewall they weren't coming for us, but I knew they would be here in the morning. They had answered my signal.

The aspirin and whisky had eased Sewall's pain. "What were you flashing?" he asked.

"SOS," I said. "After all, I was a girl scout."

"My God! SOS means ship in distress. They don't even know it's you. They'll be out looking for a ship in trouble."

I looked at him in horror. What had I done? Sending false signals at sea was a serious crime; ignorance was no excuse. I saw myself court-martialed, put in irons. I could see the head-lines: AMERICAN CITIZEN CONVICTED. POSSIBLE ESPIONAGE.

"They wouldn't expect a woman to know any signals," I said lamely.

"How do they know it's a woman?" Then he added, "Oh well, this is probably just a sprain anyway."

That did it. "Brother," I said icily, "this better be more

than a sprain. If I've lured a ship out of a safe harbor on a night like this . . ."

I tried to revive the dying fire. It was a relief to have something to poke. While Sewall dozed, I sat down and wrote the events of the past thirty-six hours in a letter to the children.

Shortly after one o'clock the wind slackened a bit and I could hear the crashing of the breakers. Suddenly a cry came out of the night: "Ahoy up there!"

I dashed outside into the blackness and followed the direction from which the voice had come off shore. Half rolling, half falling I got to the beach with my light and guided a dory in. A man jumped from the boat and said in a firm voice, "I'm John Huckle, Mrs. Pettingill. What's the matter?"

"Broken arm—pain—fever—cold," I stammered. Two more men appeared and drew the boat ashore.

"Do we need a stretcher?"

"I don't think so. Come and see."

We crawled up through the tussock. Sewall was already standing by the door, his leather case of field notes grasped in his good hand.

"We haven't a minute to lose because of the tide," John Huckle said. "Come at once. Leave everything right here."

"I can't go," I said flatly. "I can't leave the cameras here with this fire." I'd guarded the cameras too long; I'd stay alone on this horrible island rather than leave them now. "I won't go," I repeated.

"Mrs. Pettingill," he said. "You *will* go with your husband." There was no compromise in his voice. Then he hesitated. "Mac will stay. You'll stay, won't you, Mac? We'll be back for you tomorrow."

Poor Mac, he had no choice. It was apparent that one did not argue with Mr. Huckle.

Sewall passed me the leather case and went with the men.

I couldn't find my boots—the great high boots that I hated yet had to have to get into the boat. While I hunted for them, I tried to explain about the food supply to Mac who, instead of listening, kept asking me for my "torch."

"Mac," I pleaded, "Look for my boots. I can't get into that boat in sneakers."

"Lady," he assured me solemnly, "I'll devote the rest of my evening to it, if only you'll give me your torch." He pointed to the flashlight in my hand. "Please leave it with me on the beach."

I gave up on the boots and we started for the beach. My flashlight went out on the way down, but my calls for help went unheeded. Sewall was seated in the stern of the dory when I fell out of the tussock, passed the dead torch to Mac, and directed by Mr. Huckle, waded into the icy water to sit in the stern beside my husband.

"Somebody feed my little dog," Mac called as he pushed us off.

After several hair-raising false starts, we headed straight out into the breakers and total darkness. The gale had subsided but not the sea. I was on Sewall's left side, and couldn't put my arm around him. I did not dare touch him so I took a firm grip on the belt of his coat and held my breath. The stern of the heavily loaded boat seemed barely four inches above the water. So far there was no ship in sight.

The men rowed hard and finally we rounded a point and saw the ship's lights.

The rollers at the point were so big that I expected each wave to swamp the dory. Then we drew up on the leeward side of the ship and bounced against her in the darkness. Flashing beams came from the deck above.

The crew lowered a thick rope which John Huckle tied

about Sewall's waist, then a rope ladder. Supported from below by the two men, Sewall stood on the ladder and held one side with his good hand, while the crew on the deck pulled him up until they could seize his right arm and lift him over the side. I was next. The rope ladder swung out with each roll of the ship and snapped back with a bang. Mr. Cawkell caught me as I struggled over the rail and almost fell on the deck.

In the captain's cabin Stuart Booth was trying to make Sewall comfortable, and the ship's cook appeared with mugs of hot tea.

Edwin was relieved that it was only a broken arm, and that our signal had not been seen on the previous night, for at that time there had been no ship to come for us. This ship—it was the *Philomel*, the government rescue ship—had returned at six this evening. Her crew had been discharged for an annual holiday—peat-cutting week. At eight-forty-five our signal was first seen by the lighthouse keeper. He acknowledged it by stopping the light for eight seconds, then telephoned John Huckle, the harbormaster in Stanley. At nine the six men of the crew of the *Philomel* were summoned by wireless—from bath, bar, and fireside. At nine-fifteen the ship was under way.

Because of the wild sea the captain had taken her far out before attempting to enter the narrow channel between Kidney Island and the mainland. They had been four hours on the way. Mr. Booth had been sick and Edwin hadn't had a quiet moment.

"About halfway out," Mr. Booth said, "Mr. Cawkell remembered your flash equipment and suggested—only suggested—that you might be taking night pictures of birds."

"And you should have heard the language of the crew," Edwin said, grinning. "It was—shocking."

When the dory had been raised and the *Philomel* was safely

out of the channel, John Huckle joined us. "I thought that you two Americans were just out of paraffin for your primus. I was prepared to drown you on the spot." He assured me I had done no wrong in signaling, but, he added I was a failure as a girl scout.

"Not once did you send an SOS," he went on. "Better check up on the Morse code if you mean to do this often."

I tried to apologize for bringing them out in such weather; I had no way of telling them just how serious it was. I had not expected them to come at night. In fact I wished they had waited for daylight. It was wrong to risk lives.

John was consoling: "Don't worry about risking lives. They love it. They don't have excitement like this every day. It will provide conversation for weeks to come."

Sewall sat pale and silent in a corner. The effects of the mild sedative had worn off and the least movement made the pain almost intolerable. The ship crept slowly back to Stanley where we tied up at the jetty about three-thirty in the morning.

It was decided that Sewall should walk to the hospital rather than wait for Mr. Goodwin. "I couldn't stand the Land-Rover," he whispered to me. Edwin hurried ahead to alert the nurses.

"We'll not go back to Kidney Island this morning," John Huckle told me. "I'll give you a ring. Maybe Monday."

"And Mac?"

"He'll wait for us. By the way, you packed up all the liquor, didn't you?"

I knew I did. "In the camera cases," I told him. "What if he. . . ?"

"It's safe," he said. "He'll not open one thing, but . . . if it were in plain sight . . ."

The three blocks to the hospital were probably the longest Sewall ever walked. The wind cut through our wet clothes;

the stony road jogged the arm. He almost fell into the arms of the nurse who waited at the door.

When he was safely in bed, she vanished for a moment and returned with a loaded tea tray. Bless the British! Whatever the crisis, there is always time for a cup of tea. Dr. Slessor arrived and had his cup before confirming Sewall's diagnosis.

"Go home," he said to me, "and don't come back until I call you." He handed me a pill. "Take this and go to bed."

I was about to leave when I thought of something very important. "Will you try," I asked the doctor, "to get his underwear off without cutting it?"

He eyed me strangely. "What's so special about the underwear?"

I did not dare explain—not in this wool-producing colony. I was only sure that life would not be worth much without that orlon underwear. I smiled, said goodnight, and walked with Edwin into the wind. Great bunchy clouds in the east were turning pink and roosters were crowing all over town.

BIBLIOGRAPHY

Austin, Mary Hunter, *The Land of Little Rain*. Boston and New York: Houghton & Mifflin, 1903.

Bailey, Florence Merriam, *A-Birding on a Bronco*. Boston: Houghton & Mifflin, 1896.

Comstock, Anna, *Handbook of Nature Study*. Ithaca: Comstock Publishing Company, 1911.

Cruickshank, Helen Gere, *Bird Islands Down East*. New York: Macmillan, 1941.

Doubleday, Neltje Blanchan, *How to Attract the Birds and Other Talks about Bird Neighbors*. New York: Doubleday, Page & Company, 1903.

Eckstorm, Fannie Hardy. "Concerning the Bad Reputation of Whiskey John." *Bird-Lore*, IV, No. 4, July–August 1902.

Hoover, Helen, *The Long-Shadowed Forest*. New York: Thomas Y. Crowell, 1963.

Jaques, Florence Page, *Birds Across the Sky*. New York and London: Harper & Row, 1942.

———, "There Once Was a Puffin." *Childlife Magazine*, IX, 1930.

Jewett, Sarah Orne, *A White Heron and Other Stories*. Boston and New York: Houghton & Mifflin, 1886.

Lawrence, Louise de Kiriline, *The Lovely and the Wild*. New York et al.: McGraw-Hill, 1968.

Miller, Olive Thorne, *A Bird-Lover in the West*. Boston: Houghton & Mifflin, 1894.

Nice, Margaret Morse, *The Watcher at the Nest*. New York: Macmillan, 1939.

Pettingill, Eleanor Rice, *Penguin Summer*. New York: Clarkson N. Potter, 1960.

Porter, Gene Stratton, *Freckles*. New York: Doubleday, Page & Company, 1904.

Sherman, Althea, *Birds of an Iowa Dooryard*. Boston: The Christopher Publishing House, 1952.

Thaxter, Celia Leighton, *An Island Garden*. Boston: Houghton & Mifflin, 1894.

————, *Drift-weed*. Boston: Houghton & Mifflin, 1894.

————, *Poems*. Boston: Houghton & Mifflin, 1894.

Wright, Mabel Osgood, *The Friendship of Nature, a New England Chronicle of Birds and Flowers*. New York: Macmillan, 1894.

Wright, Mabel Osgood, and Elliott Coues, *Citizen Bird. Scenes from Bird-Life in Plain English for Beginners*. New York: Macmillan, 1897.